Abstinence and Holiness, Embracing Self-Deprivation

Abstinence and Holiness, Embracing Self-Deprivation

Reading Tractate *Nazir* in the Babylonian Talmud

Joshua A. Fogel

HAMILTON BOOKS
AN IMPRINT OF
ROWMAN & LITTLEFIELD
Lanham • Boulder • New York • London

Published by Hamilton Books
An imprint of The Rowman & Littlefield Publishing Group, Inc.
4501 Forbes Boulevard, Suite 200, Lanham, Maryland 20706
www.rowman.com

86-90 Paul Street, London EC2A 4NE, United Kingdom

British Library Cataloguing in Publication Information Available

Library of Congress Cataloging-in-Publication Data

Names: Fogel, Joshua A., 1950– author.
Title: Abstinence and holiness : embracing self-deprivation : reading Tractate Nazir in the Babylonian Talmud / Joshua A. Fogel.
Description: Lanham, Maryland : Hamilton Books, 2023. | Includes bibliographical references and index. | Summary: "The Talmud comprises a massive collection of rabbinical debates from late antiquity. This volume explicates one tractate within it, Nazir, concerned with self-imposed abstentions: no wine or product of the grapevine, no cutting of bodily hair, and no contact with a human corpse"— Provided by publisher.
Identifiers: LCCN 2023041340 (print) | LCCN 2023041341 (ebook) | ISBN 9780761874133 (paperback) | ISBN 9780761874140 (epub)
Subjects: LCSH: Talmud. Nazir—Commentaries.
Classification: LCC BM506.N53 F64 2023 (print) | LCC BM506.N53 (ebook) | DDC 296.1/25—dc23/eng/20230918
LC record available at https://lccn.loc.gov/2023041340
LC ebook record available at https://lccn.loc.gov/2023041341

Contents

Introduction

The Talmud is an immense collection of laws and practices derived from the Torah and the discussions among the rabbis and sages about those laws and practices of Judaism from the late antique period. While the core of Judaism in the Pentateuch before the destruction of the Second Temple in 70 C.E. was Jerusalem and the Holy Temple, if the religion was to survive, it had to be outfitted both for life beyond the Land of Israel and in the Temple's absence. In addition, the laws about the Temple and Jerusalem had to be elucidated for the coming Third Temple. As a result, the Talmud as it now stands is a mixture of theoretical and practical considerations: theoretical for matters involving the Temple and the practices requiring it; practical for all matters (e.g., household, farming, business) that do not require the Temple's presence.

It is composed of two parts: the Mishna (pl. Mishnayot) takes the laws, explicit and implied, of the Torah and lays them out by topic into six orders and the tractates within them, edited in its present form around 200 C.E.; the Gemara provides elaborate disputation and exposition of the Mishna's thirty-seven tractates. If that's not enough, there are two compilations of the Gemara, one emerging from the academies in the Land of Israel (Jerusalem Talmud) and one from the academies of Babylonia (Babylonian Talmud), edited in the first half of the fifth century C.E. Over the centuries since, the Babylonian Talmud has risen to relative prominence.

The tractates of the Babylonian Talmud are of widely varying length, altogether 2711 folio pages in all. An individual folio page or *daf* (pl. *dapim*) is by definition, then, two-sided (a and b) in the text that follows (each side, what we would now dub a "page," is called an *amud* [pl. *amudim*]), and for some (not entirely known) reason each tractate begins on *daf* 2. Over the centuries, many tractates emerged as the favorites of the rabbis and their students, while others received considerably less attention. In 1923, R. Meyer Shapiro (1887–1933) proposed a schema he had devised to read the entire Talmud one *daf* per day, a practice dubbed *dafyomi*. It requires a period of roughly seven and one-half years. Since that time, 100 years ago, this practice has caught on around the world. After each *dafyomi* is completed, a large celebration is held, and then a new cycle begins immediately.

In the way that my previous five volumes, all published by Hamilton Books, each offered a page-by-page elucidation of a tractate of the Talmud, this work turns to tractate *Nazir* in the same fashion. A *nazir* is a strange figure in Judaism. Presumably to attain a higher state of religious observance or spirituality, it denotes a person who vows three abstentions for a specific period of time: no wine or product of the grapevine, no cutting of bodily hair, and no contact with a human corpse. That would seem straightforward enough, but as we shall see it consumes a full sixty-five *dapim* and many topics directly and indirectly related to *nezirut* (the vow taken by a *nazir*), and several completely unrelated. One doesn't ordinarily think of Jewish practice associated with self-imposed deprivation. Yes, we abstain from *chametz* on Passover, and we don't eat or drink anything on Yom Kippur, but *nezirut* comes borderline close to other faiths. Indeed, as we shall see on 3a and 19a, R. Elazar ha-Kappar condemns the whole practice as sinful.[1]

His main argument does not concern hair cutting or corpse defilement, but rather the abstention from the consumption of wine which we are clearly instructed to drink on specific occasions: Shabbat kiddush (see 3b) and the Passover seder, for example. As such, he does not regard a *nazir* as comparable to a murderer or idol-worshiper, truly heinous sinners. And, in any event, his is a minority opinion. That brings up another aspect of the Talmud. Our legal codes today list and describe the laws and consequences of infractions of them. The Talmud certainly does this, but it also includes many views in the rabbinical discussions that lose out in the argumentation, as well as debates that lead to no conclusion, as if the Gemara throws up its figurative hands and "says" enough (on this topic).

What I describe as "rabbit holes" are very often the end result of these discussions. The rabbis will begin with one topic and debate it through many twists and turns, touching on numerous related topics, often altogether unrelated to *nezirut*. Although not in this tractate, elsewhere in the Talmud a leading scholar will tell one or another interlocutor that further discussion of the subsidiary topic(s) is utterly fruitless or that the likelihood of the proposed situation ever existing (and hence worth the time exploring) is way below 1%, so to speak. All of which would mean that the editors of our text were not just cutting and pasting, but trying to group discussions around topics and organize the often unwieldy material into meaningful units. To be sure, before the compilation of the Mishna, as the story goes, the texts with which we are dealing were not written down—it was all memory. And, printing in the Western world was still over a millennium away.

Until relatively recently, the Talmud was read primarily by two groups of people: the ultra-Orthodox community and the considerably smaller academic world. If the former group composed commentaries or notes on the texts they were studying, it was far more likely than not to appear in Hebrew. The latter group wrote mostly for each other in scholarly prose and venues. Recent efforts emerging from the religious world, however, have made the Talmud accessible to a far wider group than ever before. Although there were translations available before, recent decades have witnessed two completely new and full translations of the Babylonian Talmud into English—which include the original text in Mishnaic Hebrew (Mishna) and Aramaic (Gemara), though there is a heavy dose of Mishnaic Hebrew in the latter as well—and a huge explanatory apparatus.

I am by no means a member of this ultra-Orthodox community, but I have long been profoundly intrigued by the massive Talmudic text. In January 2003, I began reading in the *dafyomi* fashion. I even read through the Jerusalem Talmud as well in a similar manner. Just knowing how important this body of knowledge has been to Judaism has sustained that interest on my part, and it has now culminated in my writing the previous five volumes and now this sixth one. Even in translation and even with numerous footnotes to help understand the text, it is still an enormously daunting undertaking, and these books have as their goal to further elucidate what is being debated, discussed, argued.

The rabbis of the Talmud basically argue by two methods. They may point to a verse from the Torah to substantiate a point, and while every verse is not completely transparent in meaning, reference to authority in this way goes a long way to making a definitive case. A second way is to debate logically, a style of argumentation more familiar to us now. Logic here can mean what we would assume it to mean, but it can also mean reasoning based on the nature of the language of the Torah. Several such logic-based schemas are outlined in the text that follows, and all thirteen of them (associated with the name of R. Yishmael) are recited in the morning prayers of observant Jews. There is also an odd invocation of authority which is occasionally used, and very rarely objected to, whereby (on the basis of an extremely ancient tradition, presumably) a given rabbi simply states that his point may not be substantiated by a precise Torah verse or by logic, but it was a teaching conveyed to Moses when he atop Mt. Sinai.

One final point. While most of the text concerns men who vow *nezirut*, women were allowed to do so as well. There is a section in the text that deals with women vowing and what their husbands can and cannot do to affect those vows. I have used male pronouns, but almost all those general instances can work for women as well. Many technical terms are used throughout the text. I have translated them at their first instance and often as well when they appear much later. In addition, I have included a glossary of the more fre-quently used terms as an appendix.

JF

Toronto, 2023

NOTE

1. His condemnation is repeated in tractate *Sotah* 15a.

Chapter 1

Definitions

What Is a Nazir?

So, there are three self-denying items that an ordinary *nazir* proclaims: no wine or grapevine products; no cutting his or her body hair; and no contact with the corpse of a human being. One must also make this declaration of *nezirut* verbally. It's not something that one can simply resolve quietly to oneself. Our first Mishna (pl. Mishnayot) explains the sundry ways one may effectively invoke such a vow. The usual way is merely to say out loud: "Henceforth I am a *nazir*." If one only goes so far as to say, "I am" or "I will be," that suffices for *nezirut*, as long as the intent of the vow is clear. One can even state: "I'll be handsome." Inasmuch as the implication is that long hair may be understood as better looking, the *nezirut* intention is, again, clear. What's more, one can use terms for *nazir* which the Mishna deems "equivalent," such as *nazik*, *naziach*, or *paziach*—and the vow is accepted. There are as well a number of other terms, several quite odd on the surface, that the Mishna lists (examined below) which similarly do the trick.

The Gemara, however, does not immediately address this issue—it will, but it has some more important business to deal with. It begins by asking why this tractate of the Talmud is found in a cluster (*seder*, or "order") entitled *Nashim* (Women), a *seder* which ordinarily deals with topics distinctly addressing women, e.g., marriage contracts, divorce, widowhood, and the like. To be sure, these issues also affect men, but in ancient Israel women had less agency and were perforce in unenviable circumstances (from our contemporary point of view) in many interpersonal situations. The Tanna, or sage from the Mishnaic period, explains (citing *Deuteronomy* 24.1) that what causes a woman to commit adultery, the primary cause for a husband to initiate divorce proceedings, is a consequence of his wife's imbibing wine. The horror that a husband visits upon his wife when he attempts to expose her

1

as a *sotah* (suspected adulteress), all vividly described in tractate *Sotah*, are considered sufficiently to make one swear off wine—that is, a vow of *nezirut*.

The Gemara then turns to what it dubs "equivalent" expressions, and it adds "partial" assertions, for *nazir*. Rava boldly declares that the Mishna is effectively defective and that such partial expressions effect *nezirut*. The Mishna first stated that incomplete declarations were the same as complete ones, and then it turned to equivalent expressions, but the Gemara treats them in reverse order. Why? Because the Tanna likes to address the items more immediate and work backward from there. Just announcing this approach is apparently not enough, as the Gemara then gives three examples from elsewhere in the Talmud (all, interestingly, from tractate *Shabbat*) to justify such an approach. The Gemara won't leave this alone, as it proceeds to cite not one, but two, Mishnayot in which an ordinary one-two order is employed. So, either these two examples are extraordinary, or they are evidence of Talmudic diversity of style. (Incidentally, I swear that this tractate concerns *nezirut*, but the Talmud often, very often, digresses.) The answer here is that there is no hard and fast way that the sage in question lays out an argument.

2b

Still, though, the Tanna's choice to start the Gemara with partial declarations needs an explanation. The Gemara claims that, in order that the Tanna may elucidate what is missing from the partial, he must locate an appropriate reference from a sacred text. Thus, this part of the analysis comes first because it is, to the Tanna's way of thinking, more novel. By contrast, "equivalent" terms require no elucidation in this context, because a "synonym" has been stated, albeit an often odd one. But, this just begs the question, as the Gemara now asks: If partials are so precious to the Tanna, why didn't he start the Mishna in the partial-equivalent order? Answer: The Mishna begins as it does because it wishes to start with the primary law, proceeding then to the consequent one; when it turns to explaining them, the Tanna begins with the novel (i.e., derived) law which is deemed "precious" to him.

We turn now to those partial declarations of a vow of *nezirut*. Merely saying "I am" or "I will be" only is the same as an affirmative declaration of *nezirut* if it is beyond a doubt that such is the speaker's intent. This is, needless to say, important, as being a *nazir* is no easy or meaningless state in which to be. Perhaps, suggests the Gemara, the speaker is about to declare that he will fast. Indeed, without a predicate to "I am" or "I will be," what makes it clear that *nezirut* is the intention? The sage Shmuel avers that such a partial expression means a declaration of *nezirut* when someone is walking before a *nazir*. This must have struck generations of readers as extremely vague. Was Shmuel a mind reader? Was anyone? Couldn't one just ask the speaker to complete the thought? In any event, the Gemara states that, if it isn't definitely clear, no *nezirut*.

So, the Gemara takes Shmuel's statement apart and examines the shades of meaning in a partial vow, acknowledging that there are inherent ambiguities therein. There are basically three sorts of partial declarations: (1) totally unclear and hence irrelevant; (2) unclear, yes, but leaning in one direction; and (3) clear. How does Shmuel know that someone walking before him fits (3), or even (2)? The Gemara doesn't mention the possibility that Shmuel and the passerby may have discussed the topic of becoming a *nazir*, and the latter is now declaring, effectively, "Yes, I will be" a *nazir*, something that would be immediately clear to Shmuel, but hardly cause for asserting a general rule. If one were later to explain that, indeed, he intended by their partial declaration to be a *nazir*, then (2) or even (3) kicks in. But, this is so obvious that the Gemara wonders why it should even be considered. His answer is fairly simple: Intent for *nezirut* must either be made explicitly or such that partiality is clearly indicated. "We need his mouth and his heart to coincide." This is important, for elsewhere in the Talmud (*Kiddushin* 50a) we learn, and it applies here, that "matters that remain in the heart" (and are not explicitly enunciated) carry no meaning whatsoever; as the popular song has: "Express yourself!"

Moving on to "equivalent" expressions, how does "I'll be handsome" constitute a vow of *nezirut*? It can be understood in a number of possible ways unrelated to becoming a *nazir*, and the Gemara lays out a few involving a vow to perform various commandments in a beautiful manner such as to beautify oneself before God. Shmuel declares that such a declaration of personal beauty must be performed as one holds one's hair, indicating that he intends to allow their locks to grow, one of the main requirements of *nezirut*. No holding of hair, no *nezirut*, even if one later explains that it was what one truly intended by "I'll be handsome." Unlike the previous example of a partial expression, "I'll be handsome" is a complete expression and thus requires no further linguistic explication. So, if one is not holding one's hair at the time of his declaration of purported handsomeness, it's meaningless. The physical act of grabbing one's own hair add to the cryptic declaration, effectively explaining how one shall become good (or better) looking.

As our first *daf*, or Talmudic folio, comes to a close, it raises an important issue that will be discussed next. Is a vow of *nezirut*, in fact, sinful, inasmuch as vowing to abstain from that which is permissible, and under certain circumstances required, such as drinking wine, would seem to constitute a sin?

3a

Similarly, if such a person as a *nazir* may be dubbed "handsome," because of his long hair, can that be sinful? The Gemara goes on to identify R. Elazar ha-Kappar as the sage who argued that *nezirut* is sinful, but that was only in reference to a *nazir* who became ritually impure (*tamei*). In the case of a *nazir*, this refers to one who comes into contact with a corpse which is forbidden to a *nazir*. A polluted *nazir* must endure a lengthy process of regaining purity and then starting his *nezirut* over—this will described later in the tractate. So, as far as R. Elazar ha-Kappar is concerning, the sin is not the act of declaring a vow of *nezirut*, but of violating the proscription on contact with a corpse. An ordinary vow is for thirty days, and violation necessitates a longer period because of the requirement to start again, meaning abstention from wine for longer than the original period of thirty days. To clarify, then, a *nazir* who remain ritually pure (*tahor*) is not, according to the good rabbi, considered a sinner—and he may be handsome as well. And, there is still the matter of not partaking of wine, which has not been fully treated as sinful or not.

One of the "equivalent" statements that the Mishna states is tantamount to declaring *nezirut* is: "I am forthwith like this." Even if he were to grab his hair at the same time, still he has articulated nothing about *nezirut*. How can he be a *nazir*? Shmuel, again, says this refers to a case in which the speaker made this statement as a *nazir* walked before him. Another "equivalent" phrase: "I am forthwith *mesalsel*." This Hebrew word refers, we are told in a highly suspect story, to curled hair. Even the Gemara questions this pointing of the word in question and suggests another rendition drawn actually from *Proverbs* (4.8), but Shmuel steps forward, as it were, with the same explanation about grabbing one's hair as one makes the vow, thus ensuring that the reference is to hair and thus to *nezirut*.

Another "equivalent": "I am forthwith a *mechalkel*." This term refers after a fashion to the quicklime used as a depilatory to get rid of one's hair from the Temple area. As in the previous cases, the Gemara offers a seemingly better reference for this term, this time from the Torah (*Genesis* 47.12), to refer to offer assistance to the poor. So, maybe this person is just vowing to provide aid to the indigent. Shmuel: No, for if he makes this statement as he holds his hair, it must be a vow of *nezirut*.

Another instance: "It is forthwith necessary for me to grow strands of hair." But, as above, before we jump to the automatic conclusion that this is a valid vow of *nezirut*, mightn't the object of the verb "grow" be something else, like fruit? In fact, our text cites a passage in *Song of Songs* (4.13) which likens a bride's growing her hair to pomegranates. But, this one is even more complicated, for the same verb can mean "send" (see *Job* 5.10), meaning in this case that water is taken from Heaven and sent to the fields. No grabbing of hair here. The Tanna in our Mishna, though, pointedly claimed that this term was "equivalent" to a vow of *nezirut*. Through a complex association with a verse from *Ezekiel* (44.20), we conclude that the term in question must mean to grow stands of one's hair. And, the meaning of "remove" or "send" taken also from *Job*, really means to grow—an explanation attributed to Rav Yosef, said to be an expert in the Aramaic translation of the Hebrew Bible. After all, watering fruit trees leads to the growth of fruit.

One last instance referred to as "odd" is a statement by R. Meir in the Mishna, that one is a *nazir* if one states: "It is forthwith necessary for me an obligation to birds." What can this possibly mean? And, in fact the sages immediately negate R. Meir's assertion. Reish Lakish claims that it is a reference to birds in the Bible (*Daniel* 4.30) comparing eagle feathers and one's grown out hair. R. Meir argues that as long as one's reference is to something close to what he intends, it is a valid vow.

3b

The rabbis (meaning the sages of the Mishna) don't buy it. Why the circumlocution? It requires more than an obvious associative step to make the link to *nezirut*. No way.

A frequent contributor to the discussion of the Talmud, R. Yochanan now emerges for the first time in our tractate to note that it goes without saying that people who make vows never refer in the utterance something closely related to what he is thinking. In short, he rejects Reish Lakish's view that this is the crux of the matter. No, what R. Meir meant by birds and obligation was that one of the obligations of a *nazir* who becomes *tamei* is to offer two birds as sacrifices. So, the mention of birds indicating a vow of *nezirut*, according to R. Yochanan, has nothing to do with hair, lovely or otherwise; it refers to the birds that must be sacrificed in such an unfortunate situation. Interesting, but the Gemara now suggests that this explanation may not be definitive, for this allusive reference to birds might just mean that the vower plans to offer a voluntary bird sacrifice (two turtledoves or young pigeons)—nothing to do with *nezirut*. Remember that dubious vows to become a *nazir* don't cut it. But, if the vower simply meant that he planned to make a voluntary offering, there's a verbal formula, and it doesn't match R. Meir's language at all.

Again, the Gemara suggests that we have a case of a *nazir* walking before someone as the latter said the words as formulated by R. Meir. Maybe those words were not a vow of *nezirut* but merely offering to supply the birds for the *nazir* who happened to be *tamei*. But, the Gemara is clear that the *nazir* in this situation was definitely *tahor*.

Trying to get at the crux of the matter, the Gemara offers a hypothetical case, not mentioned by the Mishna, of someone vowing: "I am obliged regarding birds [in conjunction with] hair." R. Yochanan claims that, if someone makes such a vow while walking before a *nazir*, he will indeed be a *nazir*. If no *nazir* happens to be within earshot, then the vow is meaningless. Reish Lakish, on the other hand, is fine with the absence of a bona fide *nazir* nearby—such a statement in his view distinctly associates birds with hair and thus *nezirut*. Yet, let us not forget that this is not the statement made in the Mishna.

Plumbing the depths, the Gemara turns to the question of whether or not reference in a vow to something proximate to what the vower is thinking is required. The Gemara looks to other oblique ways in which an oath or vow might be indicated without explicitly stating what the speaker has in mind. It only considers one such expression: "Right hand." How might saying this followed by whatever one wishes to declare be the proper language for a vow? In answering, the Gemara invokes for the first time in our tractate a *baraita* (an oral law not codified in the Mishna but with the authority of a Tanna; pl. *baraitot*) which says as much, and the Gemara follows up with a citation from scripture (*Daniel* 12.7) linking raising the right hand with swearing by God (a gesture still very much in use to this day). This isn't enough for the Gemara, as it avers that *association* of "right hand" with "swearing" an oath is not the issue; it is the simple fact that "right hand" *is* itself the central term here, and another *baraita* directs us to *Isaiah* (62.8) which mentions God swearing, figuratively to be sure, by His "right hand."

Our text next turns to a new Mishna. What if a person declares forthwith that he is to be a *nazir* with respect to one of the items he is obligated to avoid—grape products, cutting of the hair, or contracting *tumah* from a corpse? Is said person a bona fide *nazir* with all the obligations intact, even though he has only mentioned one of them. Yes, claims the Mishna, he must abide by all the terms of *nezirut*.

The Gemara begins by immediately noting that this Mishna contradicts the view of R. Shimon who argues that a *nezirut* vow must involve abstention from all the prohibitions associated with the vow. In other words, if someone simply stated that he would henceforth be a *nazir*, that would suffice, but by singling out only one of the requirements of *nezirut*, the vow does not cut it. Should the vower mention all three of the items to be avoided, then, to be sure, that would suffice. The rabbis (as a general term comparable to "the sages") reiterate the statement of the Mishna that invoking a single proscription is adequate.

This dispute requires some more investigation, starting by finding the source for R. Shimon's assertion. It points to *Numbers* (6.4) which begins by forbidding "anything" to do with "the grapevine" and then specifying that this means from grape seeds to the grape skin. The Talmud can never abide a redundancy as just that—there has to be a meaning, for nothing is "unnecessary" in scripture. Here, R. Shimon would be indicating that it is an all-or-none prohibition, and he then effectively generalized this to the entire tripartite set of prohibitions that a *nazir* vows to assume. The rabbis point to *Numbers* (6.3), one verse before the one used by R. Shimon, which states that abstention from wine is sufficient for a bona fide vow of *nezirut*. R. Shimon's response is that that verse (6.3) is a reference to wine imbibed as a *mitzvah* (a commandment), from which a *nazir* must abstain just as he must from ordinary wine.

What, asks the Gemara is *mitzvah* wine? Is it the wine one drinks when blessing the onset of the Sabbath on Friday evening (Kiddush), or perhaps the wine blessing at the very end of the Sabbath (Havdalah)?

4a

No, nothing so far scripturally based. The expression "*mitzvah* wine" refers to a term used by Rava; namely, one who takes an oath to drink wine and follows by saying that he will be a *nazir*. May he still drink wine despite the subsequent vow? No, the vow of *nezirut* trumps the previous oath. The wine is out for the period of the vow of *nezirut*. The rabbis would not disagree that the *mitzvah* wine is out. The problem here is that the verse in question refers to "new wine and aged wine." Why would scripture say this and not just "wine?" Why is the latter half of this expression included in the verse?

R. Shimon explains that the term used, here translated as "aged wine" (*shechar*), allows us to compare it with the same term used elsewhere in scripture (*Leviticus* 10.9) where it is again combined with wine as obligatorily forbidden drinks for a Kohen entering the Temple. In the latter appearance, the term *shechar* might mean a strong or intoxicating alcoholic drink. (Observant readers may see the familiar Yiddish derivative term here, *shiker* 'drunk.') By associating the two appearances of this term in scripture, the Gemara claims that *shechar* must be referring to wine—not other drinks; this is admittedly a little confusing, as is often the case with this hermeneutical principle of the Talmud known as *gezera shava*. By bringing into relation the same or similar terms in scripture, the rabbis of the Talmud used them to help understand their relative meanings in their respective contexts.

There may be a problem here, for R. Yehuda doesn't accept that *shechar* is limited to wine. He sees it as anything potentially intoxicating, referencing figs from a certain region as well as honey (meaning mead in this context) or milk, which stretches the definition of *shechar* to include clouding the mind.

So, the Gemara takes another tack to explain R. Shimon, but let's move on to how the rabbis deal with his source.

R. Shimon started with *Numbers* 6.4 and explained that this involved a redundancy (see above). What do the rabbis make of this? They offer the frankly odd, but not unusual, explanation that the added phrase about grade seeds and grape skin is a warning against mixing small amounts of these two to constitute the minimum amount (an olive's volume) of grape produce punishable with lashes. That would render 6.4 not redundant but clarifying. R. Shimon doesn't buy this at all, for as far as he is concerned, there is no minimum amount of a proscribed food; any amount consumed is punishable. He knows of the olive-volume rule about consuming proscribed foods, but for a complex reason, he claims it has no bearing on *nezirut*.

Interestingly, this dispute is left unresolved, and no *halacha* (legal ruling derived from the Mishna) is averred. We move directly to a new Mishna and a new topic.

Suppose one were to state: "I am forthwith like Samson, like Manoach's son, like Delilah's husband, like he who tore off the gates of Gaza, like [the man] who had his eyes gouged out by the Philistines." Does invoking a personal parallel to this story of the most famous *nazir* in Jewish history constitute a bona fide vow of the special *nezirut* like Samson? Yes, concludes this Mishna, it does.

Why, asks the Gemara right off the bat, must the vower state all these specifics; isn't it enough just to "I am forthwith like Samson?" No, it answers what must have been a rhetorical question, for if one said only that he was "like Samson," it could mean that one was referring to some other person named Samson who has not assumed *nezirut*. Therefore, the Mishna added "like Manoach's son," but again this might be referring to another person named Samson who just happened to have a father named Manoach. Hence, the Mishna required more specificity, such as "like Delilah's husband" or "like [the man] who had his eyes gouged out." Presumably one of these latter two biographical details would clear up any possible indeterminacy regarding the identity of the figure whose name is being invoked.

The text turns to another Mishna at this point, but we're far from done with Samson and the distinctiveness of the *nezirut* he vowed (actually that was vowed by his parents before his birth). It begins with a question of how a Samsonian *nazir* differs from a "permanent *nazir*." (Remember that an ordinary vow of *nezirut* is for thirty days.) One who vows to become a permanent *nazir* (as in Samson's case) may, presuming relative youth, that their hair will continue to grow and grow, but a permanent *nazir* is allowed to "lighten" it only with a razor—this refers solely to head hair, not one's beard. If he becomes *tamei*, the required sacrifice is exactly the same as it is for an ordinary *nazir*. Additionally, he must offer three animal sacrifices at the time he trims his hair. By contrast, a Samson-like *nazir* does not have this option, and inasmuch as this commitment is also perpetual, such a *nazir* is likely to accrue quite a mop. Also, he is not required to bring sacrifices in the eventuality of contracting *tumah*.

The Gemara begins effectively: Who wants to know? Who asked about the permanent *nazir*? The answer is to address the fact that the Mishna is apparently missing something. It should have started, as did previous Mishnayot, by pointing out that the statement "I am forthwith a permanent *nazir*" is sufficient to assume such a status. It goes on to clarify the ways in which a permanent *nazir* differs from a Samsonian one, just like the Mishna had it.

4b

The Gemara homes in on the last part of the Mishna, that a Samsonian *nazir* need not bring a sacrifice if he acquires *tumah*. But, is such a *nazir* allowed to become *tamei* from a corpse? The Mishna did not explicitly permit *tumah*, just that if a Samson-like *nazir* did happen to become *tamei*, he needn't bring the sacrifice incumbent on a regular *nazir*. Now, according to a *baraita*, R. Yehuda argues that a Samsonian *nazir* may contract *tumah*, whereas the Mishna implies that, by stating no need to bring a sacrifice in the eventuality of contracting *tumah*, it is forbidden (even if not explicitly) from becoming *tamei*. Meanwhile, R. Shimon argues that anyone who proclaims that he is a Samson-like *nazir* has effectively said nothing, because such a declaration can only be divinely inspired. Actually, it turns out that the Mishna in fact follows the ruling of R. Yehuda. The similarity of wording between permanent *nazir* and *tumah* and between Samsonian *nazir* and *tumah* is, the Gemara states in resolution of this quandary, just for linguistic parallelism, because a permanent *nazir* is indeed prohibited from contracting *tumah* unlike a Samsonian *nazir*.

If all this was not complicated enough, the Gemara suggests we might understand the difference of opinion between R. Yehuda and R. Shimon by analogy with another difference of opinion. Should someone take a vow to the effect that a given loaf of bread was for him like a *bechor* (a male first-born kosher animal with innate sacrificial sanctity such that it may only be offered in the Temple), R. Yaakov prohibits the bread in question and R. Yose allows it. On the surface the parallel nature of the two disputes remains to be elucidated.

R. Yehuda accepts a vow of Samsonian *nezirut* much like R. Yaakov accepts a vow based on comparison with a *bechor*. Meanwhile, R. Shimon's claim that personal avowal of a Samson-like *nezirut* is meaningless is similar to R. Yose's requirement that forbidding oneself to something must be explicitly that which a human being can declare, meaning not something divinely sanctioned. After this propositional circumlocution, Gemara dispenses with the argument without a second thought. As an aside, the Talmud often raises, indeed frequently, lines of argumentation only to dismiss them unceremoniously. Why, one might ask, is the argument is to be deemed faulty or bogus? It would seem that it may be doing this for several reasons, of which two follow. Perhaps it is a way to cut off any suggestion that the Gemara thinks may raise its figurative head on the horizon before it gets too far. A second reason is altogether different: perhaps when the Talmud was being compiled and edited, the rabbis involved may have felt that, while certain arguments may not make the ultimate grade, they are worthy of being published for educative or even suggestive purposes. Stay tuned.

And the rabbit hole goes deeper, as the rabbis in question continue to mine this point. At one stage, it recites a lengthy *baraita* of the great Shimon ha-Tzaddik (Shimon the Righteous, see *Avot* 1.2), chief priest early in the period of the Second Temple. He tells of a *nazir* who was handsome to the nth degree and had grown beautiful hair to boot. When Shimon sees his young lad, he asks why he would shave his head; presumably he knew that a *nazir* is required to do so at the end of his period of *nezirut*, so this is probably a question as to why he chose to become a *nazir* in the first place. The young *nazir* explains that he saw his reflection in some pooled water and recognized his own beauty, and he felt his evil inclination trying to get him to use his good looks for insidious ends; he thus immediately swore a vow of *nezirut*.

What proof is there, à la R. Yehuda, that Samson himself actually acquired corpse *tumah*? Well, there's *Judges* 15.16 wherein Samson claims to have killed 1000 men with a donkey's jaw, but this is quickly rebutted, as Samson could just as well have performed the same phenomenal act by throwing the jaw at the Philistines. How about *Judges* 14.19, wherein Samson killed thirty men, then seized their clothing, and presumably touched the corpses as he did so? No, again, as he could have taken their clothing first and then put them to death. This rebuttal is deemed ridiculous, because of the order of the verses in *Judges*: he first killed them and next took their garments. A rather far-fetched second rebuttal: he brought them to the point of death, then stripped them, and then they died—hence, no corpse *tumah*. The Gemara has apparently had enough of this and just insists that it is an oral teaching conveyed mouth-to-mouth over the generations, and so ends this disputation. Conclusion: Samson was allowed to contract *tumah* of the dead.

The Gemara now turns to the permanent *nazir*. Remember that a permanent *nazir* is allowed to use a razor to trim his hair. How do we know this? We have a *baraita* here which might help. R. Yehuda ha-Nasi (Rabbi Judah the Prince, 135–200), the redactor of the Mishna, claims that Avshalom, King David's (in)famous son, was such a permanent *nazir*. He cites as a prooftext *II Samuel* 15.7 where Avshalom asks the king if he might go to the city of Hebron and "pay" his vow, which the Gemara believes is a vow of *nezirut*. Also, Avshalom only cut his hair annually, as allowed of such a *nazir*.

5a

Actually, the text here concerning his periodical hair-cutting notes that he did this every twelve months, and several verses later (*II Samuel* 14.26) it states that this took place at the "end of every year." The term used for "every year" (*yamim layamim*) leads R. Yehuda ha-Nasi to conclude that "*yamim*" implies "twelve months." Other rabbis state differing periods of time between Avshalom's grooming experiences and suggest that perhaps the son of a king had a different set of rules than ordinary folk. The Gemara also proposes that even R. Yehuda ha-Nasi may have meant not twelve months but as short as two days between trimming his hair. This can't possibly be, though, because Avshalom's need to cut his hair was due to its growth and thus its "weight." OK, then, two days borders on the ridiculous in this context, but the Gemara next suggests two years and invokes *Genesis* 41.1, wherein *yamim* appears to be used in that sense. Here an extremely interesting reason is raised to rule out this verse's reference to *yamim* and hence to its definition as "two years": All the other scriptural citations mentioning *yamim* make no simultaneous reference to *shanim* (the transparent Hebrew word for "years"), but the *Genesis* verse juxtaposes the two terms. This elimination leaves *Leviticus* 25.29 where *yamim* is by itself and would seem to mean twelve months.

This is followed by a similar effort to associate *yamim* with a thirty-day period (see *Numbers* 11.20), initially suggested by R. Nehorai, but as above the word *yamim* is juxtaposed in this verse with the word *chadashim* (months), and it is thus ruled out. In *Judges* (11.40), *yamim* appears to be used to mean a three-month period. And, once again, this objection is overruled, because here the expression (*yamim yamima*) does not find *yamim* all alone and thus cannot be used to parallel the case of Avshalom.

At this point, the Gemara essentially says: Give me a break! Many a far less clear *gezera shava* have been invoked to prove a point, so what's up here? That is, ideally, the two words or expressions need not be exactly the same to make this sort of verbal comparison, and here we have at least one case (*yamim* and *yamim yamima*) where the terms are considered effectively identical. Nu? We're not done here.

The Gemara returns to R. Nehorai's clear assertion that Avshalom trimmed his locks every thirty days and asks how he came up with this figure. There is a rule that the Kohanim were required to cut their hair once every thirty days, because they perform the Temple service and must be neatly coiffed at all times out of respect. Trimming is physically required because of the weight of their growing hair—just like Avshalom experienced. Although we did not note it above, R. Yose threw in that Avshalom cut his hair every Friday, thus weekly. Neither of these statements are debated, let alone refuted, here—just mentioned again, this time without explanations.

The Talmud moves on to a new Mishna, an extremely short one (only four words, one of them a single-letter acronym). It tells us that a regular or standard *nezirut* lasts for thirty days. To the extent that our text is well organized, a major assumption, we are basically still in a definitional phase here. The Gemara begins with a usual question: How do we know that this assertion has merit? Rav Matna (or Matana, Mattena, Mattana—different pointings of his name) avers that it's right there in scripture, *Numbers* 6.5. The phrase to which he points means: "It will be holy" (*kadosh yiheye*). What, you might justifiably ask, does that have to do with anything here? The numerical (actually, numerological) value of "it will be" (*yiheye*) is thirty; namely, *yiheye* is comprised of *yud* and *heh* each two times, so with *yud* being 10, and *heh* 5 = 30. QED. This is the first instance in our tractate of the use of what is known as *gematria* or the assignment of numerical values to each of the letters of the Jewish alphabet, a practice used for dating and many other scientific purposes as well as numerological ones. The brief phrase cited from *Numbers* refers to the hair of a *nazir*.

Next up, Bar Padda notes that in the sixth chapter of *Numbers*, the portion of the Torah concerning *nezirut*, there are thirty minus one (29) occurrences of the words rooted in *nezirut* (and never *neder* or vow). How twenty-nine can actually imply thirty will be explained below, but again this is not based on a direct statement that regular *nezirut* is for thirty days—it's a scriptural inference Bar Padda makes. The Gemara seems to like Bar Padda's analysis, as it immediately asserts that Rav Matna ought to learn from it, implicitly downgrading gematria. The latter does not take this lying down. While not decrying Bar Padda's approach, he nonetheless asserts that some of the twenty-nine incidences he counted need to be utilized for other clarifications (and implicitly should not be wasted here).

5b

Shouldn't Bar Padda have been worried about using some of these instances elsewhere? He would retort that surely not all these uses are needed elsewhere, and even just one could be employed for this purpose—I frankly have to admit confusion by this response, but presumably, if there is one such term that is free for inference, then all the others may be mustered for the larger point.

The Gemara now turns the table and suggests that Bar Padda's explanation may not hold water, just as it did just above regarding Rav Matna. After all, you don't have to be a mathematician to know that twenty-nine is not thirty, so how would his thesis be meaningful as an explanation for the *nezirut* requirement of *thirty* days? Bar Padda's response is a little light. Yes, he would aver, twenty-nine days of all the requisite abstentions, and on the thirtieth day the *nazir* cut his facial and head hair and brings the requisite sacrifices. Until the sacrifices arrive at the Temple on day thirty, a *nazir* is still a *nazir*. Waiting in the wings, however, there is another objection to Bar Padda's reasoning. As we shall see in a later Mishna, one who vows to become a *nazir* in fact shaves (and carries out the necessary sacrifices) not on the thirtieth day but on the thirty-first (see 16a below). Rav Matna laid it out that a regular *nazir* fulfills a full thirty-day period of *nezirut*, and only then may he carry out the various final rites. Take that, Bar Padda.

Actually, we are far from over with this Talmudic *pas de deux*. That Mishna we shall confront in eleven *dapim* begins by stating that, if someone went ahead and shaved on day thirty, he's cool, but if he declared himself a regular thirty-day *nazir*, shaving on day thirty is not a fulfillment of his duties. Bar Padda would cite only the first part of this Mishna, and he would assert that carrying through as a *nazir* for a full thirty days and only shaving, etc. on day thirty-one is a rabbinical sanction, not the law itself.

Where does that leave Rav Matna? How would he deal with the first part of the Mishna invoked by Bar Padda, stating that shaving on day thirty (may not be preferable but it) is sufficient. Rav Matna would offer something that looks vaguely like a compromise. He suggests that the *nazir* would surely spend at least some part of day thirty observing all the requirements of a *nazir*, and if he proceeds at that point to shave, etc., then why not accept that he has discharged his concluding obligations? He still thinks that rabbinical law requires these concluding actions on day thirty-one, but starting them on day thirty works within scriptural prescriptions. That same Mishna, though, as we have noted above, states that one who vows explicitly to be a *nazir* for thirty days may not shave on day thirty. So, that would seem to indicate Rav Matna's vague compromise solution of "part of a day is like the whole day" simply won't work. The Gemara now tells us that Rav Matna really meant that a self-declared *nazir* who vows thirty days must actually do so for thirty full days.

In its subsequent clause, that same Mishna will go on to claim that, if someone were to vow back-to-back terms of *nezirut*, he must shave for the first thirty-day term on the thirty-first day and for the second term on the sixty-first day. This works fine for Rav Matna: shaving and the requisite observances on day thirty-one and similarly on day sixty-one.

6a

This might just put Bar Padda in a quandary, as he argues for a twenty-nine-day regular *nezirut* period (followed by shaving and sacrifices). You may think the Gemara already (just above) handled this issue, but the Gemara apparently likes to deal with each confrontation individually before summing up. And, indeed, Bar Padda can resort to the second clause of the Mishna in question and say that the *nazir* can shave on day thirty and again on day sixty. The "resolution" does look very familiar.

In explaining Rav Matna's take on the counting of days, the Gemara now seeks to delineate the basis for his counting day thirty as also day one of a second period of *nezirut*. This takes us right back (see just above on 5b) to the equivalence asserted that a partial day can count as a whole day. Why is this being asked a second time? Rarely are questions posed in the Gemara this way without a ready answer. The answer is to suggest that, without the specific case of back-to-back period of *nezirut*, one might be led to believe that the ruling on 5b only refers to single periods of *nezirut*, whereas now we are speaking of this different sort of case in which a second period of *nezirut* begins immediately on the heels of the first. What we learn now is that day thirty of period one counts also as day one of period two.

The Gemara now, once again, insists on citing a Mishna on 16a which states that, if a *nazir* who is undertaking a double period of *nezirut* shaved on day sixty-minus-one (i.e., day fifty-nine), his duty in that regard has been fulfilled: the first period ended on day thirty, and the second period on day fifty-nine (which is day thirty of the second cycle). Again, it would appear as though the reckoning here makes day thirty of period one the same as day one of period of two. This works for Rav Matna, but the Gemara is curious as to why Bar Padda needs it all. Bar Padda has no trouble with this Mishna whatsoever, effectively claiming it as buttressing his view of a twenty-nine-day *nezirut* period.

Again, jumping ahead ten *dapim*, the Gemara cites that same Mishna—one can only wonder what will be left to discuss when we get there (not to worry, there's plenty there). If someone declares that, forthwith, he is a *nazir* and then becomes *tamei* on the thirtieth day of his cycle, all is lost; he has to go through the ritual purification processes and then, perforce, start all over again. This presents no trouble for Rav Matna, but what about Bar

Padda? He argued for a twenty-nine-day period of *nezirut*, making day thirty post-*nezirut*.

6b

Bar Padda falls back on another phrase from this same Mishna, namely R. Eliezer's statement that a *nazir* who becomes *tamei* on day thirty will only lose seven days, the number of days required to go through purification of one rendered impure by corpse *tumah*. What is Rav Matna to do with R. Eliezer's seven-day ruling in this Mishna? Well, inasmuch as they both believe that part of a day suffices for counting as a whole day, the *nazir* would have concluded his *nezirut* on day thirty, then become *tamei* later that same day, proceed with his seven-day ritual purification, and only then perform the last rituals of *nezirut*.

We are not quite done with the forthcoming Mishna, as it also avers that, if someone were to state that he was forthwith a *nazir* for 100 days and became *tamei* on day 100, all is lost—meaning that the *tumah* has been contracted within the time frame of the period of *nezirut* and cancels out the entire ninety-nine-plus days preceding; he must become *tahor* and start all over. R. Eliezer, as we shall see in roughly one and one-half weeks, following the *dafyomi* cycle, argues that he only loses thirty days. If, as Rav Matna did above, one presumes that R. Eliezer believes that a partial day is equivalent to a whole one, then our poor *nazir* should only have to forfeit seven days as above. In other words, where does R. Eliezer come up with thirty days in this instance? In fact, if the assumption of Rav Matna about the partial-day business being part of R. Eliezer's reasoning turns out to be incorrect, then wouldn't the latter have to conclude that the entire period of 100 days was lost? No, the Gemara states clearly, R. Eliezer did not buy into the partial-day equivalence thesis. Enter at this point Reish Lakish to defend the thirty-day loss idea. A close reasoning of *Numbers* 6.13 states: "And this is the teaching for the nazirite: When the days of his naziritehood come to term."[1] In other words, in R. Eliezer's view, no matter how long one vows to be a *nazir*, the loss for becoming *tamei* on the final day of that vowed period is the same as for a regular *nazir*: thirty days. So, 100 days or 1000 days, should one fall victim to *tumah* on the last day of his cycle, he goes through the seven-day purification, and repeats thirty days as a *nazir*.

We're nearing conclusion of the lengthy debate, and the Gemara begins to make what seem to be summary thoughts. It asks if perhaps this debate is not unlike that of a *baraita* which cites the *Numbers* requirement that a *nazir* not shave or cut his hair for all the days of his *nezirut*. Then, it reiterates that those days are thirty based on the numerological value of the term *yiheye* ("it will be"), as explained on 5a. This side of the discussion is attributed in the *baraita* to R. Yoshiya. R. Yonatan responds that we don't need this exposition, because scripture's statement of "until the completion" of the period of *nezirut* surely refers to a period of one month (either twenty-nine or thirty days). How is this in any way parallel to the debate above? The Gemara suggests that Rav Matna and R. Yoshiya both support thirty days as a regular *nezirut* period (*yiheye*), while Bar Padda and R. Yonatan go for twenty-nine, with R. Yonatan apparently stressing "until" day thirty but including it.

No, it doesn't really work, states the Gemara at this point, because Rav Matna could simply point out that even R. Yonatan would opine that a full period of *nezirut* requires a full thirty days. The debate between R. Yonatan and R. Yoshiya concerning the word "until": the former would say it means "until and including," while the latter would say "until but not including." Either way, it's still thirty days.

Every "i" must be dotted and every "t" crossed before we're done, so R. Yonatan's suspect assertion that "completion" refers to a month is now questioned. Where did he come up with the idea of a month here? Why not say that "completion" refers to Shabbat as the completion of a week?

7a

Or, for that matter, why not a year? Perhaps one senses exhaustion at this point in the extensive discussion of the length of a regular *nazir*. Be forewarned, however, that we have only just begun this tractate, barely through one-tenth of it, and the Mishna on which the discussion was based was only four words long.

Time now for a new Mishna, only a bit longer this time but still in the realm of definitions. Should someone vow forthwith a *nezirut* period of an (unstated) lengthy period, or should he do the same for an (unstated) short term, or even (*afilu*) if he should vow the bold *nezirut* period of "until the end of the world" (*ad sof haolam*), in each of such unusual cases, he is a *nazir* for thirty days.

The Gemara starts, as it often does, with the last (most proximate) of these three vows to explain how "until the end of the world" (implying until the end of one's life) in effect equals only thirty days. Such a vow is, of course, by definition undefined. Perhaps he is vowing permanent *nezirut* (see 4a above), or maybe this is just a way of equating a regular period of *nezirut* with what may seem like a lifetime. In a Mishna on the next *daf*, we learn that if someone were to vow that he forthwith was a *nazir* from the geographic point of the declaration until a certain place, one then determines how long it will take to make one's way to that place; if less than thirty days, his period of *nezirut* is thirty days, because no *nezirut* can be less, and if more than thirty days, he will be a *nazir* for that number of days. So, such vows cannot be less than thirty days but the sky's the limit beyond thirty.

Mightn't we say that a *nezirut* declaration such as "from here to a certain place" is simply a way of saying that it's really very far, perhaps exhaustingly so—much like the way in which the Mishna dealt with the *ad sof haolam*—and that we might just conclude that this is to be a *nezirut* of thirty days. Rava steps in and claims that this sort of vow refers to one who has begun his trip to that certain place, meaning his vow was meant literally. If he was not traveling at the time of the vow, then, sure, this would lead to a regular thirty-day *nezirut*, irrespective of the length of the journey.

What would be the case, asks the Gemara, if someone made a vow such as this one and set off—should there not be a period of *nezirut* for every equal segment (the Gemara uses the measurement of a *parsa*, or 8000 cubits), each such segment requiring another thirty-day *nezirut*? Rav Pappa dispenses with this pronto, though honestly his rebuttal is as vague as the suggested interpretation: The Mishna was referring to a place where they don't use the measurement of *parsaot*. Fortunately, it doesn't pursue this line any further, but it does then ask if there should be independent periods of *nezirut* for every night's accommodation enroute to that certain place, presuming that they equal the number of days involved in the trip.

This would seem to accord with the coming Mishna where we learn that, if one were to say that forthwith he is a *nazir* for as long as the specks of dust on the earth, or as many as the hairs on his head (let us assume a non-bald vower), or as many as the grains of sand of the sea, now we have someone who has effectively vowed perpetual *nezirut*, someone who shaves once every thirty days (unlike the "permanent *nazir*" on the model of Avshalom who cut his hair once every year). Every speck of dust, every hair, every grain of sand would thus engender its own thirty-day period of *nezirut*. Can this be the case? The Gemara offers a principle here that, if something is countable, it cannot produce a series of terms of *nezirut*; because we can count the number of days required to travel to a specified place, no generation of periods of *nezirut* ensue.

A couple more definitional terms follow. If one vows forthwith to be a *nazir* for all the days left in his life or if he vows to be a permanent (not a perpetual) *nazir*, in both cases he has signed up as a *nazir* for the long haul. If, however, one makes fairly or completely outrageous vows of *nezirut* for 100 or 1000 years, then he has signed up for *nezirut* for the rest of his days, but unlike a permanent or perpetual *nazir*, he may never cut his hair. Although 100 or 1000 years are certainly longer than anyone will live, the numbers are specified, unlike the previous example of hair, sand, or dust—and hence the different forms *nezirut* takes.

More debate ensues, but Rava asks (ironically? sarcastically?): "Why are you bringing up all these issues?" (Why do you ask so many questions?) The answer, he avers, is simple, and so ends the Gemara here, but the Mishna being discussed will return to center stage on the next *daf.*

The Talmud now, though, is ready for another Mishna. Three very unusual vows, at least on the surface, are raised: I shall forthwith be a *nazir* and a single day; ditto and one hour, and ditto for one and one-half. In all three cases, he has effectively vowed two periods of *nezirut*. All three of these expressions begin with "I shall forthwith be a *nazir,*" and that constitutes one period of *nezirut*. The add-on of "and a single day" is taken to mean a vow of a second term. As we have seen above, there are no one-day periods of *nezirut*—in fact, none shorter than thirty days—meaning this must be a full thirty-day term. Altogether, this means two thirty-day periods. The other odd expressions come down to the same conclusion.

The Gemara begins by asking, if these all end up meaning the same thing, why mention them all, especially inasmuch as they are so similar. This is the sort of question one encounters in the Talmud frequently. There has to be a reason, of course, and the answer comes immediately. The standard measurement for periods of *nezirut* is days, thirty of them; thus, when one adds to a regular vow "and one day," we know that a one-day period is meaningless as such, there being no such thing, and thus must mean another thirty-day term. However, "and one hour" is different, for hours are not divisions used in measuring *nezirut*; thus, an hour, being a fraction of a day, could lead one to think that the vower is saying that he is forthwith a *nazir* for thirty days and a fraction of a day, which might be interpreted to mean a vow of thirty-one days. So, our Mishna enlightens us that, no, it's in fact a vow of two full periods of *nezirut*.

7b

Just to finish this Gemara off, should someone vow a term of a single hour, that imprecision must mean *nezirut* for a regular, full period (thirty days). What could a vower have meant by "one and one-half?" It would seem to accurately denote a period of forty-five days, but inasmuch as there is no such thing, the Gemara clarifies that it in fact means two consecutive periods. In sum, then, all of the three add-ons to declaring oneself a *nazir* obligate one to take on a second period, and essentially for the same reason that a regular *nezirut* period, the term that defines one's commitment when he says that forthwith he will be a *nazir*, is thirty days (and no less).

We come now to a new Mishna, still in the definitional mode. If one explicitly declares that he is forthwith a *nazir* for "thirty days and one hour," then he is in fact a *nazir* for thirty-one days. Why? You can't extend *nezirut* by hours. But, but, didn't we just deal with this? Close, but not exactly the same, as the previous Mishna spoke of adopting *nezirut* "and one hour"; that is, it was not as precise as the present text. By stating unambiguously that he will be a *nazir* for thirty days and an hour, we translate the "one hour" into a meaningful *nezirut* unity, one day, and come up with thirty-one days. The Mishna on 7a did not state the number of days to which the vower committed, even though the regular *nezirut* is for thirty days; he declared to be a *nazir* and a fraction of a *nazir*, and that had to mean two periods of *nezirut*.

Our Mishna now states clearly that the declaration equals a thirty-one-day period of *nezirut*. Rav argues that the Mishna means to say that one is obligated for a thirty-one-day term only if one declares outright a vow of thirty-one days. If one, however, vows thirty days and one day, Rav asserts that this must be interpreted to mean two periods of *nezirut*. By dividing the two assertions in this way, the vower must have meant two separate vows of *nezirut*, at least in Rav's reasoning. The Gemara does a sort of digression here to indicate that Rav is following the great R. Akiva who explained the importance of apparently redundant language. No words are to be ignored, as the implicit message appears to be: please be forewarned, or think before you speak.

8a

We now come to the final Mishna in chapter 1 of our tractate, and it's a meaty one. It's also the same Mishna which the rabbis could not wait earlier to dig into. There may thus appear to be some repetition, but always remember that no words are lost on the rabbis. It begins with the theoretical vows of *nezirut* for as much as one's hair, dust of the earth, or sand grains. As we noted earlier, such a vow is equivalent to declaring oneself a perpetual *nazir*, one who shaves (and carries out the requisite sacrifices, though this is not explicitly mentioned in the text) every thirty days till the end of his days. R. Yehuda ha-Nasi disagrees and claims one such may not shave every thirty days and that his declaration is permanent. Who would R. Yehuda ha-Nasi state is a thirty-day *nazir* over and over again? Answer: One who explicitly vows multiple periods as a *nazir*, multiple as the number of hairs on his head, etc.

The Mishna goes on with some fresh hypothetical vows and their meanings. Should someone vow forthwith to be a *nazir* to the extent of filling a house or a pail, even the Mishna needs clarity, and we investigate what he means by such a strange declaration that lacks the precise items that would fill a house or pail. True, the number of grains of sand or specks of dust approaches infinity, but at least we know that the vow is in relation to a number, albeit a rather large one. These new vows are too obscure to proceed without clarification. If the vower responds that he meant just a really big period of *nezirut*, or that one of thirty days seems really long, then he is a *nazir* for thirty days, a regular term. If, however, he replies that he meant an indeterminate period, one about which he had no defined intention, then the Mishna offers the interesting explanation that we are to assume his pail was filled with mustard seeds, meaning his will be a *nazir* till the bitter end, a perpetual *nazir*.

The last portion of this Mishna picks up a discussion referred to earlier, the vow to forthwith become a *nazir* from here to a certain place. The text says explicitly that we ascertain the number of days needed to journey to said place; if fewer than thirty days, thirty is the length of his *nezirut*, and if more than thirty days, his *nezirut* lasts that number of days. Should a vower declare a period of *nezirut* equal to the number of days in a solar year. The specifying term "number" indicates that we read this as 365 repeating periods of regular *nezirut*, or roughly thirty years. Had he merely vowed to be a *nazir* for as much as the days of a solar year, then we would assess this to mean one period of 365 days. Be careful what you wish for (or vow). R. Yehuda is quoted at the end of the Mishna to confirm, in a way, that thirty years of *nezirut* is an awfully long time; he mentions the case of a person who made such a vow, finished his extremely lengthy period, and then died.

Inasmuch as the Gemara has already dealt with roughly half of the points raised in this Mishna, it will be interesting to see what it chooses to concentrate on now. It starts with the quandary of the declaration of *nezirut* concerning what it would take to fill a pail, and the clarification that it means the number of mustard seeds it would take, presumably a huge number. The Gemara questions the assertion of mustard seeds and asks why (the much larger seeds of) melons or gourds are not the items used as a measurement. That solution would probably enable the vower to escape a lifelong commitment to the *nazir*'s abstentions. Obviously, far fewer melon or gourd seeds would fit in a pail, even a big pail, let alone a house; if the number was fewer than thirty such items, then the period of *nezirut* would be thirty days; if more, then it would be equal to the number of days required of *nezirut*.

Chizkiya (Hezekiah) claims that the Mishna is disputed and that it effectively indicates the point of view of R. Shimon. R. Shimon argues that declarations which involve lack of certainty must be ruled upon stringently. The example offered is someone who vows to be a *nazir* if the pile in front of him is comprised of 100 *kors* (one *kor* equals thirty *se'a* or a volume of

144 medium-sized eggs, roughly nine quarts) of some produce. If he then went back to measure it and found the stack of produce missing, hence unmeasurable, and thus indeterminate, R. Shimon states that this person must abstain from all the proscriptions placed on a *nazir*. To explain further, had they been able to measure the pile, and it came to 100 *kors*, then the vower would commence a thirty-day period of *nezirut*, but because of the indeterminacy about the pile's actual volume, our poor vower may never cut or trim his locks, or drink wine; the concluding rituals following a period of *nezirut* can only be carried out when the person in question was an unambiguous *nazir*.

R. Yehuda rules the other way, namely that indeterminacy in vows may be judged leniently. In the situation of the pile of 100 *kors*, he would claim that, inasmuch as we cannot now actually measure the pile, the whole question becomes moot, and the "vow" is meaningless. A lenient take on this case, then, would mean according to R. Yehuda that the vower becomes a regular *nazir* (thirty-day period). R. Yochanan goes so far as to disagree with Chizkiya and assert that the Mishna actually follows R. Yehuda. A vow based on the size of a stack of 100 *kors* (of whatever fruit or vegetable) is, according to R. Yochanan, still conditional with respect to becoming a *nazir*. In the Mishna at hand, though, he has clearly entered *nezirut*, as just the items in the pail remain unclear (i.e., be it gourds or mustard seeds). Either way, R. Yehuda sees a declared *nazir* here, with the parameters of the period of *nezirut* to be determined over the long haul. The Gemara, though, seeks a means of rescuing our vower from endless *nezirut* based on doubt. It suggests we simply approach the pail as if it were filled with the larger items, melons or gourds, the *nazir* does his thirty days, his final rituals, and he's done with this period of *nezirut*.

8b

R. Yehuda does agree with R. Yehuda ha-Nasi that someone who vows *nezirut* as much as the hairs on his head is not doomed to perpetual *nezirut*, but just to a single thirty-day period; only if one vows multiple periods of *nezirut* (pl. *nezirot*) must repeat thirty-day periods as a *nazir* perpetually, shaving once every thirty days. If R. Yehuda's view accords with that of R. Yehuda ha-Nasi, it would then seem as though the Mishna at hand might be elucidated following R. Yehuda.

Not so fast, warns the Gemara. When the Mishna ruled that someone vowing to become a *nazir* for the "number" of days in a solar year, he will be a *nazir* for 365 consecutive thirty-day terms. And, remember that last sentence at the end of the Mishna in which R. Yehuda spoke of a case when someone in this situation completed the long *nezirut* and promptly died. The Mishna usual assumes that anyone who points to an incident in line with its ruling is corroborating the ruling. Does that therefore mean that R. Yehuda agrees with this ruling, a ruling by the way with which R. Yehuda ha-Nasi disagrees? If R Yehuda abides by the Mishna's ruling, then that would be the understanding behind his mention of such case. No, he did not refer to *nezirut* in his vow, but he still must endure a very lengthy *nezirut*. If, however, one is committed to arguing that R. Yehuda agrees with R. Yehuda ha-Nasi that, despite including a specific "number" in his vow, he must only fulfill a thirty-day term of *nezirut*, how do we resolve this dilemma?

Another problem, introduced by another colorful *baraita*. R. Yehuda claims that, if someone were to vow forthwith to be a *nazir* like the number of piles of figs, or like the number of numerous pathways through farm fields in a Sabbatical year (some texts replace pathways with aftergrowths), he is obliged to carry out the same number of periods of *nezirut*: a virtually innumerable figure. No mention of *nezirut*, just an imprecise figure, albeit a huge one. Here as well we learn from the Gemara that, by using the word "number," the vower is eschewing a single term of *nezirut* in favor of multiple, consecutive periods.

The fact of the matter is that R. Yehuda ha-Nasi does not differentiate between a vow with the word "number" and one without. The Gemara now introduces a *baraita* which both repeats the Mishna's prescription of 365 consecutive periods of *nezirut* for a vow commensurate with the days in a solar year and adds that a vow of the number of days in a lunar year obligates one to 354 consecutive terms of *nezirut*. But, the *baraita* continues, R. Yehuda ha-Nasi explicitly does not rule in this way, as he does not find the word *nezirut* there, and thus it results in a thirty-day *nezirut*.

Given these facts, how can we aver that R. Yehuda and R. Yehuda ha-Nasi would agree on this front? The Gemara tries a compromise solution. On the one hand, R. Yehuda would agree that someone who cites a specific number in a given vow has only accepted a single, regular term of *nezirut*. On the other hand, he does hold with the notion that mention of the word "number" changes everything, and this R. Yehuda ha-Nasi (as we have seen several times above) makes no such distinction.

As our *daf* and chapter wind down, a number of *baraitot* are cited seriatim, it seems to shore up any lingering doubts and in some cases to repeat points made earlier. First, if one declares that forthwith he is a *nazir* all the days of his life or that he is a permanent *nazir*, and even if he adds a number like 100 or 1000 years, he is not a permanent *nazir* but a *nazir* of the sort outlined on 7a. Second, if one declares forthwith to be a *nazir* "and one," he is obligated to observe two consecutive, regular periods of *nezirut*. If he were to add "and more," it's three periods of *nezirut*; if he adds further "and again," four periods of *nezirut*. Third, we learn, almost incidentally, that one can make a vow to be a *nazir* in Greek (or presumably any language other than Hebrew). Simply by stating he is forthwith a *nazir* followed by the term for the number X, he is obliged to observe X number of periods of *nezirut*.

Time for a new chapter.

NOTE

1. In the translation of Robert Alter, *The Five Books of Moses* (New York: W. W. Norton & Company, 2004), p. 712; Everett Fox renders it: "Now this is the Ritual-Instruction for the Consecrated-One: On the day that one's days of being-consecrated are fulfilled," *The Five Books of Moses* (New York: Schocken Books, 1995), p. 685. For consistency in the many following citations, we shall follow Alter's translation and cite them as "Alter, p. X."

Chapter 2

Cows, Doors, and Wine

Only slightly longer than the first chapter, chapter 2 begins with a Mishna, much like some of those we encountered earlier, that involves an odd declaration on the surface. If someone vows to become forthwith a *nazir* "from pressed figs" or "from dried figs," we come to our first dispute in this tractate between Bet (or the School of) Shammai and Bet (or the school of) Hillel. The former deems our vower a *nazir*, the latter does not; and part of the issue here is that figs have nothing to do with the *nezirut* vow. In any event, one who makes such a statement has not sworn off figs. R. Yehuda, in an effort to clarify Bet Shammai's affirmative response, note that they made this positive assertion of a *nazir*'s vow but only if the vower later states that figs are prohibited to him as a sacrifice would be. In other words, such a statement only works as a vow of one swearing off the consumption of figs and not a *nezirut* vow. So, R. Yehuda is saying that essentially the two schools of Shammai and Hillel agree that anyone making such a statement is not a *nazir* of any kind and that the disagreement is whether or not it constitutes a vow not to eat figs. The initial Tanna in the Mishna, though, did not see it that way; as we saw in the first chapter, if someone who made such a strange statement later explained that he was vowing to abstain from figs, at the time of the *nezirut* vow the later point was "words that remain in the heart" (meaning unexpressed), which are meaningless in this context (see 2b).

The Gemara starts with Bet Shammai's first take. How is it that Bet Shammai accept such a declaration and the vower as a *nazir*? The biblical reference (*Numbers* 6.4) says that a *nazir* swears off all grape products, nothing about figs. Any *nazir* may eat as many figs as his stomach will allow. The Gemara replies that Bet Shammai here agree with R. Meir: People don't make statements or vows for no reason at all. Even if the wording, as in this instance, is somewhat obscure or possibly contradictory, we are obliged to extract its intention as best we can. In the case at hand, the words "from figs" cannot logically be linked to a vow of *nezirut*; so, Bet Shammai assess the whole statement as two pronouncements: "I am forthwith a *nazir*" leads to a regular period of *nezirut*; "from figs" reveals that the vower was ignorant of the fact that there is no such type of *nezirut* involving figs, but the first pronouncement still holds.

As is almost always the case, Bet Hillel see things differently from Bet Shammai. They agree with R. Yose that one who makes a declaration must abide by it till its conclusion, meaning that despite the fact that he made the point about abstaining from figs later, it's all part of a whole even if the two halves don't appear to abide with one another. Thus, for Bet Hillel in this instance, by stating right off the bat "from figs," the presumed vower has demonstrated ignorance of the fact that such a vow doesn't exist, and hence the entire statement is without meaning. Indeed, as soon as the words "from figs" are uttered, this provides what the Talmud calls an "opening" (*petach*) by which a sage can release the "vower" from his meaningless "vow."

The Gemara turns things around a bit at this point and claims that Bet Shammai agree with R. Meir that no one makes a statement for no reason at all. So, no sooner has someone stated that he is forthwith a *nazir*, then that intention is clear as a bell, and he is a *nazir*. And, those final words about figs? Bet Shammai aver that these last words are an attempt to withdraw his *nezirut* vow. Thus, two intentions, both meaningful in their separate ways, are declared, and R. Meir's principle is upheld: Our speaker vowed to be a *nazir* and then immediately rescinded his vow, knowing full well that figs have nothing to do with vows of *nezirut* and that tacking the business about figs at the end might constitute release. Unfortunately, a *nezirut* vow is holy and cannot be withdrawn. The *nezirut* vow takes effect, and the added phrase about figs is in vain.

How does Bet Hillel respond to or rebut this explanation? They would agree with an argument of R. Shimon. As background, there is a Mishna in tractate Menachot (Grain offerings, 103a) which states that someone offering to donate a voluntary *minchah* (flour) of barley is stating a non-sequitur, inasmuch as all such *minchah* offerings are of wheat flour. The sage there rules that, despite such a self-contradictory vow, the person still must bring a *minchah* of wheat.[1] R. Shimon finds this ruling untenable, because the putative vower claimed to be offering something that is impossible, and hence his vow is simply null and void. And, back to our Mishna, because there is no way to be a fig *nazir*, Bet Hillel would judge such a vow similarly null and void. In this way, R. Shimon and Bet Hillel seem to agree.

9b

The Gemara turns to cite a *baraita* which describes the Hillel-Shammai difference of views differently. That *baraita* cites R. Natan who avers that, if someone were to issue a declaration to be a *nazir* from figs, Bet Shammai judge him either a *nazir* or one obliged to abstain from figs; if he says the latter was his intention, then he must abstain from figs, but if he claims that not to have been his intention, he is a *nazir*. Bet Hillel say outright that he has sworn off figs and is by no means a *nazir*. If he declares the fig business to have been his intent, then figs are off his table; if not, then under no circumstances is he a *nazir*. In this rendition of the debate, Bet Shammai's take accords with R. Meir and R. Yehuda, while Bet Hillel's accords with R. Yose.

As it turns out, there is yet another incarnation of R. Natan's explanation of this debate, one that looks a lot like R. Yehuda's explanation. Here, R. Natan claims that someone making this putative "vow" is compelled to abstain from figs but is not a *nazir*. If he then says that the aim was to commit himself not to eat figs, they are off his table, but in any event the "vow" is otherwise meaningless, a view which accords with R. Yehuda's explanation of Bet Shammai. Bet Hillel claim that neither the vows concerning figs nor *nezirut* stand—all meaningless—a view which accords with Bet Hillel's stance above. According to this version of things, Bet Shammai's take is identical to R. Yehuda's, while Bet Hillel's is just like R. Shimon.

At this point, the Gemara cites the entire Mishna from *Menachot* (103a) referred to above. The Mishna includes much more than the dispute over whether a vow to bring a donative *minchah* of barley is interpreted to mean an obligation to offer a *minchah* of wheat, because the former does not exist. The additional requirements cited in that Mishna are not of concern here, but our Gemara apparently wants it all laid out. In any event, R. Shimon discharges the "vower" of all obligations, because the latter has effectively said nothing—at least nothing meaningful.

Who would have been the Tanna of that Mishna in *Menachot*, asks our Gemara, a sage who equates a non-existent barley *minchah* with an actual wheat one? Chizkiya doesn't answer the question directly, but does offer the view that the Tanna was explaining the case following Bet Shammai. Just as Bet Shammai interpreted the initial statement vowing to be a *nazir* from figs to mean that one is indeed a *nazir*, even though the statement is self-contradictory: the vow of *nezirut* holds, while "from figs" is meaningless or an attempted rescinding of the vow (impossible, according to Bet Shammai). By the same token, a vow to bring a barley *minchah* is a dual statement: to bring a *minchah* and immediately to withdraw that vow; the withdrawal is impossible, so the offering must be made, and it must accordingly be of wheat. And, Bet Hillel would deem both statements utterly meaningless, obliging the "vower" not at all.

By contrast, R. Yochanan understands the Tanna of the *Menachot* Mishna we are assessing to be consonant even with the view of Bet Hillel. Where the Mishna there points out that, if one later effectively regrets his vow which he claims to have made in ignorance, he states that he would, had he known better, have stated "wheat" and not barley. Thus, he was first and foremost intending to make a vow, and the barley part of it was added in error. Now, there is an obligatory (as opposed to voluntary) *minchah* of barley flour, and Bet Hillel realize that such an error is understandable. However, when it comes to figs, they see no way to attach figs to *nezirut*, and thus the whole "vow" is meaningless.

Chizkiya modifies his earlier claim now by stating that, if someone made the same vow about a voluntary *minchah* offering but, instead of barley, said it was "from lentils," then certainly that is completely ridiculous and obliges nothing. But, at least barley is within the realm of the conceivable, because, as noted, there are some offerings of barley flour, just not voluntary ones. The Gemara fires back that "from lentils" is about as silly as "from figs," returning to the Mishna in our tractate proper. Both are utterly inappropriate in their respective contexts. Despite all this, Bet Shammai still deem the vower a *nazir*. So, why then does Chizkiya deem a *minchah* of lentils meaningless?

Well, Chizkiya apparently saw the light and withdrew his position that the Tanna in the Mishna from *Menachot* reflected Bet Shammai. But, why did he do this? As is so often the case in the Talmud, it comes down to language and choice of words. Why would the Mishna there use "from barley" to make its case and not "from lentils" which is the more unusual instance? "From lentils" would have obliged the vower to offer nothing, according to all parties. It fails to accord with Bet Shammai, and thus Chizkiya winds up saying that the Tanna there cannot hold a position consonant with Bet Shammai. Now, in that case, how does Chizkiya explain the position of the Tanna? He claims that Bet Shammai abide by the rule of the Tanna in *Menachot*, as per R. Yehuda's rendition of Bet Shammai. (It should be noted in passing that, far more often than not, Bet Shammai lose out to Bet Hillel in debate over *halacha*.)

R. Yochanan won't let Chizkiya off the hook and denies the latter's idea that "from barley" and "from lentils" are qualitatively different. R. Yochanan declares clearly that even a bizarre vow to offer a *minchah* of lentils would necessitate the vower to bring one of wheat. The Gemara finds this odd, for it was R. Yochanan himself who claimed that the Mishna in *Menachot* allows someone who made the "from barley" vow to correct his error once he is apprised of it and offer one of wheat. This error, as he sees it, is within the realm of conceivable errors, whereas becoming a *nazir* "from figs" is just too far out. Where does R. Yochanan then get the idea that a *minchah* may not be strictly correct but at least conceivable? The Gemara continues in this vein only a slight bit longer, suggesting that an offering of a barley *minchah* might not be so radically crazy, because there are other *minchah* offerings that are made in barley, such as the *minchah* of the *omer* (a communal sacrifice presented on Nissan 16),

10a

or the *minchah* of a *sotah* (see 2a); as such maybe a voluntary *minchah* of barley flour just might, in the vower's view, be worthy of deeming "holy." In other words, maybe the vower just really wanted to bring a *minchah* and erred in assuming barley would do the trick. In the end, let him bring a proper *minchah* of wheat. There is more intricacy to the debate, but I think we've had enough. In any event, it's time for a new Mishna.

If anyone thought the declarations in the previous Mishna were off the wall, this one sets a new standard for strangeness. If someone were to state that a cow (yes, a cow) said that it was forthwith a *nazir* should it stand up, or that a door (yes, a door) made the same statement should it open, the person reporting such an incident, according to Bet Shammai, is indeed a *nazir*, but according to Bet Hillel, he is not. R. Yehuda pipes up to attempt to clarify Bet Shammai's assertion by noting they meant someone who said that the cow here is like a sacrificial offering if it stands up. With this clarification, as in the previous Mishna, R. Yehuda has altered the understanding of what Bet Shammai actually meant, as the Gemara explains.

But, the Gemara begins with the most obvious of questions imaginable in this situation: Do bovines speak? What can the Mishna here be talking about? Rami bar Chama takes the first stab at it. We have a man looking at a cow lying down before him. He imagines it ruminating that it would much like to rise but apparently can't; if fact, it would even commit to a period of *nezirut* if that were attainable. Now, it's highly (very highly!) unlikely that a cow can become a *nazir*, but the inference of the human observer is that someone should commit to *nezirut* from its meat. So, in short, he thinks to himself that the cow is never going to stand up and that he'll forthwith be a *nazir* from its meat should it get up on its feet by itself. This still leaves the question of vowing *nezirut* from a cow's meat. There is the much bigger question as well of how anyone can know what a cow is "thinking." But, putting that rather larger assumption aside for the moment, as R. Yehuda understands Bet Shammai, the text of the Mishna means that the person reporting on the cow's thoughts is vowing to become a *nazir* from the animal's meat should it actually get up. One can only guess, but the other issue in the Mishna of an articulate door is conceivable in the same fashion. The door is jammed and the human observer imagines it swearing to be a *nazir* if only it could open itself. The person then personalizes the door's "thinking" (as he imagines it, of course) to mean that he himself is forthwith a *nazir* from the door should it be unjammed and open up.

The text then states that this Mishna is entirely parallel to the last one, with the two schools of Shammai and Hillel assuming positions very similar to this one. There Bet Shammai said a vow of *nezirut* from figs, despite there being no such thing, meant the vower was a *nazir*; here they aver that a vow from cow's meat (if one properly understands bovine cogitation) also results in one becoming a *nazir*. In both instances, Bet Hillel reject the vow as valid, as there is no such thing as either a vow from figs or from meat.

So, then, if the present Mishna is here to teach us the same thing as the one on the previous *daf*, why did the rabbis include it in the first place? Actually, the Gemara is glossing over a major difference in Bet Shammai's position on the two Mishnayot. In the Mishna here, the person is not vowing to become a *nazir* directly, as before, but only giving expression to the cow's "thinking." The Gemara's point with respect to Bet Hillel's take is the same in both: no *nezirut* takes effect.

At this point, Rava and R. Chiyya both jump in and say that you do not need one case to make a point but two or three. Examples ensue. Suppose that we only had the previous Mishna of a *nezirut* vow made from figs; someone might then read that as only Bet Shammai claiming the vow valid inasmuch as figs might easily be mistaken for grapes, meaning that the vower meant to say grapes but simply misspoke. This, by the way, was not what Bet Shammai argued on the previous *daf*. By the same token, however, nobody mistakes beef for figs. As such, it is entirely possible that Bet Shammai might well deem a vow from meat to be ridiculous, unless as the Mishna on this *daf* explains, Bet Shammai affirm the vow.

Another example has it that, if figs were out of the picture, and the person vowed solely from beef, Bet Shammai might still have deemed the vow valid, because one often puts meat and wine together. Perhaps the vower meant to say "wine" and misspoke "meat." Meanwhile, it's quite a stretch, even for Bet Shammai, to mistake grapes for figs, and thus it was up to the earlier Mishna to make such a vow from figs a conceivably valid one.

What if the Mishna had only articulated vows from figs (9a) and meat (10a), meaning no mention of the jammed door? A person might jump to the conclusion that, only in the cases of figs and meat, would Bet Shammai conclude said vower a genuine *nazir*. What possible connection is there to a door? Perhaps one might in such a situation argue that Bet Hillel had it right, as a vow of *nezirut* from a door is (on the surface, at least) utterly meaningless. By the same token, if the Mishna only explained the example of a (thinking?) door, we could fall back on the argument that Bet Shammai conclude the vower a *nazir* because he vowed to be a *nazir*, then made a quick attempt at an adjustment to his vow with an irrelevancy in the hope that it would enable him to withdraw from his vow; inasmuch as there's no withdrawing according to Bet Shammai, our poor vower is a *nazir* in spite of himself. Doors, figs, and meat might all be purposefully intended to get out of the vow, and Bet Hillel deems them all meaningless and hence futile.

Just when you thought the Mishna couldn't go further down this bizarre rabbit hole, it does just that. Rava asks rhetorically if the Mishna actually demanded that the cow stand up without assistance, as declared by Rami bar Chama. Rava restates the situation of the declaration to offer a *nazir*'s sacrifice (the cow) taking effect if the cow simply arose. Now, to be sure, one can bring a cow as a sacrificial offering, perhaps as an additional offering when a *nazir* has completed his term, but what about a door? Nobody has ever, to anyone's knowledge, offered a door as a possible sacrificial offering—let alone a door guaranteeing itself as such. Rava rewords what he meant: the Mishna posits a cow lying before one with apparently no intention of getting up;

10b

the frustrated person then says he will forthwith become a *nazir* from wine (the standard way) if the creature refuses to get up despite my best efforts to get it to do so; and then it in fact got up on its own. When the cow then rose on its own, the vower became a *nazir*. Rava twists Bet Shammai's reasoning into pretzels to come out with a valid declaration of *nezirut*, but for Bet Hillel all that matters is that the crucial point here—namely, the cow getting up, irrespective of outside assistance—has been met, and thus the vow of *nezirut* is null and void.

There follows some challenges from the Gemara laid at the feet of Rava, but they do not appreciably advance the discussion. For Rava the crucial point sees the crux of the vower's statement here to be if he can himself get the cow up with his own hands. He failed to do so, as the cow arose on its own, and thus he becomes a valid *nazir*. We have already seen how Bet Hillel assess the situation: all that matters is the cow lying or rising; if it gets up, irrespective of any help, the declaration kicks in, and the vow is nullified. Would Bet Hillel agree, conversely, that if the cow remain lounging on the ground and refusing to rise, that the vow of *nezirut* does take effect? Earlier, Bet Hillel had made ever so clear that a vow by something as bizarrely irrelevant as meat was worthless. No, because such a vow, given its eccentricity and lack of any scriptural foundation, can never take effect. The two form a reinforced basis for Bet Hillel to rule out such a vow.

This Gemara ends with Bet Shammai strongly decrying Bet Hillel's argument and reiterating that the crucial point is whether the person's declaration concerns his assistance in getting the cow back up on its feet, not simply whether or not the cow gets up. At this point at least, there is no agreed upon resolution.

11a

It's time to move beyond cows with a new Mishna. This Mishna has the advantage of relating a declaration of *nezirut* with a cup of wine, an item central to one's vow to become a *nazir*. If someone were to pour a prospective vower a cup of wine, and the latter claimed that he was forthwith a *nazir* from it, it works and he becomes a *nazir*. We then learn of a case of an inebriated woman, for whom a cup of wine was poured, and she proceeded to state that forthwith she was a *nezira* (female *nazir*), the sages of the Mishna rule that her meaning under the circumstances was effectively to say that it (presumably meaning the cup) is like a sacrificial offering; that is, she vowed that the item in question was prohibited for her, but it does not constitute a valid entry into *nezirut*.

The Gemara addressing this Mishna is relatively short. It begins by asking if the case of the drunk woman was raised to undermine the ruling that preceded it, as the usual practice is to report such cases as a way to validate a ruling. Apparently, the sages only prohibited her from just that one cup of wine presented to her. Something seems awry here, and the Gemara agrees and suggests that something essential must have been absent from the Mishna. The beginning of the Mishna has a man straightforwardly declaring himself a *nazir* for a cup of wine, but what it failed to add is that, if he was inebriated and said exactly the same thing as we find here, he has not qualified for *nezirut*, but only prohibited himself from drinking the cup of wine poured for him. That satisfies the gender equality issue.

But, what is not clear is why the vow is invalid. The Gemara claims that a claim of *nezirut* when one is intoxicated is interpreted to mean that the cup of wine is as verboten as a sacrificial offering. That merely begs the question, though. Why didn't the alcohol-imbibing person in question just say what he meant? Why must we unpack his sentence? The Gemara answers that the drunkard might think that, if I drink this cup presented to me, then they'll probably push more and more cups on me. Who needs the annoyance?! By stating it would send him directly into *nezirut*, he effectively has sworn off wine for a distinct period of time and ends with those others prodding him to drink more. The Gemara concludes by asserting, again, that there was an identical case involving a woman. Am I alone in wondering if that is how people deal with the inebriated, namely by giving them more and more to drink?

Time for a new Mishna, and it appears that we are still going to being dealing with wine. Were someone to declare that he was forthwith to become a *nazir* but only if he would be allowed to consume wine, or that he would be allowed to become *tamei* from a human corpse, he actually does enter a period of *nezirut* but is prohibited in all the standard *nazir* proscriptions. We shall see how this is possible.

The Mishna continues with someone pronouncing himself forthwith a *nazir* and then tacking on that he knew *nezirut* existed but not the prohibition regarding wine—meaning that, if he had known he was required to abstain, he never would have made the declaration—uh, it's too late: he's a *nazir* and he must abstain from wine. R. Shimon dissents and allows the putative vower to consume wine but does not count him as a *nazir*. Inasmuch as he expressed his misgivings right from the start, R. Shimon goes easy on him.

Finally, what sounds like an oddly ignorant declaration: Someone who has claimed that he is forthwith a *nazir* and then goes on to say that he was well aware of the prohibition on wine but expected the rabbis would allow him to consume it nonetheless, because life without wine is unthinkable for him, or that he believed that he could continue in his line of work as a gravedigger who inters human remains and thus contract corpse *tumah*. In both of these instances, the vower may indeed drink wine or have contact with the dead, but he's no *nazir*. R. Shimon forbids both and declares both of our vowers a *nazir*.

Three distinct pieces here for the Gemara to sink its teeth into. It starts by asking why, of the three portions of the Mishna, R. Shimon apparently disagrees with the Tanna but gives a bye to the Tanna in the first case in which the vower declares himself a *nazir* provided he can still consume wine. When the person stated that he would become a *nazir* despite knowing that wine is out, this is tantamount to attempting the impossible: declaration of a partial *nezirut*. Nonetheless, R. Shimon offered no rebuttal. Actually, avers R. Yehoshua ben Levi (a huge figure in the Talmud from whom we are now hearing in our tractate for the first time), R. Shimon did dispute the first part; when R. Shimon is cited at the end of the second part, allowing the vower to drink wine but disallowing him entrance into *nezirut*, that is meant to refer back to the first portion of the Mishna as well.

Ravina disagrees with R. Yehoshua ben Levi. As he sees it, R. Shimon's statement at the end of the second portion is not meant to dispute the first part. In fact, in R. Shimon's understanding, because the putative vower claimed he would be a *nazir* as long as he continued consuming wine, that was a self-contradictory "vow," or a declaration contradicting a law of the Torah, which by definition makes it null and void. In actual fact, both of our rabbis here agree that R. Shimon would rule out *nezirut* in the first case, with just the reasoning being different. R. Yehoshua ben Levi sees the inclusion in the case of a conditional element to the vow (*nazir* but with wine allowed) as tantamount to a declaration of *nezirut* but without the requirement to abstain from wine—there being no way to play fast and loose with the Torah, R. Shimon invalidates his *nezirut*; the Torah's laws are an all-or-nothing proposition. Meanwhile, Ravina could look at the odd statements that one would forthwith become a *nazir* conditional on being allowed either to consume wine or become *tamei* from human corpses as inserting a condition into his declaration which negates the Torah: no can do!

The Gemara goes on to cite a piece from the beginning of the third portion of the Mishna, namely that the declarer knew when vowing to become a *nazir* that wine or corpse *tumah* was out, but fully anticipated that the rabbis would cut him the necessary slack to keep his wine habit intact or his job as a grave-digger. In other words, both such statements would appear to be made from the start on the assumption that a special condition was part of the deal—in other words, *nezirut* with only some, but not all, of the proscriptions. As such, given what appeared earlier in the Mishna, one might imagine the Tanna allowing the vower to be a *nazir* but with all the prohibitions, and R. Shimon to adjudge such a vow invalid. However, it turns out to be the opposite.

In the second part of the Mishna, addressing someone who vows to become a *nazir* but then states that he was unaware of the prohibition on wine, the Tanna claims that his vow of *nezirut* is accepted but the ban on wine remains intact. There R. Shimon allows him to drink all the wine he wants but disallows his vow. This seems to conflict with the first portion of the Mishna. The Gemara does something at this point that it rarely does: It instructs us to amend the text to bring it into alignment with the rest of the text.

That is a striking resolution, but the Gemara apparently also felt that way and now offers another approach that does not necessitate changing the text of the Mishna. Maybe we don't have to reverse rulings of the rabbis involved. In the second case, where the declarer claimed to know about *nezirut*

11b

but not the requirement to abstain from wine, he has effectively vowed *nezirut* but without all the required conditions pertaining. The rabbis of the Mishna deem him a *nazir* nonetheless, but insist he follow all the restrictions placed on a *nazir*. R. Shimon, by contrast, lets him drink to his heart's content, but does not allow him to become a *nazir*, because you have to abide by all the requisite abstentions to become a bona fide *nazir*.

What about this third case in which the declarer vowed to adopt all the proscriptions but then sought for the rabbis to let him off the hook for one of them because he simply couldn't do without wine? Now, the sages of the Mishna state that you can vow to be a *nazir* with regard to just one of the proscriptions, and indeed you'll be a *nazir* but, as soon as you request to be let off from that one proscription, sure, you can drink wine, but your vow is nullified. R. Shimon, by contrast, avers that no vow of *nezirut* is acceptable unless all the proscriptions are to be observed; thus, there is no release for any one of them, unless he seeks to be let off all of them. Thus, the Mishna states that R. Shimon prohibits a kind of niche *nezirut*, making the request out of the question but the vow to become a *nazir* stays in place (with all the proscriptions).

But wait, as they say, there's more, a third possible resolution. Maybe, the difference of views between the sages of the Mishna and R. Shimon is really about what are known as vows beyond one's capacity to change. It apparently, we are told, maps nicely onto a disagreement between Shmuel and Rav Assi. First, the Gemara must elucidate the clash of views, and only then explain how it helps us understand the point at hand. The Gemara tells us of four types of vows delineated in tractate *Nedarim* (Vows), all four of them void, and the last of them being a vow beyond one's control. Rav Yehuda reports in the name of Rav Assi that, to be released from any one of these four, one must put in an appeal. In fact, all four are unquestionably rejected and need no one to appeal for release. Rav Yehuda reports this reply from Shmuel. What does this have to do with our debate? In the case of someone who declares a vow of the fourth sort, the rabbis of the Mishna resemble Shmuel's ruling here: one who articulates such a void is not a *nazir*. R. Shimon's position resembles that of Rav Assi: the person in question becomes a *nazir* until such time as he appeals to a sage for release from his vow.

New Mishna time again. Should one declare forthwith to be a *nazir* and go on to say: "And I," adding that he must also be responsible for bringing offerings of a *nazir* who shaves, presumably another *nazir* who has concluded his *nezirut* period. If at the same time a colleague *nazir* makes the same declaration with respect to another *nazir*, then they will ready the necessary offerings for each other, if they are astute. If they aren't quite so astute, then such a declaration requires that they prepare their own and someone else's sacrificial offerings.

This Mishna will keep the Gemara busy for a while. What, asks the Gemara, if the colleague (*chaver*) of the person declaring himself a *nazir* had only said: "And I"? What would the law adjudge him to have actually said or committed? That is, do these two words (only one word, *va'ani*, in Hebrew) carry the entire duty to both become a *nazir* and ready the offerings for another *nazir*, or does it merely obligate the vower to perform only one part of his statement? The Gemara begins with my personally favorite expression, *ta shma* (Come, listen), an expression that appears a total of forty-six times in this tractate alone (and hundreds of times throughout the Talmud as a whole). The Gemara is telling us that it has an answer to the question. By reading the actual word of the Mishna, the Gemara states that "And I" alone would only constitute a partial affirmation. The rabbis accept that this is a partial affirmation, but which part? It concludes, without going into great detail, that it fulfills both parts of the Mishna's declaration.

If that all seemed just a little bit too neat, the Gemara itself questions its own proof now. Rav Huna, son of Rav Yehoshua, presses Rava by claiming that "And I" would work for the entire declaration. The additional words at the end of the Mishna's statement, where the vower says bringing another *nazir*'s offerings is "on me" to perform, is superfluous, whereas the "proof" immediately above it was adduced to satisfy both parts of the Mishna. But, nothing is ever superfluous—perish the thought!—for the Talmud. The Gemara wriggles out of this one by claiming that "on me" is just a restatement of the first part of the Mishna ("And I"). So, Rav Huna will attempt to prove his assertion by looking to the next Mishna (see below, 12b) wherein someone states that it is required of him to shave one-half of a *nazir*; upon hearing this, his colleague replies: "And I" must also shave one-half a *nazir*. In this instance, the speaker must cough up half the costs related to shaving a *nazir*. The Gemara there is said to make the same point as it does here: the latter "on me" is only there for emphasis, with the "And I" being the crux of the matter.

Rava isn't quite ready to give up on his proof. He doesn't like the idea of attributing declarations to superfluity, but before he can get very far, the Gemara commences its first real dig into a digression worthy of a rabbit hole. Rav Yitzchak bar Yosef says in R. Yochanan's name that, if a person were to tell his agent

12a

to betroth a woman on his behalf but without saying whom, and the agent then died before letting the man who sent him to whom he was now betrothed, the poor man may never marry anyone ever. Why so tough? We assume the agent has done his job as instructed, meaning that some woman was betrothed to him, but because the original sender didn't identify whom he wished to betroth, he can now never know whom the agent found for him to enter *kiddushin* (betrothal). Ultimately, that makes all (Jewish) women in the world potentially relatives of his betrothed, whoever she might be, and thus prohibited to him.

Reish Lakish for his part looks to a seemingly unrelated Mishna in tractate *Kinnim* (Nests) to dispute this ruling of R. Yochanan. The reference is to section 2.1 concerning the sacrificial offering of a pair of birds that are brought as part of certain rituals of purification: one of the birds for a *chatat* (sin offering) and the other as an *olah* (burnt offering). If one did not indicate which of the birds is which offering, and one of the two flew off into the wild blue yonder, or flew off and joined a group of *chatat* birds that perforce are left to die (for any one of several reasons), or even if one of the two just died, the person who brought the original pair finds another bird to join the remaining one. In other words, the remaining bird is not stuck in limbo, as a match can be found which is appropriate in this situation.

How does Reish Lakish, then, sum up the disagreement he is articulating vis-à-vis R. Yochanan? If we were to follow a parallel line to the latter's argument, then all birds in the universe would be off limits, because somewhere out there the designated avian is flying around. No, we can't ban all birds, because we must follow the majority, and the overwhelming majority of birds have not been so designated for sacrifice. Interesting argument, comparing birds to betrothed women, but R. Yochanan isn't buying it. He notes the obvious: The woman in his ruling was not flying around like a bird, but stationary. There is a tried-and-true Talmudic principle that anything stabilized in a place is considered a 50–50 probability, which means that half the women in the world might just be the unknown betrothed, and the rule of the majority does not apply. And, in an effort to forestall a potential line of argument, R. Yochanan effectively says: Don't tell me that the agent caught up with the woman to be betrothed as she was walking along the street, implying that the principle of majority rule (as with birds) kicks in. Why? Because she will in short order be returning to her stable place (her home or residence)—can birds be counted on to do the same? The argument is much more complicated than the above explanation, but the point should be clear. One question that almost suggests itself but is not even mentioned here is: Don't birds build nests, and aren't nests fixed sites to which (at least, some) birds regularly return?

Rava now returns to the discussion to elaborate a bit on what R. Yochanan has stated. He claims that R. Yochanan would add that, if a woman had no female offspring, grandchildren, mother, grandmother, or sister—or, if she did have a sister who may have been married at the time of the betrothal but later became a divorcée—such a woman may marry the man who dispatched the agent. Such a woman could never be one of the prohibited relatives of his mysterious betrothed.

What if all this panned out for a prospective alternate betrothal and then a sister suddenly popped up out of nowhere? The Gemara tells us that the key point is that when our prospective groom sent his agent off to find him a bride, this sister was married, meaning she was off limits at the time. So, if all the female relatives of the prospective bride were all married at the time the agent caught up with the sender's future betrothed, none of them would be in a position to spoil the betrothal. The agent was not, as the Gemara stresses, sent to find something (or someone) who was legally off limits at that point in time. If this sister later became divorced, this was unconnected to the agent's work, because he would not have considered her as a potential partner when she was married.

This elaborate debate was aimed at explaining Rava's idea that an agent can only be assigned to do what it is within the realm of possibilities at the time his agency is retained. While this may seem obvious, there is the ancillary point involved that the person hiring the agent is not expected to be concerned with what is not now practicable. The Gemara, though, is not at all ready to accept Rava's point, and to respond to him it reiterates the entirety of the Mishna on 11b. How does this move the discussion forward? Well, as the Gemara relates, the second person in this Mishna will have no problem, because he offers to bring his offerings for the first person when the latter has already committed to *nezirut*. How, though, can the first person ready the offerings for the second if the latter had not at the time vowed to be a *nazir*?

12b

That first person is effectively declaring that he will ready the sacrificial offerings for a second person down the road among those who will commit to *nezirut*. In other words, whoever that second person might be would not necessarily at the time the first person agreed to "shave a *nazir*" as yet have made the commitment. And, that contradicts Rava's principle. There would, then, appear to be no good reason for the agent to have been assigned only to line up someone available at the time of his agency. The Gemara proceeds to refine Rava's ruling but it does not develop the point further.

Where then do we stand vis-à-vis Rava's intervention? The Gemara wants to take another look at how an agent's job will be altered by it. To do so, however, it asks us again "to come listen" to a *baraita* (attributed to R. Yoshiya) that appears to be taking up a wild goose chase, but let's see. A man is about to set off on a trip and tells someone he has hired to look after his household: Do me a favor and, any vows that my wife commits to, from this moment of my travels to where I am going until I come home, annul them all. Now, a husband is empowered by the Torah (*Numbers* 30.14) to annul his spouse's vows, and he is now hiring someone to watch his home and in particular his wife. So, the *baraita* continues that the caretaker does as requested and annuls the man's wife's vows. You would think this does the trick, but the biblical reference says the husband can uphold and the husband can annul a wife's vows, repeating "her husband" as if to make this point crystal clear that it is only he, but he cannot enable someone else to perform this role. R. Yonatan, though, states an important and obvious point, namely that everywhere in the Torah we find the principle that a person's agent is a stand-in for the person.

The Gemara must be going somewhere with this line of thought, though *nezirut* hasn't been mentioned for a while. R. Yoshiya has noted that the double mention of "her husband" rules out an agent's annulling another's wife's vows. Now, it would be possible if this emphasis were not so apparently explicit, and otherwise he appears to agree with R. Yonatan's statement of the Torah's general principle as valid. In tractate *Nedarim* (75a), we learn that, if a man setting out on a trip were to say to his wife that any and all vows to which she might commit in his absence are upheld, no dice. One cannot uphold a future vow before it has actually been made. Interestingly, R. Eliezer does permit a husband to annul his wife's vows in advance of their being made, while the sages of the Mishna do not.

Where does that leave us? The Gemara here concludes after a fashion that a man may authorize an agent to do things for him that it is not now feasible for him to do, and that would refute the point that Rava was trying to make. As the Gemara winds down, it becomes a question of whether R. Yoshiya's words in the *baraita* are close to the sages of the Mishna or to R. Eliezer, and ultimately the resolution seems to be like betting on all horses, *mutatis mutandis*, in a given race.

A new Mishna now offers some claims that are closely related to the last one. R. Meir rules: Person A states that forthwith he is obliged to shave one-half of a *nazir* (whatever that may mean, see 11b). His colleague, person B overhears him and says, "And I" must do the same. The Mishna rules that person A is required to ready the sacrificial offerings to shave a full *nazir*, and person B must do the same. The sages read the text more literally and oblige both persons to cover one-half of the costs of the requisite offerings accompanying the shaving of *nazir* as the completion of *nezirut*.

Rava is the first to offer an explanation, and he claims that both parties here, R. Meir and the sages, actually agree. While that may strike one as fully in contrast to the wording of the Mishna, Rava's point is that half a *nezirut* is meaningless. How can there be one-half of a *nazir*? In the previous Mishna, the term "half" unmistakably referred to the sacrificial offerings, and ditto here. The only difference is the wording used by each party. As soon as either person A or B assumes he must supply sacrificial offerings for a *nazir*, the business about "half" is a fiction for R. Meir who indicates that it must be a full provision, there being no such entity as a semi-*nezirut*. In other words, R. Meir breaks the statement in two parts: the declaration to pay for a shaving and the odd phrase "half a *nazir*." The latter is an impossible effort to affect the former. Meanwhile the sages somewhat cryptically argue that the phrasing here is such that commentaries cannot fully understand.

A new Mishna completes this *daf* and carries over to the next one. Should someone state that he is forthwith a *nazir* when his wife gives birth to a son, and a son is then born, he enters *nezirut*. If, on the other hand, his wife produces a daughter, or a *tumtum* (an infant whose gender is unclear), or an infant with both sets of genitalia (an androgyne or hermaphrodite), he does not enter *nezirut*. If he vowed to become a *nazir* if his wife gave birth to a child, then any of the three results ruled out in the previous statement (daughter, *tumtum*, androgyne) enable him to be a *nazir*.

13a

The Mishna continues with the unfortunate result of a vow concerning the birth of a child. If the man's wife gave birth but the child died—miscarriages are not referred to a "children"—he will not be a *nazir*. In this case, and informed by many other rulings, the Mishna is referring to a child born prematurely died within thirty days of its birth, and it is impossible to say if it passed through a full period of gestation. R. Shimon claims that the vow does fly, as the man is deemed a *nazir* out of doubt, inasmuch as we simply do not know if the infant was carried to full term and can thus be considered a "child." The Tanna of the Mishna obviously disagrees, and we can expect the Gemara will take this issue up. There is a problem, because two of three required rituals upon completing a full period of *nezirut* are forbidden to a non-*nazir*, and indeed our vower is definitionally in doubt. So, R. Shimon tells us that the "father" should declare that, if it was viable and died, he is a *nazir*, as previously vowed, and if not viable he vows a voluntary *nezirut*. Pretty crafty work-around.

Moving on, then, if a woman were to then give birth to a viable child that lives, her husband's *nezirut* commences, because in the Tanna's conception of things, the vow preceding the infant that died was never carried out—and the Tanna doesn't buy the "doubt" business—so the husband must become a *nazir* now. R. Shimon, though, claims that the husband is for the second time a *nazir* out of doubt. He must say that, if that first infant was actually viable, then the first *nezirut* was required of him, and the present one is voluntary; if, however, that child was not viable, then the reverse situation should kick in: first *nezirut* voluntary, second required.

Why, begins the Gemara, do we need the first judgment of this Mishna? Seems quite clear that, if a man's wife bears a son, his vow is valid and he's a *nazir*. Well, maybe it's there to lay the groundwork for the more legally complex cases that follow—and the Gemara likes little more than balance and completion—about his wife bearing a daughter, a *tumtum*, or an androgyne, consequences which do not result in his becoming a *nazir*. But, the Gemara question if this is also as patently clear. Why? The term in Hebrew for "son" (*ben*) is related to the verb for "to build up," and perhaps that's what the text meant when it used *ben*, which in turn would include other kinds of children. The Gemara quickly overrules this possibility and states clearly that the Mishna means "son" here—other outcomes of the man's wife's birth do not result in him being a *nazir*.

Again, the Gemara's first response to the next piece of the Mishna—if a man declares he'll be a *nazir* if his wife bears a child (not specifically a son), his vow is accepted—is that it, too, seems pretty obvious. Like the previous question, this rhetorical point suggests that a statement such as this one might be understood as a declaration of *nezirut* if his wife produced a "child" of significance or prominence, and that could presumably be seen as meaning only a "son" and not of some other or indeterminate gender. (It is, of course, important to remember that this text was compiled many centuries ago when these sorts of issues were not considered in the same way that they are today.) As before, though, the Gemara states clearly here that the text means "child" (*valad*) of no specific gender.

If the newborn dies within thirty days of its birth, and its viability remains in doubt, the Mishna ruled that the vow of *nezirut* would not take effect. This time, the Gemara asks who made such a ruling, and it answers that it was R. Yehuda and his ruling back on 8a. In a *baraita* there concerning one who vows to be *nazir* if a pile of produce before him amounts to 100 *kors*, and then the pile disappeared, R. Yehuda ruled that indeterminacy in vows may be judged leniently. Thus, if there is doubt about the circumstances surrounding a vow to become a *nazir*, and in this case that would mean about the infant's viability, the vow does not take effect.

Now, R. Shimon (who incidentally disagreed with R. Yehuda back on 8a) argues that the man doing the vowing should specifically declare that, if his late infant was viable, then he is (already) a *nazir*; if the child was actually not viable, then he is (already) a voluntary *nazir*. The Gemara restates this only to address further cases not posed in the Mishna. R. Abba asked R. Huna about someone who declared forthwith to be a *nazir* when his wife gives birth, but the wife loses the newborn, while he has already prepared his offerings for the conclusion of his *nezirut* by consecrating the required animals. Now, with this weighted situation placed before R. Huna, for how should we rule if the wife were the very same day to give birth to another child who lives, presuming of course that she was carrying infants. The consecrated animals were prepared with respect to the first infant, meaning that the ritual standing of those creatures is tied to the first infant. If his vow holds, the animals' sanctification does as well, but if he is judged as not a *nazir*, that sanctification is also ruled out.

The Gemara wonders which sage R. Abba was thinking of when making this inquiry. If R. Shimon, then R. Shimon (back on 8a) made it quite clear that the presence of doubts in a vow of *nezirut* is understood as a satisfactory vow, and vower in a *nazir* and his offerings (again, out of doubt) are consecrated. But, R. Abba, we learn, was actually asking with respect to R. Yehuda who, as we have seen, rules differently. What is the ritual standing of the prospective sacrifices? In practical terms, if the animals have not effectively been sanctified, then one may shear them and put them back to work, an option utterly unavailable if they have been sanctified. In this instance, the Gemara decides to leave the question unresolved for now.

It now turns to pick up a related issue and introduces in this tractate two other authorities. Ben Rechumi asked Abaye about what the judgment would be in a case when a man vowed forthwith to be a *nazir* if his wife bore a son, and at that point in time a friend of his heard him make this vow and declared the same vow for himself ("and me"). It is unclear if the second man declared his vow should his friend's wife bear a son or if his vow refers to his own family. Now, if the latter, then the Gemara proceeds down a rabbit hole, for what would happen if the second man makes a declaration to be a *nazir* if his wife bears a son, and a friend of his (a third person) makes a similar vow as the second man did when the first person here made his vow.

13b

After tying itself in knots over how to resolve this situation, the Gemara decides to leave this complex of queries unresolved and move on to a new Mishna.

As we have seen, the Mishna has a way of building upon previous rulings to ever more complex articulations. This one fits the bill for complexity: Someone declares forthwith to be a *nazir* and that, when his wife bears a son, he will again be a *nazir*; then, the son emerges (viable) prior to completion of his first period of *nezirut*. He must finish his first period, then shave and bring the required offerings, and then proceed to carry out the second term, due to his vow based on his son's birth, and finish with a second set of sacrifices and a shaving. A second ruling has slightly, but significantly, altered wording: Should he vow forthwith to be a *nazir* when his wife bears a son and also that he will serve a period of *nezirut*—meaning the *nezirut* linked to the birth of a son is articulated prior to a standard vow—what happens when he starts the standard *nezirut* and a viable baby son emerges before he finishes that first vow? The Mishna says he must discontinue his personal vow as a *nazir* and move on to carry out the vow related to his son's birth, because he assumed that vow tied to his son first, meaning that no other vow can interpose in its fulfillment. When he has discharged the son's *nezirut*, he returns to complete his personal one. Many possible complications ensue, and the Gemara will address quite a few of them.

Rava gets the ball rolling by raising a possible scenario. Someone declares himself forthwith a standard thirty-day *nazir* to begin in twenty days. He then adds that he is forthwith a 100-day *nazir* "from now." How would this be possible? Obviously, he can't squeeze his 100-day commitment into the twenty days before his first vow is set to begin. So, "from now" in the second vow can't be meant literally, but it is meant to begin just as soon as the first vow is completed (fifty days down the road). Perhaps, though, he did mean to launch the longer *nezirut* vow immediately, halt it at day twenty, do his standard thirty-day *nezirut*, and then complete the remaining eighty days of the longer commitment. Rather than adjudge which of these scenarios takes effect, the Gemara asks why Rava had to raise such a complex situation. Why not simply just pose a thirty-day *nezirut* set to commence in twenty days and then another regular one to start whenever? That, of course, would have been way too easy.

The Gemara states that Rava was posing two periods of *nezirut*—one long and one regular, shorter—that interrupted each other.

14a

He worded the query (#1) in such a way that a regular, thirty-day *nezirut* is stated before the longer, 100-day one. The Gemara suggests that the key factor in resolving how we understand the Mishna is the question of when it would be appropriate for the vower to shave. The problem is that, if we allow for interruptions in vying vows, there may not be enough head-hair growth to warrant a shave. If he cuts the 100-day term into twenty- and eighty-day periods, then there is no issue with accumulated growth after eighty days. But the Gemara ends this discussion by averring: "Or not" (*o lo*), sounding very contemporary and colloquial.

Rather than try to come to a conclusion of this question, the Gemara asks another (#2), related one. Should someone vow forthwith to be a regular *nazir* in twenty days, and "from now" to become a permanent *nazir*, how are we to rule? Here, as above, "from now" need not mean immediately for his permanent *nezirut*; the thirty-day period definitely begins in twenty days, and no hard-and-fast date for the start of the permanent one. Again, no resolution is offered, though a complementary issue (#3) is raised. The thirty-day *nezirut* can potentially be annulled by either a qualified sage or a group of three lay persons, and then the permanent *nezirut* can, indeed, begin then and there. However, what about someone who vows to forthwith be a Samson-like *nazir* (perennial and no annulments) in twenty days' time and "from now" to be a regular thirty-day *nazir*? This would constitute a reversal of the order of the previous case. What does one do about the regular period?

Another question (#4) follows on the heels of the previous ones, and this one requires a little explanation. How are we to rule on someone who declares, "like Moses on Adar 7?" Has he become a *nazir*? That date was Moses' birth and also his death date, making it both a possibly celebratory as well as a mournful day. The former possibility has nothing to do with *nezirut*, the latter vaguely so inasmuch as we often abstain from certain practices in mourning, but something has led the authorities to deem it most likely unrelated to the question at hand and thus probably an error of the editors of the Talmud to have placed it here.

Finally, the Gemara now starts to try to determine conclusions to this series of questions. Question #1: the vower serves twenty days of his 100-day term, then interrupts this to serve his vow of thirty days as a regular *nazir*, and finally he completes the remaining eighty days of his much longer period.

The Gemara breaks its discussion resolving the dilemmas above by asking about the issue of *tumah* on an interrupted period of *nezirut*. Suppose a vower is serving a period of *nezirut* when his wife gives birth to a son, and the second commitment kicks in; his regular, personal period is halted so he can start the term committed to his son. What if in this latter period he contracts corpse *tumah*? R. Yochanan claims that, of course he loses all his accrued days from the *nezirut* devoted to his son, but he also loses all his earlier days from the regular *nezirut*; he must go through the purification rituals, become *tahor*, and then start all over again. Reish Lakish, by contrast, states that he only loses the number of days he was into the *nezirut* before his son's birth interrupted his count.

Explanations of these two sages ensue. R. Yochanan avers that he loses the days of his personal *nezirut* as well, because it as well as the period devoted to his son was interrupted, and our prooftext, *Numbers* 6.12, would encompass both: "And the first days shall fall away because he defiled his naziritehood." (Alter, p. 712) R. Yochanan sees the two vows forming one long, continuous *nezirut*, and all of it thus far observed is for naught. Meanwhile, Reish Lakish separates the two *nezirut* periods and treats them as distinct entities. The impurity incurred affects, in his view, only the period of *nezirut* currently in play, and the personal regular period is unaffected at this point.

14b

There are several different kinds of *tumah* discussed frequently throughout the Talmud. *Tzaraat* (discussed on several *dapim*) is a skin discoloration, and one afflicted with it is known as a *metzora*. However, as we shall see, a *nazir* who contracts *tzaraat* does not lose accrued days of *nezirut*; he halts his count, goes through the ritual purifications for this condition, and then resumes where he left off. Corpse *tumah* is different, however. R. Yochanan rules that if a *nazir* who is a *metzora* were to contract corpse *tumah*, he loses all the days he accrued even before becoming a *metzora*, whereas Reish Lakish claims that he does not lose those earlier days. The *tzaraat* affliction compels the *nazir* to interrupt his period of *nezirut*, although these days as a *metzora* do not count toward completion of his period of *nezirut*. Reish Lakish argues that the *nazir* who finds himself in this situation does not loses any days; for this sage, *tzaraat* is separate from *nezirut*.

Lest you believe the last two rulings, the differences between R. Yochanan and Reish Lakish, are making the same point—namely, that when *nezirut* is suspended and the *nazir* contracts *tumah*, whether or not the accrued days during the days of suspension are lost—the Gemara continues to explain why both were necessary. The Gemara frequently reiterates what appears on the surface to be the same point being made in comparable situations, but upon a closer look it turns out that there are significant differences. Without going into that here, that is precisely what it does.

One thing we learned in passing over the last two *amudim* is that a *nazir*'s final shaving cannot take place if he has less than thirty days of growth; if a term comes to an end before thirty days, actually part of the term that has had to be separated from the rest because of an interruption, he must wait until he reaches thirty days of growth and only then shave. This issue now is what a *nazir* is to do if he becomes *tamei* in the extended days necessary to fill out thirty. Rav says it affects nothing—no lost days—and R. Yochanan actually agrees. Earlier, we noted that R. Yochanan rules a loss of days but only if *tumah* is contracted during *nezirut*, not during its interruption. However, Rav's perennial interlocutor, Shmuel, comes down on the side of a loss of days, and Reish Lakish supports this position. The reason is that these are not two separate periods of *nezirut*, as above, but one continuous period.

What about a *nazir* who contracts *tumah* while performing the final rituals of purification (shaving and offerings). Rav Chisda opines that all parties, meaning Rav and Shmuel, are in consonance insofar as ruling that, if he had as yet not shaved at the point when he was applying the blood of his sacrificial offerings to the Altar, and then he contracted *tumah*, he is in deep trouble. According to Rav Chisda, he is trapped in an impossible situation in which, to make a complexity simpler, he can never escape *nezirut*. What stage or action in the final rituals is key to permitting a *nazir* out from the proscriptions associated with *nezirut*? The Gemara comes to answer this question by trying to discover what Rav Chisda was following in making his fairly harsh ruling. The Gemara suggests it was R. Eliezer who claims the key action is the head shaving. So, if the *nazir* contracts *tumah* at the end of his period of *nezirut* when he has made his offerings at the Altar in the Temple but before he has shaved himself, there is no way to go back and not be *tamei*. Much later in our tractate, a *baraita* offers a possible resolution, but not as yet.

Perhaps Rav Chisda is following the rabbis, but how can that be, as they do not deem shaving to be the crucial stage in the final process. For them it's the sacrificial offerings before the Altar that seals the deal. Once the *nazir* (even with a full mop) applies the blood in the appropriate way to the Altar, his *nezirut* has concluded. So, where is Rav Chisda coming from? Now, the Gemara does a major switcheroo and reassesses what Rav Chisda was trying to say when he claimed that there was no way out for a *nazir* in such a situation. What he was referring to was that he has no solution to the fact that he will not be satisfying the mitzvah of a *nazir*'s shaving. Once the sacrifices have been made at the Altar, he's good to go, according to the rabbis and thus to Rav Chisda as well.

What happens to a *nazir* who, for whatever reason, delays his final rituals—usually on day thirty-one after a regular period of *nezirut*? R. Yose, son of R. Chanina, states a *nazir* who finds himself in such a situation is flogged for contracting corpse *tumah* but not for consuming wine or for shaving. How, asks the Gemara, is it that, even after his thirty days are over, he is still susceptible to flogging for contracting corpse *tumah*? Probably, this is a consequence of the verse (*Numbers* 6.6) that directs a *nazir* for "all the days" of his *nezirut* he must not come into contact with a corpse, and "all" leaves little wiggle room. Only when all the final rituals have been completed is the *nazir* free from the self-imposed proscriptions.

What about the other proscriptions attached to *nezirut*? If he shaves or drinks wine before day thirty-one, before the completion of all the concluding rituals of a *nazir*, he should be subject to flogging (see *Numbers* 6.4–5).

15a

But, no, there is a distinctive ruling regarding the contraction of *tumah*. As it turns out, the head-shaving part of the final rituals of a *nazir* is crucial, and a *nazir* who puts off those rituals after the period of his *nezirut* has been completed and who has occasion to contract *tumah* from a corpse contravenes a

Torah proscription (*Numbers* 6.9) for which he is to be punished. How does *tumah* in this case differ from the other proscriptions of a *nazir*? The Gemara cites a *baraita* which reiterates that the three main proscriptions (shaving, wine, and corpse *tumah*) remain firmly in place after the *nazir* has concluded his term of *nezirut* right up until he performs those rituals. It goes on to state clearly that if the *nazir* at this point were to violate any of the three proscriptions, he will be the recipient of a flogging of forty (actually thirty-nine) strokes. In sum the ruling of R. Yose, son of R. Chanina is brazenly repudiated. And, our Gemara comes to an end on this high point, and without resolving the many queries numbered above.

A new Mishna and the last one in this chapter deals further with the issue of overlapping *nezirut* periods. Should someone state that he will forthwith be a *nazir* if his wife bears a son and, as well, that he is forthwith a *nazir* for a period of 100 days, that would appear to be a regular, thirty-day period and a much longer 100-day one, altogether 130 days. The Mishna is about to suggest a special situation which might allow for overlapping terms, making the entire period only 100 days. If his wife gives birth to a viable son at any point of his 100-day period up to day seventy, he may carry out the regular *nezirut* synchronously with the longer one. The Mishna actually states that in such a situation, "he loses nothing" by which it means that he need not add the thirty-day commitment pledged to his son's birth onto his own 100-day vow. Should his son emerge after seventy days of his personal vow, then he interrupts his own vow, proceeds to observe the shorter vow dedicated to his son's birth, and then returns to complete the personal vow; altogether 130 days. The key point here is that he can't shave at a time shorter than thirty days. This may take some work.

Rav notes that in the special case, day seventy is reckoned in both periods of *nezirut*, as it also is day one of the vow for his son and saves the vower a day. The Gemara is troubled by some of the language of the Mishna. So, it repeats that portion of the Mishna about "up to seventy days" and then adds Rav's calculation that, should his son be born at that time, it is reckoned toward both periods of *nezirut*. The Gemara, however, is slowly mounting a dispute with Rav's view. The problem comes down to the Mishna's language, but ultimately it leads to a ruling that a proper understanding of the Mishna disagrees with Rav's take on it.

As it so frequently does, the Gemara now is curious where Rav might have come up with his interpretation. In other words, which earlier authority would lay out the notion that one day in a *nezirut* period could be reckoned as two. Its first candidate is Abba Shaul, concerning whom we learn the following from a lengthy *baraita*. If one inters a deceased relative three days prior to one of the major Jewish holidays, then *shiva* (seven days of mourning) is abrogated,

as the holiday effectively terminates the rest of his *shiva*. Similarly, if inter-
ment took place eight days prior to a major holiday (namely, *shiva* plus one
day), the second period of mourning, *sheloshim* or thirty days of mourning,
is abrogated; he may also get a haircut on the day prior to the holiday, but if
he fails to do so, *sheloshim* returns in spades, no abrogation, no haircut. The
daylong permission for a haircut is due to respect for the holiday.

15b

Enter Abba Shaul who disagrees with the last piece of the *baraita* and permits
a haircut after the holiday. He reasons analogously that, if fulfillment of three
days toward *shiva* serves to abrogate the remaining days, so too does fulfillment of seven days for *sheloshim*.

   How does Abba Shaul's thinking in this *baraita* relate, let alone work to
authenticate, Rav's position. Perhaps Abba Shaul's notion that the seventh
day of mourning, the last of *shiva*, may also be reckoned in the *sheloshim* as
well, thus one day counting for two. This possibility is promptly rebuffed,
as the Gemara rules the two are not comparable. *Shiva* is a rabbinic decree,
while *nezirut* is clearly laid out in the book of *Numbers*. Thus, Abba Shaul's
ruling regarding periods of mourning can't be used to buttress Rav's ruling
of days of *nezirut*.

   Perhaps R. Yose might fit the bill. In a *baraita* concerning women's
menstrual cycle, a topic of inordinate complexity for the Talmud and fully
explored in tractate *Niddah* (concerning laws relating to women's menstruation) R. Yose rules that, if a woman seems to be completing her period
and shows no blood after a previous day in which she did, and her family
proceeded on that clean day of hers to slaughter the Passover sacrifice, but
she then experiences a secretion of blood, she becomes *tamei* (again), is not
permitted to join her fellow celebrants in eating from the Passover sacrifice,
and she is released from the obligation to bring that sacrifice a month later.
Ordinarily, those *tamei* men and women who are not permitted (or physically
unable) to bring the Passover offering on Nissan 14 must do so one month
later on Iyar 14. R. Yose relieves a woman in the above situation of the obligation to bring a Passover sacrifice on the second Passover as well.

   As it did with Abba Shaul's ruling, the Gemara now wants to find common ground between R. Yose and Rav. Perhaps R. Yose takes part of a day
as equal to a full day. How so? She began the day apparently free of any
signs of blood, purified herself in a *mikveh*, and had the Passover sacrifice
made by her family including her. She has now been adjudged *tahor*, but
then she experienced the flow later that same day. The reasoning here is that

until the point of unexpected discharge of blood, she was *tahor* for part of the day, and that exempts her from the obligation to bring a second Passover sacrifice. In other words, the new blood does not take effect ex post facto. The possible parallelism with Rav's ruling would be that a single day might be reckoned doubly.

Don't hold your breath, suggests the Gemara. It cites another *baraita* which includes a man who experiences a seminal discharge (though not blood), like the woman in the previous *baraita*, after the Passover sacrifice has been slaughtered and its blood applied to the Altar in the proper manner. Without getting too deeply into the weeds here, the *baraita* rules that, while such a person may not partake of the Passover offering, he is released from the obligatory second Passover, although the *tumah* such a person is capable of spreading may be counted ex post facto.

Intriguingly, this ruling is also stated in R. Yose's name, so he has some explaining to do. Maybe at the rabbinic level, *tumah* might be accounted after the fact, but on the Biblical level it is only from the moment of the emission forward. This just might work to allow R. Yose to have it both ways, albeit at different levels. The reasoning runs as follows. When the sacrifice was made and the blood applied from it on the Altar, the previously *tamei* woman was *tahor*, meaning she was biblically purified of *tumah* and there is no retroactivity with respect to *tumah* at that level.

We have now seen two views proffered by the Gemara to explain R. Yose's position. It now further supports part of R. Yose's argument with one from R. Oshaya who agrees that any talk of retroactive *tumah* must be rabbinic. Again, without getting too deeply into the weeds here, R. Oshaya invokes a ruling of R. Yochanan, which is oddly worded, the Gemara restates the latter's wording, and

16a

we conclude this lengthy discourse where the Gemara was taking us: When R. Yose averred that *tumah* can be retroactive, he meant rabbinically.

Tacked on to the tail end of the Gemara is a very brief discussion of a major or total *zavah* (a woman who experiences bleeding on three successive days), and how such an unfortunate woman would be when it came to bringing her offerings. It gets all caught up in how the language is stated, but it has little to do with the main issue preceding it. It is also interesting that we seem to have completely forgotten about Rav who set this whole discussion in motion going back several *dapim*. And, thus, chapter 2 comes to a close.

NOTE

1. See Joshua Fogel, *Grains of Truth: Reading Tractate* Menachot *of the Babylonian Talmud* (Lanham, MD: Hamilton Books, 2014), pp. 347–48.

Chapter 3

Graveyard Vows and Outsized Vows

The first Mishna in this new chapter is a long one—actually four separate pieces—although it is still concerned primarily with statements of vowing to be a *nazir* to which a variety of additional terms are added—and what in each case that means. We begin with an already familiar Mishna, effectively previewed on *dapim* 5a-6b. Should someone declare that he is forthwith a *nazir*, then he would shave thirty-one days later, although if he actually shaved on day thirty, that would be fine. Earlier, we noted a difference of opinion on this issue between Rav Matna and Bar Padda; there the *nezirut* vow did not indicate the number of days to which the vower was committed, and Rav Matna stated it would be thirty days, while Bar Padda claimed twenty-nine. (Spoiler alert: Rav Matna's opinion has been accepted as *halacha*, the law.) Now, strictly speaking, he should wait to shave until day thirty-one, but Rav Matna made the case that part of a day can count for a whole day; so, part of day thirty can count for the final day of his term of *nezirut*, and he may then proceed with his shaving and ritual offerings later that same day. We're not quite done here, for if someone were to declare that forthwith he would be a *nazir* for thirty days, clearly specifying that period of time, then shaving on day thirty does not satisfy his commitment. Here "thirty days" means thirty complete days of hair growth, and partial days do not count.

The second piece of our Mishna concerns a man who vows two successive periods of *nezirut*. He must shave on day thirty-one, after his first period, and on day sixty-one for the second period. So, he has fulfilled the requisite thirty complete days as a *nazir* before shaving and bringing sacrifices on the next day. That thirty-first day counts as the first of his second period of *nezirut.* Now, for whatever reason, should he shave on day thirty (accepted retroactively), he then would shave on the sixtieth day for his second period. In such a case, day thirty becomes the first day of his second period, and day sixty is day twenty-nine of period two, so he shaves and brings his offerings the next day (day thirty-one). The Mishna goes on to say that, if our *nazir* shaved on day "sixty minus one" (i.e., day fifty-nine), that is fine and he has fulfilled his duties—not ideal but acceptable, again, retroactively. It's not entirely clear why the Mishna has the odd locution of "sixty minus one," though it's probably to indicate that doing this is one day short of ideal. The Mishna offers this ruling in the name of a little-known sage, R. Papyas, who clarifies that, when someone has made such a vow of two successive periods of *nezirut* and then concluded period one by shaving on day thirty, he ends period two by shaving on day sixty; however, if he shaved on the fifty-ninth day, that's acceptable because day thirty works both as the end of period one and the start of period two.

The third piece of the Mishna at hand concerns someone who has vowed forthwith to be a *nazir* but then contracted corpse *tumah* on day thirty. He thus loses all the days accrued due to the fact that the *tumah* afflicted him within the period of commitment. We just learned that part of a day can stand in for a whole day. Would that not mean that for at least part of day thirty he was *tahor*? Not here, for one must first perform all the final rituals (shaving and sacrifices), and only then if he contracted *tumah* will he not lose his accrued *nazir* time. R. Eliezer takes exception here and deems any part of a day a full day, meaning that if a person is *tahor* for even a short time on day thirty and even if he has not performed the final observances of *nezirut*, the only consequence of contracting corpse *tumah* is a "loss" of seven days. In fact, this is not a "loss" in the same sense as the Tanna of the Mishna meant it, as everyone who contracts corpse *tumah* must undergo a seven-day sequence of purification. Should someone declare forthwith to be a *nazir* explicitly for thirty days and then contract corpse *tumah* on day thirty, he loses all his accrued days, for the same reason we noted above: When you specify the number of days of a period of *nezirut*, those are complete days and partials don't count as such.

The fourth and final piece of this Mishna concerns someone who declares that forthwith he will be a *nazir* for 100 days—and then he contracted *tumah* on day 100. Bad news—all 100 days are lost. R. Eliezer claims that only thirty days would be lost, though if he contracted *tumah* on day 101, only seven days are lost. The reasoning for R. Eliezer's take on these matters was dealt with somewhat prematurely back on 6b. A *nazir*'s contracting corpse *tumah* on the final day of a lengthy cycle does not impend total loss, but only the forfeiture of a regular thirty-day *nezirut*; similarly, after the committed

100 days are fulfilled, a vow of *nezirut* has been completed, head shaved, and ritual offerings brought to the Temple, so that contracting *tumah* the following day (101) means one enters a standard seven-day purification process (not strictly speaking a "loss").

That's a lot of meat for the Gemara to handle, and in fact much of the analysis was already accomplished earlier. Actually, the Gemara will deal selectively with portions of this lengthy Mishna. It begins with the third piece about someone who vows to become a *nazir* and then contracts corpse *tumah* on day thirty, for which he loses all thirty accrued days, while R. Eliezer only penalizes him seven.

16b

As we noted above, R. Eliezer reasons that *tumah* contracted after a full period of *nezirut* means the vower loses but seven days. In his assessment, the vower must interrupt his final ritual observances, go through the week-long purification process, and then perform those final rituals. The assumption here is the Gemara is referring to a case in which the *nazir* contracts *tumah* on day thirty, and according to R. Eliezer the man's *nezirut* will already have been fulfilled at that point.

The Gemara next looks at the next portion of the same third part of the Mishna, in which someone vows a *nezirut* of thirty days and contracted *tumah* on day thirty. The Mishna dinged him all thirty days. In this instance, R. Eliezer would agree with the Tanna, because when the vower stated the number of days explicitly, he meant full days, not partials.

Finally, the Gemara examines the fourth piece of the Mishna about a declared *nezirut* of 100 days and the unfortunate contraction of *tumah* on day 100. The Mishna claims it will cost him all 100 days, but R. Eliezer is effectively more forgiving and claims he loses only thirty, a regular term of *nezirut*. And, the Gemara then abruptly tells readers that it has really dealt with all these issues back in Chapter One, where it discussed the extensive debates between Rav Matna and Bar Padda.

The next Mishna takes us in a related direction. If someone states that he will forthwith be a *nazir* while he is in a cemetery, meaning he has most certainly contracted corpse *tumah*, and he stayed there for as long as thirty days after his initial vow, all the time spent in the cemetery cannot be reckoned toward his fulfillment of the period for which he vowed. Also, inasmuch as he was never *tahor* during his *nezirut*, he is not obliged to bring any of the ritual sacrifices associated with purification from *tumah*. Now, should he depart the cemetery and then return after undergoing the seven-day ritual purification, the number of days from the required *mikveh* immersion (part of the purification) until his re-entry may be counted toward his fulfillment; he is thus a *nazir* who is *tahor* who then becomes *tamei*, so he is required to bring the sacrifice required for corpse *tumah*. R. Eliezer opines that he loses nothing if he leaves and returns to the cemetery on the same day. To explain: The *nazir* becomes *tamei* on day one, but he may still count that day toward completion of his period; he then leaves and becomes *tahor* which counts as day two; so, if he returns to the cemetery on the same day as his immersion, he has effectively banked two days. This understanding requires a rigorously close reading of *Numbers* 6.12, and we shall return to it below in the Gemara.

The Gemara begins with two opposing views on the question of *nezirut* and cemeteries. R. Yochanan argues that a vow to be a *nazir* while in a cemetery is effective, while Reish Lakish claims that it is not. For R. Yochanan, our *nazir* must still avoid wine and other grape products and he must not cut his hair, but because he is *tamei* from the get-go, he will not be required to bring the special sacrifice required for corpse *tumah*. For Reish Lakish, none of the proscriptions apply because he is not a *nazir*, but he must nonetheless get out of the cemetery, go through the purification ritual, and then adopt a proper term of *nezirut*. R. Yochanan basically tells us that, as long as the *nazir* remains in the cemetery, he may count no days, and as soon as he exits the graveyard and undergoes purification, he has begun his period of *nezirut*. Reish Lakish requires this person to make his vow explicit once more, only this time after becoming *tahor*, and he may then begin his *nezirut*.

R. Yochanan raises a quibble with Reish Lakish's understanding. The Mishna was clear that, a declaration of *nezirut* while in a cemetery—even for thirty days—does not enable the vower to count those days, and he need not bring the *tumah* sacrifice. But, in such a case, the vow of *nezirut* is not operative. Reish Lakish responds that the Mishna's point is to completely rule out all the days the vower spent in the cemetery, despite a vow of *nezirut* there, in his count; should he become *tamei* once again before even declaring himself a presumed *nazir*, there is no requirement incumbent upon him to bring the sacrifice for *tumah*.

R. Yochanan offers another point of criticism drawn from a *baraita*. If a *tamei* person pronounced himself a *nazir*, he is obliged to follow the regular three abstentions: hair-cutting, wine, and corpse *tumah*; if he violated any of these three proscriptions, he is flogged forty times. Now, if one were to argue that *nezirut* while *tamei* is effective, then the flogging is a consequence of this person's purposive flouting of an interdiction. If, by contrast, one claims such a vow is ineffective, why would he have to endure a flogging? We will get Reish Lakish's response on the next *daf*, though I for one find it interesting that the text has not, at least not as yet, asked why someone would make a vow of *nezirut* while in cemetery, or why he would stay there for a month.

17a

Reish Lakish points out that the case at hand is not about a person who vowed to be a *nazir* while already *tamei* and went on to violate the proscriptions of a *nazir*, but to a person who was *tamei*, became *tahor*, again committed to a period of *nezirut*, and then became *tamei* again. R. Yochanan's response is to cite a *baraita* arguing that the only difference between someone afflicted with *tumah* who vows a period of *nezirut* and a *nazir* who is *tahor* who contracted *tumah* is that for the former, when he goes through the seven-day purification process, that seventh day post-purification may be counted also as day one of his *nezirut*. For the *nazir* who is *tahor* and become *tamei*, there is no such way to use the seventh day twice, because he brings his special offering on day eight. R. Yochanan thus claims that a vow to become a *nazir* while one is *tamei* is indeed effective.

The Gemara now assumes that Reish Lakish's view here is down for the count, so it takes a second look at what distinguishes his position from that of R. Yochanan. Mar bar Rav Ashi notes that both of our sages agree that a vow of *nezirut* while *tamei* nonetheless is effective as soon as it is made. The difference between them concerns the flogging. R. Yochanan's point is that, because he had declared to be a *nazir*, when he then intentionally transgressed the proscription against corpse *tumah*, presumably after becoming *tahor*, he is to be flogged. Reish Lakish claims that such a person is not flogged, just as he is not required to bring the special offering.

R. Yochanan still doesn't buy it. He reiterates the first part of the Mishna—about someone vowing to be a *nazir* while in a cemetery, even for as long as a month, who is not required to bring the offering for corpse *tumah*—and notes that this last point is the crucial one, but the man still is subject to a flogging. Reish Lakish does not take this rebuttal sitting down. The Mishna does not mention anything about flogging, but it does specify that such a person is not required to bring the special offering, and this was its way of also indicating a balanced non-requirement regarding flogging.

The Gemara now turns to a *baraita*, and things are not looking good for Reish Lakish's argument. This *baraita* is basically the same as the one cited by R. Yochanan directly above. The implied suggestion is that this is the only difference between the two sorts of *nazir*, meaning that when it comes to being flogged, both sorts fall victim. Reish Lakish doesn't buy it. There follow some deep-in-the-weeds debate over precise verbiage, but the final word comes with a *baraita* (which was actually cited on 16b above). There it explicitly says that a *tamei* person who vowed a term of *nezirut* may not do either of the other two things that are proscribed for a *nazir* (consume wine or cut hair); if he did either of these or contracts corpse *tumah*, he receives a flogging. And, Reish Lakish's argument is summarily vanquished.

In a closely related query, Rava posits a *nazir* in a graveyard and asks what should happen to him. Does he have to remain there for a certain protracted period of time to incur a flogging? The answer is somewhat complex, though little in the Talmud isn't. If the man declared himself a *nazir* after he had already entered the graveyard, and he was warned not to make such a vow because contracting corpse *tumah* could lead to severe consequences, why should the amount of time he was there matter. We should note that to incur a flogging, one must be warned with two witnesses present that he is about to violate a law or ruling that will lead to a flogging. Because of the warning, his entrance into the graveyard was clearly deliberate; had he unintentionally stepped in it, that might be a different case. So, as soon as he does step foot in the graveyard, out comes the whip. His declaration of *nezirut* in the cemetery was no different from the act of a non-*tamei nazir* stepping inside.

17b

The Gemara now refines what it was that Rava really wanted to know, though it does so while rubbing up against the absurd. We are now told that Rava meant a *nazir* whose entry into a graveyard was a consequence of his being brought there while in some sort of container or chest, conveyed by others; while there, he is still *tahor*. But, then along came someone else and, unbeknownst to our *nazir*, literally pulls the floor out from under him and lets the *tumah* in. So, now the issue of how long our unsuspecting and newly *tamei nazir* has to remain in the graveyard before he incurs a flogging. If it were the Temple, where one is also prohibited from entering while *tamei*, then he incurs a flogging if stays there as long as it takes to demonstrate self-abasement. So, if our *nazir* lingers longer than such a brief period, and after being warned, he should ready himself for a flogging; if he scurries pronto, he should be safe. The Gemara decides not to resolve this quagmire, and it chooses not to resolve Rava's query.

Rav Ashi turns the discussion at this point to the issue of a *tamei* person who takes a vow to become a *nazir*. He also places the vow to be a *nazir* for someone already in a graveyard, and he goes on to ask if that person must shave when later undergoing purification. We know from the Mishna that he does not bring the special offering. Rav Ashi is just asking about the shaving requirement, and this will keep us busy for some time.

To lay out the parameters: if a *nazir* departs *tahara* (state of being *tahor*) and becomes *tamei*, he must shave his head to rid his body of the desecrated hair of a *tamei nazir*; however, if he declared to be a *nazir* while in a graveyard, he was never a *tahor nazir*, and thus never desecrated his locks, meaning no special reason to shave. One again the Gemara reiterates the opening lines of the Mishna at hand, and it would appear to indicate that it is only the special *tumah* offering that he must bring—no mention of head-shaving. This line of argument is quickly dismissed. We know that the shaving and the bringing of the special offering enjoy a kind of symbiotic bond. So, if the special offering is not to be brought, then clearly the shaving is not required either.

Another effort to answer Rav Ashi's query looks to a *baraita*. "Ta shma," as the Gemara now says for the fifth time. This is a slightly different riff on the only difference between someone *tamei* who vows to be a *nazir* and a *nazir* who goes from *tahor* to *tamei*: the former may count the seventh day of his purification ritual as he resumes his period of *nezirut*, while the latter may not do so. We've been down this road just one *amud* above. Would one conclude from this that, in both of these cases, head-shaving should take place on the seventh day as well? Not at all, as there may be some parallel areas, but all that one may take away from this is that they both lead to a flogging.

The Gemara needs some clarification. When it comes to the shaving of the head, does this mean that the latter person would do so, while the former would not? And, if so, why does the *baraita* not say so explicitly? It was explicit about only one difference; if there are actually two, what's up? The response is to emphasize that the *baraita* focuses on the seventh day and all the requisite obligations on that day as a unit.

Not satisfied, the Gemara turns to another *baraita*. Knowing from *Numbers* 6.12 that a *nazir* who contracts corpse *tumah* must give up all accrued days reckoned toward completion of his period of *nezirut*, why is it that a *nazir* who contracts *tzaraat* must also forfeit accrued days? Maybe it runs parallel to the *nazir* who contracts corpse *tumah* and must during purification shave and bring an offering; a definite *metzora* might be required to do the same. Similarly, as a *nazir* such as ours may not count the days during which he was *tamei* in his reckoning toward completion of his term, so too would a definite *metzora* not be allowed to do so. It turns out that the *baraita* only raised the issue this way to shoot it down. While we do revoke all accrued days for a *nazir* who contracts corpse *tumah*, such is not the case for a *metzora* whose days remain in the count.

The form of analogous reasoning fails in our case at hand, so the Gemara will now try a *kal vachomer* (*a fortiori* reasoning) argument. Should someone become a *nazir* while in a graveyard, then although his head is ready for a pair of clippers befitting *nezirut*, he may not count accrued days that he was *tamei* toward completing his period. Thus, when it comes to his days as a *metzora*, a time when his head is unlikely to be ready for those clippers, wouldn't it be a better bet that his days not be counted? The *baraita* is working from the assumption that one who became a *nazir* while in a graveyard has a head ready to be shaved. Does this mean to say that shaving the head is a consequence of the purification rituals from *tumah* acquired in the graveyard? So, anyone who takes a vow of *nezirut* while in a graveyard must, while becoming *tahor*, shave his head—and Rav Ashi's issue is settled.

Or not. The point about shaving in the *baraita* is that it is to be done in *tahara* at the end of a period of *nezirut*. The Gemara thinks this a more acceptable accounting,

18a

but the issue remains unresolved, and to do so requires yet another look at yet another *baraita*. Referring to *Numbers* 6.9, wherein we learn that a *nazir* who finds himself next someone who passes away unexpectedly becomes *tamei* and must shave his head on day seven of the process of purification. The *baraita* clarifies that this is a case of a *tahor nazir* who in this manner becomes *tamei*; he must shave off the hair on his head and bring the special offerings requisite of someone in his situation, referred to here as "birds" but in fact comprising two birds and a sheep. The *baraita* notes that this excludes someone who vows *nezirut* while in a graveyard, and such a person requires neither a head-shaving nor "bird" sacrifices. The key verse here is: "and he defile his nazirite head" (Alter, p. 712); it is taken to be superfluous and therefore ready to be used to explain something else—nothing is purely superfluous. By virtue of the presence of this verse, we are informed that the Torah wants us to know that this refers to a person who was *tahor* and became *tamei*, and also that such a person requires shaving and "birds" as parts of his purification. By the same token, it excludes someone who vows *nezirut* while in a cemetery from these requirements. And, now the text tells us definitively that the case has been proven: QED.

Oftentimes, the Gemara attempts discursively to establish the provenance of a *baraita* or a Mishna. It now looks back to a *baraita* on *daf* 17 (which we discussed at length) and wants to know who authored it. This is the *baraita* which stated that the only difference between someone *tamei* who declared he would become a *nazir* and a *nazir* who was *tahor* and became *tamei* was that the former counts day seven of his purification toward the number of days in his initial *nazir* commitment, while the latter could not and must wait until day eight. Rav Chisda thinks he knows: R. Yehuda ha-Nasi, who announced at some point that a *nazir* who went from *tahor* to *tamei* does not begin his period of *nezirut* until day eight of his purification. By the same token, this should rule out R. Yose, son of R. Yehuda, who said of the same case that the count begins on day seven.

How was the basis of Rav Chisda's declaration that sees R. Yehuda ha-Nasi as the author but certainly not R. Yose, son of R. Yehuda? It may seem a bit circular, but Rav Chisda points to another *baraita* which itself cites *Numbers* 6.11: "he shall consecrate his head on that day." (Alter, p. 712) Here, the *baraita* affirms, "on that day" refers to the day the *nazir* who has contracted corpse *tumah* completes his purification by bringing his offerings and starts to grow a head of hair as part of his vow of *nezirut*, and that must mean day eight. And, the *baraita* concludes, R. Yehuda ha-Nasi is its author, while R. Yose, son of R. Yehuda, claims "that day" means day seven.

If this *baraita* strikes one as somewhat self-referential, the Gemara must think so as well, because it proceeds to cite a Mishna from tractate *Keretot* (plural of *karet*, the punishment of being "cut off" from the Jewish people for the commission of certain sins) which simply states that, if a *nazir* becomes *tamei* more than once, he is required to bring only one offering to expiate the *tumah*, rather than the usual set for each and every case of *tumah*. Rav Chisda does not directly say that the author of this *baraita* was none other than R. Yose, son of R. Yehuda, but he does note that it reflects that sage's point of view. This explanation is not exactly transparent, but Rav Chisda insists it does. He does point out that it is decidedly inconsistent with R. Yehuda ha-Nasi's view. Suppose someone contracted *tumah* on day seven and then again on the same day; these are not considered separable violations for which the *nazir* must make restitution but are all part of one extended *tumah* desecration. Inasmuch as the *nazir* cannot complete his purification until day eight, then the Mishna must be referring to the *nazir* becoming *tamei* (on day eight) after cleaning up his act on day seven, necessitating another offering to accompany the second purification. Even if he fell victim to *tumah* on day eight but before his sacrifices were presented, according to R. Yehuda ha-Nasi, he still must bring a second set.

If it is becoming less clear where this is all heading or even tautological, the Gemara at this point decides that it now wants to state clearly what the basic point of difference is between our two rabbis. It begins by asking how R. Yehuda ha-Nasi came to determine that the purified *nazir*'s count picks up again on day eight. Answer (again): *Numbers* 6.11, "the priest . . . shall atone for him, as he has offended through the corpse"; and it then goes on with "he shall consecrate his head on that day." (Alter, p. 712) Thus, returning to the count as a now *tahor nazir* (based on the latter quotation) follows atonement, and that must indicate day eight. By the same token, R. Yose, son of

R. Yehuda, rebuts this argument by saying that, if it is meant to be day eight, then the added words "on that day" (*bayom hahu*) make no sense.

18b

Had the Torah not added the words "on that day," day eight would have been crystal clear, but their presence in the Torah appears superfluous—and, once again, there are no superfluities in Torah, so they must indicate something else. He says they mean the day, day seven, when the *tamei nazir* shaves his head toward the end of his purification.

What does R. Yehuda ha-Nasi make of those words? Does he consider them "superfluous" as well and thus available for interpretation? He would agree that, should the words "on that day" have not been in the *Numbers* passage, it would have indicated day eight but only if the required sacrifices were brought on that day as well. So, the apparently superfluous expression is there to inform us that, even if the offerings are not presented then, the count resumes on day eight.

If this isn't specific enough for you, the Gemara now seeks to determine if, when R. Yehuda ha-Nasi refers to the day the offerings are brought, he means from the night before, as Jewish law has each day beginning just after sunset and continuing through the next evening. The Gemara now goes back to Rav Chisda's citation from Mishnaic tractate *Keretot* and asks why he only built an explanation of the Mishna using the reasoning of R. Yose, son of R. Yehuda. He could have used R. Yehuda ha-Nasi and started the count from the night before *day* eight, and sacrifices may only be offered during the daytime. Had the *nazir* contracted *tumah* again that night, it would constitute a separate incidence, and atonement would not be available until the following daytime—hence, no need for a separate offering. Seen from this perspective, the Gemara argues that the Mishna would work with R. Yehuda ha-Nasi's view that the count picks up on day eight.

The Gemara now suggests a couple ways that Rav Chisda might skirt this conundrum, and he will eventually fall off this grid completely as newer rabbinic authorities enter the discussion and the last part of the Mishna which began this whole debate is brought up for analysis. First, sure, one cannot offer a sacrifice until daytime of day eight, and sure, the night before is counted as day eight, perhaps the time for the sacrifice can be said to have arrived on the night before, even if it can't actually be offered. This one is easily shot down. Rav Ada bar Ahavah argues that the time when a *nazir* may take up his count and the timing of sacrificial offerings are mutually determined. Ultimately, Rav Chisda's effort to understand the Mishna in line with R. Yehuda ha-Nasi is thus deemed unsuccessful, and it now begins to move away from this collection of rabbis to other sages' views on *tumah* affliction on days seven or eight of a purification process.

Immediately above on 18a, the Gemara cited a *baraita* about contracting *tumah* on day seven of purification and then becoming *tamei* again that same day. He is required to bring only one offering for both *tumah* afflictions together. If he were to contract *tumah* on day eight of the purification process and then again became *tumah* the same day a second time, he must bring an offering for each incident; he also may commence his *nezirut* count from day seven right after his immersion in a *mikveh*. This is R. Eliezer's viewpoint. Now, the rabbis argue that one offering suffices for all incidents of *tumah*, until he offers his *chatat* sacrifice. Should he contract *tumah* after having offered his *chatat*, he must bring another, and every time thereafter. Thus, as soon as he offers the *chatat*, he may then commence his count, even if the *asham* (guilt offering) has not as been brought. The rabbis here, incidentally, are disagreeing with the view, noted above, of R. Yehuda ha-Nasi who accepts a start for the count on day eight, irrespective of whether any offerings have been brought. R. Yishmael, son of R. Yochanan ben Beroka, injects a slightly different view by arguing that not only the *chatat* but also the *asham* must be offered before the count may commence.

How do these three new positions—R. Eliezer, the rabbis, and R. Yishmael— jibe with the biblical passage on which we have been focused? R. Eliezer had pointed to day seven ("on that day") as the start of the resumed *nezirut* count, whether or not offerings had been brought, so he should be fine with scripture; the rabbis would stress that, whether he brought the *asham* or not "on that day," the count may begin; that leaves R. Yishmael who insists we wait until after the *asham* is offered up. What is he to make of "on that day?" The response invokes the third of the three sacrifices, the *olah*, and suggests that the *nazir* being purified may starting counting "on that day" even if the *olah* has not been brought.

This begs the question, as the Gemara assiduously notes, for how are the rabbis knowledgeable that offering the *olah* is not crucial; they are clear that the *asham* is critical here, but what about the *olah*? As it turns out, the *olah* is different from the *chatat* or the *asham* sacrifices, offered to atone for sin and guilt respectively, in that it is a gift (*doron*) to the Altar and needs no scriptural mention before resuming the *nazir*'s count. (R. Yishmael would disagree, as he insists that we wait until the *olah* is brought.) The Gemara still wants a better explanation from the rabbis about how we need "on that day" to justify waiting for the *asham* offering. The Gemara implies that the order of the verses in *Numbers* 6.11–12 makes clear that "on that day" is unnecessary to articulate their point. The reply submitted by the Gemara is to draw on another *baraita*. Verse 6.12 reads in part: "And he shall keep apart [i.e., dedicate] for the Lord the days of his naziritehood [*nezirut*], and he shall bring a yearling lamb as a guilt offering." (Alter, p. 712) The first words of this line of text refer to the *nazir*'s count. Now, as the *baraita* continues, all *asham* sacrifices are essential to atonement and purification. One might assume that that would be the case here as well and that without bringing the *asham* the *nazir*'s count cannot resume.

19a

So, the Torah first mentions dedication (namely, resuming his count of days) and then notes the bringing of the *asham* ("yearling lamb") afterward. The count resumes before any mention of the *asham*. R. Yishmael would insist on waiting for the count to pick up again after the *asham* is brought.

At this point the Gemara quotes from yet another *baraita* and asks who its author might be. This time it specifies a woman making a *nezirut* commitment and then becoming *tamei* from a corpse; she proceeds to ready her birds and lamb which will be brought as offerings. Then, her husband decides to rescind her vow, something he is biblically allowed to do within certain bounds. So, she offers the bird *chatat* but not the bird *olah* nor the lamb *asham*, because once her vow of *nezirut* has been vacated, she was effectively never a *nazir* at all, and never was in a situation in which the corpse *tumah* desecrated her vow, putting the *olah* and *asham* off the table. The *chatat* remains necessary, as will be explained below. Rav Chisda opines that this *baraita* is in accord with the view of R. Yishmael, the son of R. Yochanan ben Beroka, who argued that the *olah* and *asham* are brought as part of the *nazir*'s atonement.

Why would R. Yishmael distinguish the *chatat* bird from the *olah* bird? Arguably, once the husband has rescinded his wife's vow to be a *nazir* after the fact, the *chatat* which is part of the ordinary purification process should also disappear, as she was never a *nazir*. If, by contrast, the husband's act only causes his spouse to cease being a *nazir* from the moment he voiced his annulment of her vow, then would she not be obliged to bring the *olah* (and, incidentally, the *asham*) as well? The Gemara states that, once the husband rescinds his wife's vow, it annuls it entirely after the fact, meaning no offerings should be necessary, as no *nezirut* ever took effect. As for that odd *chatat* she must offer up, the Gemara declares that R. Yishmael agrees with R. Elazar ha-Kappar who claims that declaration of a vow to become a *nazir* is a sin and necessitates a *chatat* (sin offering). The woman may never effectively have been a *nezira* but she did deprive herself of wine, and that R. Elazar ha-Kappar considers sinful, along with all self-denial.

R. Elazar ha-Kappar's views in this vein were laid out briefly on 3a and now they get fuller treatment. He focuses on *Numbers* 6.11 which states that, in the purification process of a *nazir* who has become *tamei*, the Kohen atones for the *nazir* who has "sinned with respect to the soul" (*chata al-hanafesh*). Ordinarily one takes the "soul" mentioned here to be the corpse with which the *nazir* accidentally came into contact, but R. Elazar ha-Kappar claims that the "sinned against" party and the sinner are the same (in an odd conflation of the title character in *King Lear*). The *nazir* denied himself wine, and add to that the other items of self-deprivation, and we have a major sinner. The Gemara comes back with the obvious rebuttal that the verse in *Numbers* is focused on a *nazir* who contracted corpse *tumah*; if vowing to abstain from wine is a sin, it should also apply to a *nazir* who remains *tahor*. Actually, R. Elazar ha-Kappar would agree, as he lumps all those who take vows of *nezirut* in the sinners' bag.

It's been a while, but the Gemara now returns to the Mishna, discussed near the top of 16b, and cites a snippet. If someone who vowed to be a *nazir* while in a graveyard left the graveyard and returned to it, the time from leaving to returning may be counted as days of his *nezirut*. On the surface this seems odd, for wouldn't he have been *tamei* when departing the cemetery? What about the presumably requisite purification preceding resumption of his reckoning of days? Shmuel tries to provide cover for this reading of the Mishna by stating that the case at hand involves someone who did go through purification concluding with immersion in a *mikveh* on day seven (all of which explanation is clearly read into our text).

Another puzzling issue: From the Mishna's brief recital, one might think that resumption of one's count comes only if the purified *nazir* returns to the graveyard. What if he somehow kept away from a place full of corpses? This seems awfully strange. The Gemara responds that, of course, if he remained *tahor* outside the graveyard, he may go on with his counting of days, but should he return to said graveyard, a purified *nazir*, he may also do so—and that's the point. In an almost humorous addition to this string, we read in the Gemara of Rav Kahana and Rav Assi asking Rav: How come you never taught us this business the way Shmuel (Rav's perennial interlocutor) just taught it to his disciples? Rav: I thought you wouldn't need to be taught this.

Back to the Mishna and R. Eliezer who claims that, if the graveyard *nazir* departs and returns on the same day, he loses no accrued days in his count. This is based on a close reading of *Numbers* 6.12 which states that he does lose "the first days," because until there is more than one day, you don't have "days." And, as will become important momentarily, until you have "days" you don't bring the special offering for a *nazir*'s *tumah*, according to R. Eliezer. Ulla, a prominent sage of the Talmud, now makes his first appearance in our tractate, and he attempts to explain more thoroughly what

R. Eliezer was arguing: If a *nazir* who is *tahor* becomes *tamei*—even if on his first day out of the box—he may not count that single day in his count toward his commitment.

19b

Rava doesn't appear to like Ulla's take on R. Eliezer. The Gemara turns to Abaye who does Rava's bidding by contesting Ulla's take via a lengthy *baraita*. Should a person declare himself forthwith to be a *nazir* for a period of 100 days, and he then became *tamei* on the first day of this declaration, it would be conceivable to assume that he loses this first day in his count, and that following purification, he would have to complete 100 days to fulfill his vow. As we just noted, however, the Torah states clearly "the first days" will be lost to the count, implying that you need more than one day to constitute "days." That being the case, our *nazir* would be allowed to count the first day before he contracted *tumah*, and he would thus only need ninety-nine more. Now, should a person become *tamei* at the very end of his count, day one hundred, it would be conceivable to assume that he loses the entire kit and caboodle (all 100 days). Again, the Torah states that he loses "the first days," and this indicates that there must also be last days (plural), meaning that the *tumah* hit at a time when only a single day (not days) remained in this person's period. So, he does not lose everything, because he does not have "last days." Should our *nazir* contract *tumah* on day ninety-nine, meaning lots of preceding days and one more (day 100), he would presumably have violated the terms of his vow, both explicit "first days" and implied "last days." He loses everything accrued. The thrust of the *baraita* is thus to affirm R. Eliezer's position by its continued stress on the constraints imposed on one's count by "the first days." And, although it was never entirely clear what Ulla was expressing, the Gemara regards his position as fully rebutted.

Our Mishna's citation of R. Eliezer is now to be discussed, and Rav Pappa asks Abaye if the "days" mentioned there—meaning more than one day necessary prior to *tumah* leading to one's loss in his count—implies one day completed and a second just begun, or does it mean two full days and a third beginning. On the surface, any time on day two that a *nazir* becomes *tamei* would mean loss of two days in his count. Rav Pappa would not have been asking such an elementary question. However, how does "first days" jibe with inferred "last days?" Must they be precisely parallel? If, for example, *tumah* was contracted anytime on day ninety-nine, all is lost; that would not, though, comprise two full days. By the same token, we don't know precisely when a given vow of *nezirut* was declared, but it was likely sometime during day one—again, not a complete day in a count. Interestingly, Abaye draws a blank.

Rav Pappa takes his question to Rava. Rava answers in a vaguely cryptic manner by stating just one word—or so the Gemara recounts things—from *Numbers* 6.12: *yiplu* 'shall fall away' (Alter, p. 712), in reference to "first days." The idea here is that even partial days do count in contracting *tumah*, meaning that loss of accrued days can occur on day two.

The Gemara concludes its lengthy disquisition of this Mishna with an assessment of R. Eliezer's reading of the verses from *Numbers* that we have been so closely examining (considering Rava's rather brief explanation). Just as we have seen that we needed the Bible to explicitly spell out "days" (plural form), we also needed it explicitly to state *yiplu* (plural form). Had scripture stated "days" but not *yiplu*, one might assume the need for two complete days to be over and a third to begin before a *nazir* loses accrued days due to contracting *tumah*; scripture's use of *yiplu* confirms that partial days are sufficient. By the same token, had scripture only stated *yiplu* without mention of "days," one might assume that loss of accrued time could commence with but a single day on which one contracted *tumah*. The inclusion of "days," thus, clarifies that a second day must have begin.

We now turn to a lengthy Mishna which is followed by a relatively short Gemara, the reverse of the preceding section. We turn in this Mishna to a largely new area, vows of *nezirut* of more than a standard, thirty-day length, asserted outside the borders of the Land of Israel and fulfilled in their entirety there. The problem is that the rabbis declared such terrain entirely filled with corpse *tumah*. If such a vower were to make his way to the Land of Israel after his period of *nezirut* and there bring his offerings to the Temple, what sort of situation would he then find himself facing. Bet Shammai state that he must undertake a thirty-day period as a *nazir* in the Land of Israel; the Bible makes no reference to the country in which a *nazir* commits himself, but the rabbis were certain that there were unmarked graves all over heathen lands, and thus such a person has been adhering to his *nezirut* on rabbinically *tumah* terrain. Bet Hillel, by contrast, declare that he has to start all over again—all for naught, this being a case, as we saw above, similar to someone who vows to be a *nazir* in a graveyard.

The Mishna then introduces us to the fascinating Queen Helena (mid-first century C.E.), sovereign of Adiabene who converted to Judaism and often puts in cameos in the Talmud. When her son, presumably referring to Munbaz who also converted, went off to war, she vowed that, if he returned safely, she would then become a *nezira* for the hefty period of seven years. And, both happened. When her period of *nezirut* was fulfilled, she traveled to the Land of Israel, only to find that Bet Hillel judged that she had now to undertake another seven years as a *nezira*. She did this as well, and on the final day of this second seven-year period, she contracted *tumah* which meant that the second period was also lost. So, she then undertook and complete a third seven-year commitment, and she was as such a *nezira* for twenty-one years in total. R. Yehuda states that she was "only" a *nezira* for fourteen.

Usually, we find Bet Shammai stricter in their interpretation of the law than Bet Hillel, but that is clearly not the case here. Their contrasting views in this instance center on what constitutes *tumah* as decreed by the rabbis in terrain outside the Land of Israel. So, in the case of someone who vows to be a *nazir* for more than thirty days and fulfills it, all while outside the Land, Bet Shammai rule that he must undertake a thirty-day period inside Israel, while Bet Hillel demand he start all over from scratch. As is often the case, the Gemara begins by posing possible explanations which it must know will be shot down immediately, often starting from the least viable. So, it rhetorically asks if Bet Shammai's reasoning is that only the ground (as opposed to the air above) outside the Land of Israel is polluted with corpse *tumah* for the reason noted above, and Bet Shammai thus rule more leniently than usual, as the rabbis would have been easy-going vis-à-vis the air outside the Land.

20a

Completing this line of reasoning, Bet Hillel would possibly rule both ground and air *tamei*, and this stringency demands a complete redo on the vow.

But, the Gemara claims that, in fact, there is no difference between the schools of Shammai and Hillel on the issue of countries outside the Land; they agreed that the ground there, not the air, was *tamei*. The difference was that Bet Shammai argue that we discipline someone who vows to be a *nazir* outside the Land of Israel by making him adopt a thirty-day *nezirut* when he returns; Bet Hillel argue that we discipline him by demanding he return and redo his entire period of *nezirut*.

The Gemara now turns to the piece of the Mishna concerning Queen Helena and R. Yehuda's dissenting view that she was "only" a *nezira* for fourteen, not twenty-one, years. How does R. Yehuda come to this calculation. He reasons that she contracted *tumah* at the end of her seven-year term outside the Land, and it was thus deemed necessary for her to observe a standard, thirty-day *nezirut* à la Bet Shammai in Israel; another thesis has it that R. Yehuda postulates that she did not contract *tumah* at the end of her term, meaning that her behavior accorded with Bet Hillel. Even if we follow the first of these two scenarios, would Queen Helena not have altogether observed a total of fourteen years and thirty days, although the Mishna says only fourteen years? If we take this as a rhetorical question, then R. Yehuda must have doubted that she ever contracted *tumah* at all. She was punished with a second term of seven years, à la Bet Hillel, although maybe in the context of a whopping fourteen-years of *nezirut*, thirty days is easily forgettable.

This Gemara concludes with a *baraita* in which we find R. Yehuda citing a ruling in the name of R. Eliezer. The latter cites *Numbers* 6.13: "And this is the teaching for the nazirite: When the days of his naziritehood come to term." (Alter, p. 712) He interprets this to mean that, if one contracts *tumah* on the final day of his period of *nezirut* ("naziritehood"), he is punished with a thirty-day term.

We move immediately to a new Mishna, the final one for Chapter Three, and look at a wholly new topic, one that can be found in many tractates of the Talmud. It postulates two pairs of witnesses presenting opposing testimony about a given individual. One pair state that the individual in question vowed two periods of *nezirut*, while the second pair state that he vowed five periods. Unnoted here is that the man himself must have denied ever having made any vow. Silence is far from golden; it's effectively a confession, and five periods of *nezirut* would ensue for him. Under such circumstances, Bet Shammai rule that, because the two sets of witnesses completely disagree, they effectively cancel each other out, and no *nezirut* is Bet Shammai's judgment. Bet Hillel, by contrast, rule a vow of two periods may be considered a portion (actually, 40%) of five, resulting in a judgment of two periods of *nezirut* for the person in the dock.

In an interesting move, the Gemara starts by citing a *baraita* that offers us another rendition of the differences of views from this Mishna. The *baraita* has R. Yishmael, son of R. Yochanan ben Beroka, ruling that the houses of Shammai and Hillel actually agree on this one, and that the subject must undertake two periods of *nezirut*. In this take on things, Bet Shammai follow the reasoning of Bet Hillel. They do, though, disagree about something (they always do), and that concerns a situation in which we have a pair of witnesses in which one claims he heard two periods of *nezirut* vowed and the other claims five. Here, Bet Shammai declare that the witnesses' disagreement makes both testimonies null and void, whereas Bet Hillel conclude two periods of *nezirut* incumbent on the subject.

Rav adds to R. Yishmael's reading of this difference of the two houses by noting that both concur that, when the witnesses dispute one another, no *nezirut* ensues. To this he introduces a new concept of "counting," which the Gemara goes on to explain. Rav Chama asks Rav Chisda what this "counting" means, before going on to answer. Explanation: One witness states it was five periods, not two; the other states it was two periods, not five; conclusion: we have a clear conflict. So, the situation must be such that one witness states that the subject vowed one and two periods of *nezirut*, while the second witness state that the subject vowed three, four, and fives periods. If this was what transpired, then we can see that the witnesses were not disagreeing as to what the subject actually vowed, but were counting out what they heard. It follows that one of the witnesses must actually be lying. Under such circumstances, we do not merge the two testimonies and rule the subject not a *nazir* at all.

20b

Rav Chama doesn't buy Rav's argument that the second witness's testimony of three, four, five—without citing the first witness's one, two—actually constitutes a negation of the first witness's testimony. He claims that starting with three merely assume one and two, and to support this perspective the Gemara concludes Chapter Three by declaring that "in the West," meaning the Land of Israel, the rabbis all agree with Rav Chama's disputation of Rav in this instance.

Chapter 4

"And I," Women, and Sacrificial Animals

20b (CONTINUED)

The new chapter begins with a meaty Mishna, back to definitional issues, that will keep us busy for the new few days. So, a man vows forthwith to become a *nazir*, and someone else, upon hearing this vow, declares: "And I" (*vaani*); then, a third person also tags along by saying: "And I." What is the result? They all enter a period of *nezirut*. (We have seen the first two segments of this on 11b, and now it's a bit more complicated.) If, for whatever reason, the first person's vow is annulled, then all three are as well. Once vow one is vacated, the others' vows vanish, contingent as they were on the preceding one. Now, should the vow of the final person in such a string be annulled, none that preceded are affected.

New case: Should a man vow forthwith to become a *nazir*, and then another person avers (rather less directly): "My mouth is like his mouth" or "My hair is like his hair," again the second vow is affirmed. Third case: If one were to vow forthwith to become a *nazir*, and his wife heard him and declared: "And I"; as the husband, he is empowered (see *Numbers* 30.14) to annul her vow at the same time that it has no impact on his own which preceded it. In the reverse situation in which the woman first vowed a period of *nezirut*, followed by the husband vowing: "And I," he may not annul his wife's vow. In this case, revoking his wife's would necessarily annul his own, because it follows in the string, and one may not unilaterally cancel one's own vow. Fourth and final case: If a person declared forthwith to become a *nazir*, and then turned to his wife, asked if she would like to join him, and she replied "Amen," she has effectively said "yes." He can here annul her vow, as he wishes, without affecting his own. In a reverse situation, she declares a

69

period of *nezirut*, asks if he'd like to join her, and he replies "Amen" (= yes), he likewise is not empowered to annul her vow.

The Gemara begins with a slight limitation of the first case of the Mishna about a string of vowers stating "And I" after one person declared to be a *nazir*. Reish Lakish stated to R. Yehuda Nesia (grandson of R. Yehuda ha-Nasi)[1] that this piggybacking (you should excuse the metaphor) to a previous vow of *nezirut* by stating "And I" only works if made within the time frame of uttering a short expression. How would we accurately characterize such a period of time? Reish Lakish says: The length of a greeting to another person. This only begs the question, for we then need to know how long a greeting requires. We still don't have a response in seconds or even minutes, but we are told the greeting being referred is not just a passing hello to a friend but that of a student to his teacher (*shalom alecha rabbi* 'peace unto you, my teacher'). This would probably cut short a string of "And I" declarations to three.

After hearing all this, R. Yehuda Nesia doesn't go for it. He thinks Reish Lakish has overly foreshortened the time allowed for "And I" to be uttered and to be effective. He gives the example of a student prepared to reply "And I" to someone's audible vow of *nezirut*, but just then he sees his teacher and greets him with the requisite three-word salutation, by which time his window to declare "And I" would have passed, according to Reish Lakish.

21a

While R. Yehuda Nesia's reply may certainly seem justifiable, the Gemara won't allow Reish Lakish's assessment of such a situation disappear so easily and so brings possible backing for his reading. It cites a *baraita* which basically reworks the segment of the Mishna we are addressing and agrees with Reish Lakish that, if someone heard a vow of *nezirut*, waited the amount of time required for a salutation, and then said "And I," his vow is accepted but none thereafter are. And, when it raises the question of the length of such a salutation, it answers the same way as above.

The Gemara next directs our attention back to the Mishna where it adduces more support for the position articulated by Reish Lakish. The string of one *nazir* declaration followed by two persons stating "And I" says nothing about a fourth person tagging on. The Mishna only ruled out, by implication, a fourth person joining in (the third to state "And I") after the time is takes for a three-word utterance. Had it allowed for that fourth person, it would have explicitly said so, and that would make R. Yehuda Nesia's position tenable.

The rebuttal sounds like a contemporary, satirical remark. Is it the respon-sibility of the Mishna to count out every conceivable case, "like a peddler" hawking his merchandise? The ordinary Tanna of a Mishna never says more than necessary. But, if that is true, then shouldn't the Tanna only have indi-cated one person stating "And I," and the rest would be understood without expressly communicated. The Gemara finds this reasoning specious. Sure, the Tanna could have cut short his statement at one "And I," but what follows in the Mishna about the subsequent persons—if the vow is annulled, all that follow are automatically annulled; if the last vow is cancelled, it has no effect on those preceding it—indicates that there is a middle vower. The Mishnaic text refers to a "first one" (*rishon*), a "last one" (*acharon*), and "all of them" (*kulan*), which implies altogether three.

Before the Gemara moves on to other section of the Mishna, it focuses much more closely on the apparently simple expression, "And I." Are we to assume that every person who makes such a vow in this manner is referring to the person who said "And I" just before him, or is everyone who says "And I" referring to the initial person who made his claim of *nezirut*? If one heard a vow of *nezirut*, followed by someone saying "And I," he can of course join the string and explicitly say to whom he is linking his own vow. The Gemara, though, wants to know what we are to understand when subsequent vowers of "And I" are not explicit. Can the string go on forever, as long as each sub-sequent vower says his "And I" within the three-word time limit? If, though, all must be linked to the initial articulator of the vow to be a *nazir*, the time limit will expire after the equivalent of a mere three words, *shalom alecha rabbi*, can be spoken. How is this to be resolved?

"*Ta shma*," says the Gemara for the eleventh time in our tractate, the first of four on the *amud* alone. It reiterates out Mishna again in stating that the case is of one initial vower and two "And I" responses. It concludes simply that the respondents are referring to the first person; if it were to be understood as each referring to his antecedent in the string, the Mishna would have pointed out the possibility of numerous respondents. This is summarily dismissed with the same satirical comment asking if a Tanna is obliged to itemize each and every likelihood like a peddler hawking his goods. But, why then, the rebuttal goes, does the Mishna have two respondents with "And I" and not one. And, again we come to the same conclusion we did just moments ago.

Two more tries to resolve the present conundrum ensue. First, as the Mishna states, if the original vower has his vow vacated, all that follow in the string of "And I" also find their vows evaporated. This might mean that, only when the *rishon*'s vow is annulled, do the subsequent vowers find theirs annulled as well. If a middle person finds his vow annulled, it has no effect on anyone else, as the Mishna would, in this reading, be obliged to articulate specifically that the middle vow's annulment has the same effect on those that follow. The Mishna only refers to the initial vow in this regard, which would mean everyone who states "And I" is referring to that initial vow. No way, as the Gemara promptly rebuts this line of reasoning and reasserts that one "And I" signifies its immediate antecedent.

It then attempts one last time, this time emphasizing the piece of the Mishna which states that, if the last person has his vow vacated, this has no impact on the vows of those before him; if the middle person has his vow annulled, then the last person endures the same result. Wouldn't this mean that each person vowing "And I" is only referring to his immediate predecessor. The Gemara doesn't buy this at all either and moves on to attempt to finally resolve this particularly thorny issue.

We have another *baraita* introduced here. If the *rishon* has his vow vacated, all that followed him with "And I" also find theirs vacated as well. If only the *acharon* has his vow annulled, he alone is affected while those preceding him in the string are unchanged. Now, the *baraita* continues, if the middle person has his vow vacated, anyone thereafter who stated "And I" also has his vow vacated; anyone before him in the chain remained committed to his vow. This has been stated several times. The lesson, the Gemara states clearly, is that the claim of "And I" refers specifically to one's direct antecedent, not all the way back to the initial vow. As if to stamp its approval before moving on, the Gemara notes as indication of its proof: *Shma mina* (Learn from this!).

We move now to look at the second section of the Mishna, in which one person declares a period of *nezirut*, and then a second hears him and states "my mouth" or "my hair" is "like his"; verdict: he does enter a period of his own *nezirut*. The Mishna begins with a fairly obvious question: How can he make such a guileless statement about his mouth or hair and have become a *nazir* by it?

21b

The Gemara attempts to seal the deal by comparing this piece of the Mishna with a *baraita*. This *baraita* claims starkly that, if one were to claim that his hand or leg were a *nazir*, nothing of legal import has been proclaimed. By contrast, the *baraita* goes on, if one were to claim his head or his liver were a *nazir*, then (oddly?) he has indeed begun a period of *nezirut*. Before we can so much as stare into space on this one, the Gemara explains that, only when a declaration of *nezirut* is placed on an organ critical to life itself, does one then enter *nezirut*. As one's mouth or hair do not fit the bill, the *baraita* disputes the Mishna. R. Yehuda straightens things out by clarifying that the Mishna meant as follows: Vowing that one's mouth be "like his mouth" (namely, one who vowed to become a *nazir*) should be understood as regarding refraining from drinking wine; and "like his hair" understood as regarding refraining from cutting it.

The next piece of the Mishna is the first to deal specifically with women vowing a period of *nezirut*, except for the special case of Queen Helena in Chapter Three. If a woman so vows and her husband responds "And I," he then may not annul her vow (again: no man can unilaterally vacate his own vow). When a man wishes to have his vow vacated, he must appeal to a sage or a group of three laymen, and they must be able to cite some element of the vow or its potential effect that could not have been known. When a husband vacates his wife's vow, he does so on the basis of a special law in *Numbers* 30. The Gemara asks now if his cancellation of her vow is thorough, all the way to its commencement, or if it breaks off the vow at the point of cancellation. From a practical point of view, why do we need to know? The Gemara answers its own question by noting that, if a woman took a vow of *nezirut* and then another woman said "And I," and at that point the first woman's husband cancelled his wife's vow, what happens to the second woman. If it's a thorough cancellation the second woman's vow becomes null and void as well, because the first woman never became a *nezira*; however, if it merely blunts the force of the first woman's vow, her vow does indeed come to a sudden halt, but the "And I" woman's vow is unaffected.

The Gemara now asks why, in this piece of the Mishna that we are considering, the husband cannot merely cancel his wife's vow from that point on (that is, not in retroactive fashion) and remain steadfast in his own vow. The Mishna states that this is impossible, and this must therefore mean that when a husband vacates his wife's vow, he does so in the thorough way. Nope, states the Gemara, as the husband's annulling his wife vow is only from the point he utters it so. He should, it would appear, be able to do so in the case at hand, but the Mishna forbids it. Why? The reason is that he responded to her declaration of *nezirut* with "And I" which is equivalent to his saying that he upholds or validates her vow. He may appeal his validation and have a sage or group of three laymen do the annulment, but otherwise he is legally impotent.

Another go at this piece. The Gemara now cites a Mishna we shall come to in about three days (24a). A woman takes a vow of *nezirut* and sanctifies the requisite animal offerings that must be brought at the conclusion of the period for which she declared. Her husband than steps in and vacates her vow. What is the fate of her animals? Now, if the animals belonged to her husband, they return to the flock and are simply divested of their sanctities. If they belonged to her, a rare enough state of affairs, the *chatat* is simply left to die, because it cannot be used any longer, and it cannot be sacrificed. Her *olah* and *asham* can be sacrificed as donative offerings to the Altar, something impossible for a *chatat*. If we understand a husband's annulment of a wife's vow as total, even the *chatat* should return to its ordinary state before being set aside as a prospective offering. Because we know this cannot happen, it must be the case that a husband's vacating his wife's vow only picks up from the point at which it was made. The Gemara again discards this attempt at a proof by demonstrating that there are other instances in which a *chatat* is left to die, and they are not a consequence of the above case.

One last try at settling this problem, this time citing a Mishna we shall come to soon (23a). A woman declares to become a *nezira* and then purposefully drinks some wine or comes into contact with a corpse. The Mishna rules a punishment of flogging, forty strokes. The Gemara then explains that, if her husband hadn't vacated this vow of hers, there would have been no requirement for the Mishna to state any punishment—it's obvious. So the husband must then have vacated her vow. If, though, his annulment was throughgoing, why would she incur a flogging? She was effectively never a *nezira*, meaning that the wine or the corpse would have no bearing on her behavior. This should provide further proof that a husband's vacating a wife's *nezirut* only kicks in at the moment of annulment.

And, once again, the Gemara doesn't buy it. OK, it is obvious that no flogging would have been administered as punishment if the husband's annulling his wife's vow was thorough and retroactive, as the Mishna on 23a states that, if her husband annuls her vow, then even if she is unaware of his doing so, she goes ahead and consumes wine or makes contact with a corpse, no flogging is decreed for her.

22a

The Mishna's earlier statement that she is subject to such a flogging is there for artistic contrast.

Apparently having had enough of all this, the Gemara now decides that it must resolve this issue. It cites a *baraita* which in turn draws from the Mishna at hand. When a woman vows to be a *nezira*, then is afflicted with corpse *tumah* and brings the requisite offerings in such a case, at this point her husband vacates her vow. She must still offer the *chatat* (bird) but not the *olah* (nor the *asham*, though the *baraita* doesn't mention it). If his annulling of his wife's vow only picked up from the time he issued it, then she should bring all three offerings, because she would still have been a *nezira* at that point in time.

The Gemara quickly retorts that, if the husband's annulment was thorough and retroactive, meaning she was never a *nezira*, she would arguably be under no obligation even to offer the *chatat* (or any of the other sacrificial offerings). Yes, that would seem to be so, so why must she bring a *chatat* in this instance? As it frequently does, the Gemara begins its reply by determining who authored such a ruling. It points to R. Elazar ha-Kappar, whom we have encountered several times thus far, who issued a ruling in a *baraita* running as follows. Through an intriguing reading of *Numbers* 6.11, which was mentioned previously, he addressed the problem of a *nazir* whose vow was vacated but indeed did sin regarding abstention from wine—required for a *nazir* but absolutely not for any other adult. Through the linguistic devise of a *kal vachomer*, he argues that it is for abstaining from wine that she is deemed a sinner, and a sinner is obligated to offer a sin offering (*chatat*).

The Gemara now presents further evidence for its ruling with yet another *baraita*. Should a woman vow to be a *nezira*, followed by a second woman who heard her and stated "And I," and then the husband of the first woman vacated his wife's vow, she is no longer a *nezira*, but the second woman is unaffected by this action. This would indicate that the husband's action only took effect from the moment he vacated his wife's vow. The *baraita* goes on to cite R. Shimon who averred that, if the second woman were to have said "I am like you," then both her vow and that of the first woman are vacated when the latter's husband annuls his wife's vow. The "like you" indicates that, just as the first woman has had her vow now annulled, so too is the second woman's.

22b

On the basis of the first part of this *baraita*, the Gemara tries to settle an ancillary issue. It does this by reference to a possibly comparable case of a *shelamim* (peace offering); before it is ritually slaughtered and its blood sprinkled on the Altar, but after it is set aside to be an offering, the *shelamim* is still proscribed for consumption. After the rituals of its sacrifice are completed, it is permitted to be eaten. The link to the ruling on a husband's vacating his wife's *nezirut* vow is very difficult to follow. The Gemara, though, is convinced that the two are comparable.

We noted the difference between a second woman, after hearing a woman declare a vow of *nezirut*, stating "I am like you" as opposed to "And I." The Gemara now turns to other utterances a second might state and what their consequences would be. If she stated "I am forthwith a *nezira* in your footsteps" after hearing the first woman, the Gemara asks if her vow is also vacated when the husband of the first woman annuls his wife's initial vow. To settle the matter, the Gemara returns to the Mishna and the phrase about a husband who hears his wife make her vow and himself says "And I." In this case he cannot annul her vow, because in so doing it would vacate his own vow, which is impossible. But, the Gemara does rule that a husband's "And I" is tantamount to a second woman's "I am forthwith a *nezira* in your footsteps." This would clearly indicate that such a statement ties the second woman to the first in all respects. Thus, once the husband vacates his wife's vow to become a *nezira*, the second woman's vow is similarly annulled.

If you think that line of reasoning was just too easy, you would be right. What it attempts to deflate is the argument about a husband's "And I" linking his own vow to his wife, and then his inability to vacate hers because it is impossible to annul his own. In fact, the Gemara tells us that his "And I" is an effective affirmation of his wife's vow. To now vacate her vow requires appeal to a sage or panel of three layman. Does that undermine the analysis we have just outlined? I'm frankly not entirely sure.

In this case, the Gemara will not let the grass grow beneath its feet and turns to the next piece of the Mishna. This concerns a husband who vows forthwith to be a *nazir* and asks his wife: "And you?" (*ve'at*). If she responds "Amen," then he can vacate her vow while his own remains unaffected. The Gemara now cites a *baraita* which would seem to contradict the Mishna. It poses the same brief marital conversation and concludes that both vows of *nezirut* hold fast; if she did not reply "Amen," both partners are absolved of their vows. Why? Because by offering his wife to join him in *nezirut*, he effectively made his own vow contingent on hers; if she either said no or said nothing at all, he too was off the hook.

Now, when this *baraita* noted that, after the marital exchange, the vows of both husband and wife hold fast, and this in turn would mean a husband would be unable to vacate his wife's vow (because it would lead to vacating his own, and that, as we have seen many times now, is simply impossible solely on his own authority). All true, except that the Mishna says that he can vacate her vow. Rav Yehuda steps into the fray and suggests a small change to the wording of the *baraita*: Yes, he can annul her vow, and his own vow is unaffected. Now the *baraita* is in consonance with the Mishna. Abaye presents another way of settling this apparent conflict without rewriting the *baraita*. If the husband's statement to his wife that he is forthwith a *nazir*, and "And you" is not a question but a declarative sentence, then he has tied his own vow to be a *nazir* to his wife's. As his vow is now contingent on hers, if he annuls her vow, his is automatically gone.

23a

Abaye, though, knows that it must be read as a question—incidentally, there was, of course, none of the modern punctuation in the original text. The husband takes his vow and then asks his wife is she would care to join him in *nezirut*. As such their vows are separate entities. He can vacate hers and have his own be unchanged.

A new Mishna now continues on the general theme of women and vows of *nezirut*, and we have already seen mention of this Mishna on 21b. If a woman commits to becoming a *nezira* and then purposefully drinks wine or comes into contact with a corpse, she is punished with forty stripes (though it always is turned to a flogging of thirty-nine). Should her husband vacate her vow, even if she is unaware of his doing so, and she proceeds to consume wine and have contact with a corpse, she is spare the rod. Once he has spoken, then whether or not she knows it—even if she still thinks she's a *nezira* and flaunts her vow—she no longer is legally under the strictures of *nezirut*. R. Yehuda agrees that she does not incur the forty stripes of the rod, but she is still flogged for rebelliousness.

The Gemara begins by citing a *baraita* which in turn cites *Numbers* 30.13: "Her husband has annulled them [i.e., her *nezirut* vows] and the Lord will forgive her." (Alter, pp. 839–40) The *baraita* clarifies that the Bible here is pointing to his annulling her *nezirut* and her lack of knowledge of this act; she still requires some sort of penance and absolution. It offers an interesting parable of sorts from the famous R. Akiva who, apparently, argued that if a Jew were to purposefully consume what he took to be pork, but instead was fed kosher lamb, he has not violated *kashrut*, but he still requires penance and absolution; and if that same person were actually to have been fed pork, all the more so does he require forgiveness. Now, if someone unwittingly violates Torah law, he must still "bear his punishment" (*Leviticus* 5.17; Alter, p. 562)—not lashes but an offering. An example presented in the *baraita* is of someone who fully intended to eat kosher lamb but was served and consumed pork. By comparison, once again, a person who sought out a nice pork chop, got it, and ate it is in for a more serious penalty. Isi ben Yehuda, from whom we are now hearing for the first time, uses another case to make a similar point: If someone is served two pieces of fat, one kosher and one not, and he ate the one he thought was kosher, only to learn *après le fait* that it was *treyf*, he must "bear his punishment." All the more severe must the purposive pork consumer be treated. In other words, unawareness of a sin may reduce the severity of the consequences, but it does not eliminate the need for some sort of punishment.

Quite a *baraita* that, and the Gemara questions the need for all the citations to texts. Of course, they were all necessary, as the Gemara proceeds to demonstrate. If we were only to learn that purposeful violation of a law requires penance and absolution, but that one is home free for and inadvertent violation while trying to do the right thing, the various citations from Torah should put that mistaken reading to rest. By the same token, if we only learned of an inadvertent violation requiring some form of penalty, but not of the woman whose vow was revoked by her husband, making her purposeful violation of

Torah law irrelevant vis-à-vis any need for forgiveness, as she was effectively never a *nezira*, again we would get a skewed view of things.

The issue of intentionality, present in many tractates of the Talmud, is too important here for the Gemara not to continue analysis. Rabba bar bar Chana asks in the name of R. Yochanan about the meaning of a passage from *Hosea* (14.10) which gets the ball rolling. The prophet states clearly that God's paths are straight, and the righteous (*tsadikim*) walk along them while the violators (of the law) stumble. In fact, this is so apparently clear on the surface that the suspecting reader knows much more will be derived from it. The Gemara suggests a reading that links it to the topic of intentionality. We have here a story of two parties preparing their Passover offerings; one party consumed it as a consequence of the mitzvah to do so, while the other party stuffed himself despite already satiated. Obviously, the former party qualify as "righteous," and the latter would be represented as the "violators."

As transparent as that allegory might seem, Reish Lakish doesn't like it, and he asks rhetorically if we are to take the latter party as evil. Sure, he may not have carried out the mitzvah as it arguably should have been, but he did eat his offering. He then offers his own reading of the allegory, but it is so quickly rejected in concept that we should probably move on, as another allegory which will garner extensive consideration is raised.

This one comes straight out of *Genesis* and the tale of Lot and his daughters. Under the impression that the world was being obliterated, his two daughters thought the only way for humanity to continue was, yes, to become pregnant and procreate with their own father, who they believed was the last man on Earth. So, they got him drunk on successive nights, each lay with him on one of those nights, and both became pregnant. The Torah accepts their behavior as the intentional commission of a mitzvah, and the Gemara here sanctions their actions as "righteous." By contrast, it is simply assumed that Lot intended the commission of a sin, thus making him fit the category of a "violator." But, asks the Gemara, what evidence do we have that Lot behaved in an wicked manner?

For this, the Gemara has lots of evidence, drawn from *Genesis* and elsewhere, to prove beyond a doubt that Lot was mired in depravity. The verse cited (*Genesis* 13.10) reads completely above board, but the explanation of its virtually every word is fleshed out to demonstrate what a wicked, immoral person he was in reality. And, this is how the tradition has treated him. Somehow, his cohabitation with his own daughters is posed as them being righteous and him debauched, and the Gemara suggests that his drunkenness placed his behavior as beyond his capacity to effect. Yes, he may have had a generally depraved personality, but how can we decide if that was behind his act of cohabitation with his daughters? The Gemara cites a teaching by R Yose, son of Rav Choni, but dismisses it so fast that it is hardly worth another word. Maybe what it all comes down is, after Lot learned what had happened with his first daughter, upon waking up the next morning, he probably should have refrained from drinking that second night, a night in which his other daughter connived to cohabit with her own father. This may be where he truly "stumbled."

Rava offers his own view of things by citing a verse from *Proverbs* (18.19).

23b

Without extensively examining the verse, the Gemara regards Lot as someone who rebelled, as it were, against Abraham and caused dissension in the family and ultimately led to eternal strife between the Israelites on the one hand and the Ammonites and Moabites on the other. Rava piles on with another verse from *Proverbs* (18.1) to make exactly the same point.

Ulla now poses another famous act of apparent incest against one of adultery to make the overall point (somewhat) clearer. Tamar (in *Genesis*, chapter 38) cohabited with her father-in-law Judah, an act deemed upright by virtue of her intentions to enable the family of Jacob to multiply, and the result was (generations later) the Davidic dynasty. Zimri, by stark contrast, committed adultery with Cozbi, and the result was the deaths of 24,000 due to plague (*Numbers* 25.9). Again, the contrast is between a transgressive act for a noble aim versus straightforward transgression.

Rav Nachman bar Yitzchak states that an intentional violation of the law for a morally higher purpose ranks superior to the performance of a commandment with underlying, personal motives. How does he know this, or how did he come to this conclusion by reasoning? Before it addresses Rav Nachman's important proposition, the Gemara interjects a ruling that appears on several occasions throughout the Talmud (such as in tractate *Sotah* 22b). In the name of Rav, Rav Yehuda opines that Torah study and mitzvot should always be on everyone's agenda, even if for personally advantageous ends, because one may start with questionable aims, but he will sooner or later come to Torah and mitzvot as objectives in and of themselves. So, with this in mind, the Gemara rewords Rav Nachman's statement to be that a purposeful violation of the law for a morally positive end is not superior but equal to mitzvot for private reasons.

Meanwhile, we have lost track of what Rav Nachman bar Yitzchak, no slouch as a rabbinic authority himself, adduces for such a positive assessment of an upright violation. He cites a verse from *Judges* (5.24) in which Yael (Chever's wife) is adjudged to have perpetrated a moral but upright offense, and she is to be blessed as superior to the matriarchs. The Gemara goes on to have R. Yochanan describe, following *Judges*, just what Yael did. The evil

Sisera apparently had sex with her seven times; he clearly enjoyed himself, but the Gemara wonders if she did as well, which would call into question her aim. But, before this gets too pornographic, the Gemara adjudges her a victim of sorts and her objective altogether upright.

The Gemara then returns to the interjection immediately above by Rav Yehuda (in the name of Rav) and repeats it verbatim. To verify the veracity of this proposition, the Gemara notes that ("the evil") Balak had forty-two bulls and rams sacrificed at an assortment of altars with the aim of tormenting the Israelites, but as a result among his progeny several generations later was Ruth who converted to Judaism.

Back to Lot and his offspring. In the name of R. Yochanan, R. Chiyya bar Abba makes an interesting linguistic point, though his intention was surely not just that of language. Lot's older daughter named the son of her incestuous union "Moab" which R. Chiyya notes could (possibly) mean "from father." Many generations later, God tells Moses (*Deuteronomy* 2.9) neither to "besiege Moab . . . [nor] provoke them in to battle." (Alter, p. 887) The Gemara understands this to mean not to engage Moab militarily but that it was OK to cause them trouble. Meanwhile, Lot's younger daughter named her son Ben Ami which means "son of my people," and we learn that God also instructed Moses (*Deuteronomy* 2.19): "You shall not besiege them and you shall not provoke them." (Alter, p. 888) Here no troubles may be foisted on the Ammonites.

As our *daf* comes to an end, R. Chiyya bar Avin reports a teaching (in the name of R. Yehoshua ben Korcha) also concerned with Lot's children. Always, he rules, one should aim at performing a mitzvah as soon as he or she can, and he gives as an example the case of Lot's older daughter who bedded her father on the first night, one day before her sister.

24a

What was the older daughter's reward? Her descendants rose to the throne of Israel (the Davidic dynasty) four generations prior to her sister gained her reward. One might have forgotten that the theme (and, in fact, the title) of this tractate of the Talmud is the *nazir*, and now we turn to a new Mishna.

As we have seen, a husband can vacate his wife's vow to be a *nazir*, and we will soon learn that he can do this all the way until she is ready with her final offerings to be sacrificed and their blood placed at the appropriate place(s) on the Altar. If a husband does annul his wife's *nezirut*, this Mishna addresses what is to be done with the animals—ordinarily, a male lamb for the *olah*, a female lamb for the *chatat*, and a ram for the *shelamim*—that have been sanctified in advance (we had a taste of this Mishna back on 21b). If the animals belonged to him, they simply return to the flock and are divested of their sanctity. Once the wife had set aside her animals, they would no longer be allowed for use; once her vow is annulled, their sanctity evaporates, and the animals can rejoin their brethren. Because they were her husband's to begin with, she is (retroactively) in no position to have sanctified them. True, he did give the animals, but only if she used them for her concluding rituals as a *nezira*. With her vow vacated, she does not perform the final ritual sacrifices, and the animals go back to her husband.

If, in fact, the animals were hers to begins with (as noted above, not a routine circumstance), then the animal set to serve as the *chatat* is "left to die," while the *olah* and the *shelamim* are sacrificed but as voluntary offerings. As we shall see, the more challenging question concerns the *chatat*, because there is no voluntary option for a *chatat*; it only is offered when the one offering is so obligated. If an animal is sanctified to serve as an obligatory sacrifice, and then that obligation disappears, the Mishna states that the animal is "left to die"—meaning that it is confined in a pen and left to starve. The meat from the *shelamim* may be consumed but only for one day, just as in the case of a *nazir*, but the *nezira* need not bring the accompanying breads required of a *nazir*. There are other differences between the voluntary *shelamim* of a *nazir* and a *nezira*, as well as between the *shelamim* brought as a voluntary offering and as part of a concluding ritual of *nezirut*.

The Mishna now turns to how the money prepared for use in purchasing the three final offerings is to be dealt with. If the wife had one amount of cash, as yet not having stipulated how much would go for each of the three, the entire sum is to be used for voluntary offerings on behalf of the community, at times when the Altar is not in use. If, on the other hand, she had designated the amounts, or the actual coins, of her money that were to be spent on each animal, and then her husband vacated her *nezirut*, the money reserved for the *chatat* is taken to the Dead Sea and tossed in, or in some other way destroyed. Nothing may be gained from it, although the Mishna makes clear that, if someone were to use it to his or her advantage, this is not considered misuse of sacred funds. The money reserved for the *olah* goes to the purchase and offering of it as a voluntary *olah*, and in this instance using these funds for anything else is considered misuse. The funds reserved for the *shelamim* similarly go for the purchase of a voluntary offering; and, as noted, it must be consumed within one day's time and no breads need be part of the sacrifice.

Lots to discuss here, and the Gemara will focus on this material for the new four *dapim*. The Gemara begins by attempting to elucidate the Mishna's differentiation between animals belonging to a husband and those belonging to his wife. Now, the husband is under no requirement to give his wife the requisite animals for her final ritual sacrifices, but if he does so on his own, this is what the Mishna means by "his." We learn immediately that the Tanna who declared that the husband is under no compulsion to give his wife the animals was Rav Chisda; once he vacates her vow, those animals never belonged to her and may simply be led back into the company of their fellows. We shall see momentarily how he came to make this statement which accords with rabbis in refutation of R. Yehuda. A *baraita* explains that R. Yehuda argues that a husband is obligated by virtue of the marriage contract (*ketuba*) to provide his wife's sacrificial animals and in fact all of her sacrifices. Rava adds something on the order of an *amicus* brief, noting that R. Yehuda specifies that the husband must afford his wife sacrifices needed by her, but Rava points out that, if her *nezirut* has been annulled, she no longer "needs" things that were never really hers in the first place.

24b

The Gemara now looks to the interesting passage in the Mishna about a *chatat* that must be "left to die," if the animal was hers from the start. I say "interesting," because it addresses the question of women enjoying property rights, something modern readers might find thought-provoking in a document over 1500 years old. It begins with a rhetorical question basically asking how it is possible for a woman to possess property, inasmuch as we have been led to believe that anything a woman acquires becomes her husband's property. Rav Pappa takes a stab: Maybe she saved it up by squirreling away bits and pieces of her food allocations, a provision of the *ketuba*. Perhaps someone simply presented her with the animals and specified at the time of presentation that they were hers (and not her husband's).

The Gemara seems happy with such explanations and moves on to the part of the Mishna noting that the *olah* and *shelamim* are offered, despite revocation of her vow, but there's that thorny bit about the *shelamim* of a *nezira* being offered without the breads required of a *nazir*. At this point, Shmuel firmly asks Avuha bar Ihi to explain this without so much as sitting down; namely, in what cases is a ram offered without breads. The latter replies that there are four such rams: (1) "hers," as just delineated above; (2) "his," which we shall address in the Mishna on 28b; (3) "after death," to be analyzed in detail momentarily; and (4) "after atonement," to be analyzed after (3).

Getting ahead of itself, as we have seen is frequently the case with the Gemara, we get something of a précis here of that Mishna on 28b (greater detail to follow when we actually reach it in a few days): a father is empowered to commit his son to a period of *nezirut*; a mother is not so empowered; if the son or other relatives shave the boy's head, or if either objected to this, his *nezirut* is annulled; and the other provisions, concerning the itemized allocation of funds, follow precisely what we have seen in the case of a wife whose *nezirut* was vacated.

Now, as for "after death" as a basis for the ram of a *nazir* without breads, the Gemara directs us to another Mishna in tractate *Meila* (Misuse of [sanctified] property). It runs as follows. A *nazir* reserves moneys for his concluding offerings without specifically stipulating how they should be divided; it is now sanctified and unavailable for anyone's personal use. Despite that, using such funds personally is not a *meila* violation which would require a guilt offering (*asham*). If he should then die with the moneys that he set aside unstipulated as to their use, it all goes for voluntary sacrifices. If he had designated amounts to the various requisite offerings, then we find rulings much like those on 24a: the *chatat* money is taken to the Dead Sea and tossed in (or somehow destroyed); again, using it for some other purpose does not rise to constitute *meila*. The *olah* money is used to purchase an *olah*, and here using the funds so designated does constitute *meila*. The *shelamim* money is used for a *shelamim*, available for consumption for one day and no breads as accompaniment.

Finally, "after atonement" as a basis for the "no breads" specification. This time the Gemara turns to its other major tool in the toolkit (after a biblical or biblically derived source): reasoning. As we just noted, a *shelamim* that is offered even after the death of the *nazir* is still sacrificed without bread. Why? Because, once the *nazir* is gone, the offering is no longer appropriate for use in atonement.

If this list and analysis is not sufficiently complete, the Gemara now suggests other instances of a *nazir*'s ram brought without the accompanying breads. A *baraita* teaches that any other *shelamim* of a *nazir* that underwent *shechita* (ritual slaughter) but not following the mitzvah properly—namely, without requisite intent specifically for a *shelamim*—are suitable, but they do not pass muster in terms of fulfilling the *nazir*'s final ritual obligation. They are, though, available for consumption for one day and no breads need apply. Avuha apparently neglected this last case, because he only listed instances in which proper intent was preserved.

The Gemara next addresses the question of how unstipulated funds for offerings would, after the *nezirut* is vacated, all go for voluntary offerings on behalf of the community.

25a

But, wait a minute. We learned above that *chatat* moneys can't be used to buy a voluntary offering, so can all the moneys formerly set aside in an undivided lump be spent on offerings? The *chatat* is part of the lump total. R. Yochanan begins the Gemara's answer by claiming, despite the apparent illogicality of the situation, that this is one of those cases of the law concerning a *nazir* that was communicated to Moses when he was atop Mt. Sinai. This explanation which appears a fair number of times throughout the Talmud strikes me as not really a response—just: it is so because it is so, for how can anyone say that it was *not* conveyed to Moses? Reish Lakish has another possible explanation, this one based more explicitly in scripture. He cites a verse from *Leviticus* (22.18) which he reads as saying that the leftover amount from vows, as would be the case in a revoked *nezirut*, are to be spent on voluntary *olah* sacrifices.

The key distinction that now comes to the fore is between itemized funds (X for a *chatat*, Y for an *olah*, Z for a *shelamim*) and lump-sum non-itemized funds. R. Yochanan's reading of the situation makes perfect sense in the case of the latter, though certainly not to the former. That's just the way Moses (presumably) heard the law when he was on the mountain top. But, Reish Lakish's understanding, based on the verse from *Leviticus* makes no such distinction.

As we have seen, however, this law must reject the use of itemized moneys. Rava claims that excess itemized funds may not be used to purchase animals for voluntary sacrifices, and he brings to the table a *baraita* taught in R. Yishmael's academy. This *baraita* is concerned with the animals themselves, not with the funds to purchase them, but apparently Rava believed they should be treated in the same manner. It also involves some seriously complex reasoning, but the conclusion is that an excess *chatat*—such as one belonging to a person who has died—does not get sacrificed, and any moneys used to acquire it are not available for sacrificial offerings either.

The Gemara goes on now to further explain this *baraita*,

25b

taking it apart phrase by phrase. Intrinsic to this analysis is the Gemara's separation of arguments based on scripture and those ascribed to teachings derived from tradition (namely, laws initially believed to have been imparted by God to Moses on Sinai and then down through the ages with the same sanctity as if carved in stone). Rava makes his case with such an ascription, while R. Akiva believes he has a biblical verse that can serve as a source for the practice of how the various offerings are to be treated.

When referring to the *chatat* that we earlier learned in the sort of case with which we are dealing must be "left to die," because it can't be sacrificed, Rava's citation of the explanatory *baraita* from R. Yishmael's academy makes explicit what the euphemism "left to die" truly entails. The poor creature is to be brought to the Temple and there deprived of food and water until it starves to death (see 25a). This practice surely won't sit well with modern sensibilities, but the period about which we are writing is not modern.

After this digression, the Gemara now goes back to pick up the discussion of R. Yochanan's view that the *halacha* that excess *nezirut* moneys not specifically itemized are available for voluntary sacrificial offerings for the community comes from the oral tradition. The implication is that this *halacha* is applicable only in the case of offerings of a *nazir* or *nezira*. But, now we get some pushback from another *baraita* (there sure a lot of these) introducing another instance which might contradict this reading. It begins by presenting a case of anyone required by law to offer a bird pair

26a

and has reserved the necessary money to purchase the birds. In such a situation, he is allowed, if he so desires, to use those funds to buy an animal for a *chatat* sacrifice. He can even make that animal an *olah* offering. If he dies with his money not itemized for use, though, it all goes for voluntary offerings for the community—this despite the fact that his original requirements included a *chatat*. All of this goes to prove that a *nazir* is not alone as one whose excess unitemized moneys are to be used for voluntary offerings. The *baraita* thus suggests that R. Yochanan's exclusive assignment of this law to a *nazir* may have been hasty.

The Gemara seeks to clarify the issue, stating that the "*halacha* to Moses from Sinai" was used here unambiguously with respect to a *nazir*, but it applies as well to anyone who finds himself required to bring bird offerings inasmuch as their cases are similar to a *nazir* (insofar as they are required to bring a *chatat* and an *olah*). The reason R. Yochanan's phrasing focused on the case of a *nazir* is that he wished to exclude the case cited in the following *baraita*. As a result of some sin, a man must bring a *chatat*, and he then adds that he would like to offer a voluntary *olah*. He then allocates the requisite funds specifically for his offerings but does not indicate for which (or both) this money should go. So, if he now wants to make use of that money to buy and offer an animal as a *chatat* or as an *olah*, he can't. In the previous example, his action required that he bring both sacrifices, but in this case the two sacrifices are separate entities, separate obligations. And, in the present case, if he dies with his money still in one lump sum (in which the funds for the *chatat* are included), it must be transported and dumped in the Dead Sea.

We have been referring to itemized funds and indeterminate ones. The Gemara now explains the former more clearly. Rav Ashi repeats that leftover funds that have been stipulated for a given offering are not available for voluntary *olah* offerings. He wants us to know that designating one's money for X, Y, and Z (as a whole) is sufficient to qualify as itemization; in other words, one doesn't have to say this amount of cash if for my *chatat*, etc. If one just states that this pile of cash is for my requisite sacrifices, then that qualifies as indeterminate funds.

Now, back to money not designated to specific sacrifices, and Rava reminds us that they must be directed to voluntary offerings for the community, but if any of that money was set aside to be used for the *chatat*, the whole amount of his money for the *nezirut* offerings is regarded as itemized. Clearly, the *chatat* is the piece of the pot that determines that much of its allocation, especially if he dies before he can bring the offerings.

26b

Sometimes, when the Gemara tries to clarify or offer proof for what one sage has stated, it makes things more, rather than less, murky. Allegedly to buttress what has just been attributed to Rava, the Gemara adds that, should a *nazir* state something like: This is my money for my *chatat* and the rest goes for the other required offerings; then, he dies before the money can be used to buy the animals. What do we do? The money allocated for the *chatat* goes right to the Dead Sea; the leftover, undesignated funds are split with half for the *olah* and half for the *shelamim*. If all his money was unitemized, then it would be used for a voluntary *olah* sacrifice for the community. Tagged on at the end of this ruling from the *baraita* is the note that the sin of *meila* is only considered committed if one mishandles all these funds; partial misuse of the unitemized money does not constitute *meila*. (Incidentally, one would think with all these moneys being tossed into the Dead Sea that it would hold a Swiss Bank account's quantity at its bottom. But, that's the point of using the Dead Sea in this way. Because of its high salt content, the coins were expected, more likely than not, to disintegrate.)

The Gemara now turns to a *baraita* which focuses on a case in which one designates a piece of his funds for the *olah* (rather than the *chatat*) and whatever is leftover for his other (unitemized) requisite offerings (meaning his *chatat* and his *shelamim*). Then, he dies before he can offer his sacrifices, so the money he designated for the *olah* in fact goes to purchase an *olah*; mishandling the money for an *olah* does constitute *meila*. The unitemized leftover funds are to be spent on voluntary offerings for the community; and only mishandling of all this money constitutes *meila*.

We have thus far been speaking only of actual money allocated to the purchase of animals, but the Gemara now directs our attention to items of value which may be allocated in the same way. In the name of Rav, Rav Huna claims that the ruling about leftover undesignated funds does not apply exclusively to cold cash. It would include valuables of one sort or another, even animals themselves, that might be used when sold to support a *nazir*'s offerings. In the case of an animal, should the *nazir* dies, the animal must be "left to die," and under no circumstances sold to fund any offerings. It's actually a little more complicated (as always). Rav Nachman notes that the animal in such a sad situation must be unblemished. If the animal had one of a number of blemishes, it can be exchanged for and is thus regarded as comparable to money.

What else is not regarded as comparable to money? The Gemara first rules that a metal ingot (some claim this to mean a silver bar) does not rise to comparability, because it can't easily be converted to ready cash. Rav Nachman bar Yitzchak disagrees about an ingot, but he does rule out an assemblage of construction beams. Presumably the beams would not work here, because they are only of immediate value to someone requiring construction material and thus not easily turned into cash.

Rav Shimi bar Ashi apparently doesn't like all this ruling out of objects of clear value which may not be easily converted into cold cash. So, he asks his colleague Rav Pappa why the rabbis have privileged money over ingots or construction beams or certain animals. What he actually argues is much more complicated, but we shall address that when we come to Rav Pappa's response on the next *daf*.

27a

The crux of Rav Shimi bar Ashi's point was that sacrificial offerings such as the pair of birds ought to be regarded as indeterminate. Thus, he's arguing basically that money can't buy everything, it's true; the *halacha* in question is not, therefore, limited to money and similar items (e.g., jewelry). Rav Pappa replies by asking his colleague how he jibes such a reading with a Mishna still eighteen *dapim* away in our tractate (45a). There we find Rabban Shimon ben Gamliel claiming that, should a *nazir* ready his three animals for the offerings required at the conclusion of his *nezirut* but not designated which was for which sacrifice (*chatat*, *olah*, *shelamim*), then the following procedure is to be followed: the animal appropriate to the *chatat*, the female lamb, indeed goes for a *chatat*; similarly, the male lamb for the *olah* and the ram for the *shelamim*. But if animals like the two birds are considered indeterminate, then how do these three beasts pass muster? Rav Shimi's retort is that the Torah grants the person offering the birds or the responsible Kohen to specify the birds in question as the sacrificial offering, but beforehand the avian creatures exist in a limbo of indeterminacy.

27b

Clearly, according to Rav Shimi, the appropriate animal is always assigned to the appropriate offering—no indeterminacy there.

The Gemara now jumps back a *daf* to the point at which a blemished animal is to be treated similarly to undivided moneys. Rav Hamnuna questions this and cites a *baraita* which poses the issue from another angle. For the twenty-first time, "Come, learn." It starts with a rhetorical question asking when a *nazir*'s shaving (meaning his offerings at the end of his *nezirut*) can be funded by his father's *nezirut*. This involves a Mishna (see 30a) dealing with a case of a father who was a declared *nazir* himself and had allotted funds to purchase his concluding sacrifices but then died before he could offer them. If the son later declares to be a *nazir* with these undivided funds formerly accrued by his late father for his own offerings, he may do so. Now, if the son and father took vows of *nezirut* at overlapping times, and the father allotted an undifferentiated sum for his final sacrificial rituals and died, then the son's desire to use his father's unused money for his own final offerings is for naught. Those funds are to be spent on voluntary *olah* sacrifices for the community. If the father, however, had made clear prior to his passing which animals were to go for which offerings, then the *chatat* is "left to die," while the *olah* and *shelamim* are sacrifices as per usual. This extensive citation of a *baraita* having nothing (on the surface) to do with blemished animals is somewhat puzzling, to say the least. The apparent implication is that animals, blemished or otherwise, are all to be regarded as determinate.

Before it resolves this assessment, the Gemara turns to an extensive *baraita* regarding shifting a *chatat* from a father to his son or from the penance for one sin to another. It begins by citing the relevant term from the Torah, *korbano* 'his sacrifice' (it actually appears three relevant times), which the *baraita* takes to mean that it is one's own and that one cannot fulfill his duty with his father's (or anyone else's) sacrifice. Immediately we're in territory that the previous Gemara argued in an opposite direction. The Gemara now tries to tease out a place where a son might be able to make use of his late father's sacrificial animal. So, it suggests that if the father's sin was less severe than the son's—and there is a wide gamut from mild to extremely serious offenses against *halacha*—or even the reverse, or for that matter if the sins were at comparable levels, that might work. But, the *baraita* won't budge on this one. The passage mentioning *korbano* makes crystal clear that one only expiates his own obligations with "his" own sacrificial offerings and not his father's (or anyone else's).

The *baraita* is not done yet. It has tested whether animal transference was possible and rejected that option. Now, it asks if the son might access for his own sacrifice a father's money allotted (for his own sacrifice) but not expended on an animal. We now know for sure (and the *baraita* actually repeats it) that a son cannot use his father's *nezirut* animal for his own concluding *nezirut* offering. How about money in this context? We learned above that a son is permitted to use undifferentiated funds left over from his father's *nezirut*,

28a

but not if the father has designated which of his moneys were to go for which animals. But, all of this aside, the Gemara again makes crystal clear that, if we're talking about father-to-son, *chatat* transference, the key word (again) is *korbano* 'his sacrifice'; the point would be to emphasize that the *chatat* is different from other offerings.

So, the *baraita* takes another angle and asks if one who had allocated his *chatat* to make amends for a given transgression might possibly use it to do the same for a different transgression—either mild to serious or vice versa. Same answer comes back, as if to say: Didn't you hear me the first time? The Torah is clear: *korbano*! A designated *chatat* to account for a given transgression must be used for that one and no other, irrespective of their relative severity or whether intentionally or unintentionally committed, even if the same person committed both offenses against the law. OK, how about transferring money dedicated to atone for one offense to another committed by the same person? Namely, it speaks of using money dedicated toward buying an animal to be sacrificed as a *chatat* and using it for another *chatat*—is money different in terms of transferability? The simple answer that concludes this long *baraita* is that the Torah clearly states that, be it an animal or money, whatever has been set aside "for his sin" (*al chatato*) must go to atone for that sin and no other. The *baraita* has now made this case several times—no switching allowed—and its length is due as well to several examples of transgressions and to repetition for clarity's sake of the mild-vs.-severe question.

The point of laying out this *baraita* was to set up the issue raised on the previous *amud* regarding its statement that a son may not use his father's animal for his own concluding sacrificial rituals—no mention about blemishes. The thrust of this *baraita*, and how the Gemara wishes to understand it, is the comparison between blemished-unblemished animals and designated-undesignated funds left by a deceased father when a son is preparing his final sacrificial offering incumbent on a *nazir*. There is more to this consideration than what I have included above, but it is frankly beyond me.

Time for a new Mishna, and this one will take us in a new direction, or back into a direction more closely related to an older consideration. We looked earlier at many of the consequences of a husband's revocation of his wife's vow to become a *nezira*, and now we address what transpires when he vacates her *nezirut* at the time that her final sacrifices are being offered. An essential part of the ritual of a sacrificial offering is sprinkling or applying the animal's blood on the Altar. As soon as the blood of any one of a *nazir*'s offerings is applied to the Altar, the *nazir* is released from all abstentions. If his timing occurs at this moment, then he cannot vacate his wife's *nezirut*; actually, if he wants to vacate her vow, he must do it the same day that he learns that she has made her vow, and if that day coincides with the day of her final offerings and the blood of one of them has been applied to the Altar, it's already too late. R. Akiva even predates the inability of the husband to vacate his wife's vow to the moment any one of the animals is slaughtered—that is, before the blood is actually collected and applied.

Now these regulations are all find and good, but we have seen in earlier Mishnayot that other considerations may intercede to make this more complicated, specifically the contracting of *tumah* at a late stage of this process. The Mishna here notes that it is speaking of a *nazir* who had shaved his head (in conjunction with the animals brought as offerings, these constitute his final rituals) without becoming *tamei*. Now, if his wife has contracted *tumah*, she must cut her hair and then resume her *nezirut*, but in this instance, the husband is permitted to vacate her vow, even if she has brought the requisite offerings for a *nezira* who has become *tamei*. It is there that the husband may step in and declare that he doesn't want her in a state in which she denies herself wine. R. Meir takes a contrary position and argues that, even after she is released from the proscription of *nezirut* when the blood of one of the offerings has been applied to the Altar, the husband is within his rights to vacate his wife's vow. Here the husband can declare that he doesn't want his wife to appear in the unattractive state (for a woman) of being bald following the head-shaving, apparently a big turn-off even many centuries ago.

The Mishna here made a blanket statement at its outset that, once one of the sacrificial bloods is applied to the Altar, all the *nezirut* abstentions evaporate. The Gemara effectively tells us to hold our horses, because R. Eliezer for one raises a problem. In an upcoming *baraita*, he is cited as arguing that those abstentions only vanish once all the final rituals have been carried out. Thus, if the *nezira* sprinkles the blood on the Altar prior to shaving her head, she is still proscribed from consuming wine; as a consequence, because she is still in a state of self-denial, her husband is within his rights to vacate her vow.

The Gemara goes on to assess the position stated by R. Akiva in the Mishna vis-à-vis the Tanna of the *baraita*.

28b

As stated clearly in the Mishna, the Tanna argues that, as soon as any blood from her sacrifices has been applied to the Altar, she is free to consume wine, meaning she has been released from all her vows of abstention—no self-denial remains and thus the husband's capacity to vacate her vow is itself vacated. R. Akiva, by contrast, argues that as soon as any of her sacrifices has been slaughtered, before any of their blood has been applied to the Altar, the husband's powers have been curtailed in this arena, and the Gemara adds by way of explanation that annulling her vow after the animal was slaughtered would squander a sacrifice—the meat would be wasted, the animal could not be burned on the Altar, and thus the rabbis declared it verboten.

R. Zeira is the first to take up the gauntlet here, asking why R. Akiva assumes annulment of a vow between slaughter and blood application leads to waste. He claims that, once the husband has vacated his wife's vows, one might use the slaughtered animal not for its initial purpose but for some other end, apply the blood, and the meat is allowed to be eaten. This has been dealt with right at the beginning of tractate *Zevachim* (Sacrifices); there we learn that, aside from the Passover and *chatat* offerings, a sacrifice offered not for its own sake (*shelo lishmah*) may be slaughtered to satisfy another obligation.[2] To support this argument, he cites a *baraita* which raises the case of lambs slaughtered on Shavuot, and he adds all the permutations about intent and timing to cover all bases, including the outlawed slaughter on Shabbat which is deemed OK. Conclusion: No waste, as R. Akiva feared, for the animal slaughtered can be re-assigned a designation other than an obligation of the original *nezirut* and all is OK.

Attentive readers will already see the possible hole in the fabric of R. Zeira's argument. Yes, if the question is an *olah* or *shelamim* slaughtered, followed by a revocation by a husband of his wife's vow of *nezirut*, no waste ensues. But, the issue concerns a *chatat*, which is always the sticking point. If it is the first offering to be slaughtered, and the husband then vacates his wife's vow, this would lead to waste. This was R. Akiva's object with his prohibition. One simply cannot slaughter a *chatat* and then apply its blood for another designation. If the husband annulled his wife's vow after her *chatat* had been slaughtered, there is nowhere else for its blood to go and no one else may consume its meat.

The Mishna next dealt with a *tahor* head-shaving associated with the final *nezirut* rituals, after which the husband may no longer annul his wife's vows, though if the head-shaving is performed because his wife became *tamei* during *nezirut*, he is in this instance authorized to vacate her vow. It was here that R. Meir allowed a husband the right to annul a wifely vow even if she was *tahor* and doing her final rituals. He supports this by stating on behalf of a husband who finds himself in such a situation that he abhors a bald wife. The Tanna of our Mishna states the obvious: She can wear a wig. R. Meir still finds this abhorrent, as it is not his wife's own hair and thus hideous to have her wearing something made from another's hair; what is hideous to her is unacceptable to him.

A new Mishna now looks at other cases in which people other than the one actually entering *nezirut* can potentially control one's life. A father, we learn, can commit his son to a period of *nezirut*, but a mother is not so permitted. Various qualifications will ensue in the Gemara, and while the son must observe the three abstentions of wine, hair cutting, and corpse *tumah*, if the son makes it to the end, the father is responsible for purchasing his son's sacrifices. Interestingly as well is that neither parent can commit a daughter to *nezirut*.

Now, if the son is unamenable and shaves his head or relations of his do, or if the son just rejected in words the commitment to *nezirut* or (again) relations of his did so on his behalf, while the father went and readied the requisite animals for sacrifice at the end of the period of *nezirut*, we may have a problem. Those offerings are now left over and they go as follows: The *chatat* is "left to die"; the *olah* is sacrificed as a voluntary *olah*, and the *shelamim* is similarly sacrificed as a voluntary *shelamim* (see 24a for a very similar assignment of leftover animals). The *shelamim* may be consumed but only for one day, as would be true of a *nazir*'s *shelamim* but without breads as would be required in the case of *nazir*.

If the father allotted a lump sum of money to buy his son's final sacrifices, only to have his son reject the vow, it all goes to purchase voluntary *olah* sacrifices for the community. And, if he specified his funds to each of the offerings, then whatever had been allocated for the *chatat* must be hauled off to the Dead Sea and tossed in. No advantage may be gained from this money, though no *meila* attaches if one does gain something. By contrast, the specified fund for the *olah* must be spent on a voluntary *olah*, and this time any personal benefit taken does rise to *meila*; and the *shelamim* money goes for a voluntary *shelamim*, permitted for consumption for one day (without the breads).

The Gemara begins what probably would intrigue a modern reader about the opening words of the Mishna. Why does a man have control over his son in this way, and why does a woman not? Two answers ensue. First up, R. Yochanan asserts that this is simply one of those laws communicated to

Moses when he ascended Mt. Sinai, a stance we saw this venerable rabbi take several *dapim* back and meaning that he had no easily ascribable source in scripture. Second, R. Yose, son of R. Chanina,

29a

channels Reish Lakish to effectively agree that there is no obvious *halacha* for this ruling, but that it is a rabbinical sanction to help a father teach his son proper observance of the mitzvot.

Sounding proto-feminist, the Gemara retorts that, if the intent of this rabbinic sanction was pedagogical, oughtn't women be accorded the same instructional capacity to have a son become a *nazir*. Reish Lakish responds by not really addressing the retort and just saying that only men are duty-bound to teach their sons the mitzvot; women are not. R. Yochanan accepted this parental division of labor as a law transmitted to Moses at Mt. Sinai, but he asks why it is that Reish Lakish's reasoning of the obligation of a father to instruct his son in the mitzvot does not extend to daughters. Again, Reish Lakish responds by verbally putting his foot down and reiterating that it's a father's duty to teach his son, but he is not so compelled with respect to his daughter.

That was the second challenge to Reish Lakish's interpretation, and five more are on the way. This time the Gemara starts by asserting that R. Yochanan's view makes it understandable that such a ruling works for vows of *nezirut*, though not for other similar commitments. If a father's power to have his son become a *nazir*, however, is a consequence of peda-gogical imperatives, then one would expect those other commitments to be included in his rabbinic sanction. The Gemara, apparently taking up the cause of Reish Lakish, affirms that *nezirut* is stricter than other vows in terms of self-denial (in the interest of education), and would therefore be subsumed without need for mention.

Next, R. Yochanan or his surrogates want to know the following. If the Reish Lakish's claim, as relayed by R. Yose, son of R. Chanina, that the intent of the Mishna is pedagogical, how is it that the son's relations have the power to reject the imposition of *nezirut*, effectively telling the father that he must not educate his son in the mitzvot. Reish Lakish would reply that, if a son's relations find the father's pedagogical approach objectionable, that would certainly signal that the son also would find it so.

Again, according to R. Yochanan's understanding of the Mishna accepts that a son would conclude his *nezirut* with the head-shaving, even clipping off the "edges" of his hair which is ordinarily outlawed; this has been interpreted to mean the sidelocks (H. *peot*; Y. *peyes*) that ultra-Orthodox Jewish men allow to grow from their temples. Now, scripture forbids shaving this area of the head, but Reish Lakish claims this is all rabbinic and part of a father's educative mission. But, can the rabbinic trump the biblical? Now, Reish Lakish points out that the proscription of a full head-shave is itself rabbinic, as the Bible does not ban it as such. It thus resembles the father's duties to educate his son, which is also rabbinic, and Reish Lakish simply asserts that this education in the mitzvot transcends the ban on a full shaving of the head.

R. Yochanan's view of things accepts that, when the son performs the ritual hair cutting at the conclusion of his *nezirut*, his father is empowered to provide the animals for his ritual sacrifices. Now, if the purpose of this practice is pedagogical, why would the father provide the animals and not the son? And, inasmuch as the sacrifices themselves are not scriptural in the original, but rabbinic (like Reish Lakish's understanding), would this not entail commission of a transgression: conveying unsanctified animals into the Temple domain? This one is simple for Reish Lakish. He simply asserts that the ban on unsanctified animals within the Temple grounds is also not biblical, but rabbinic.

Finally, R. Yochanan's view would accept that, if the *nazir* son became *tamei*, he is required to offer up a bird pair, and the presiding Kohen is allowed to consume these birds if they are slaughtered in the distinctive way reserved for birds. In this case, however, inasmuch as the bird pair obligation is rabbinic, those birds on the Temple grounds would be biblically unsanctified; would Reish Lakish's disallowing the Kohen to consume them be based on the eating of unkosher food? Reish Lakish's reply would be that, in addition to his having already dealt with the problem of unsanctified animals on the Temple grounds being rabbinic, the same applies to methods of slaughtering birds.

Reish Lakish has drawn this last argument from R. Yose, son of R. Yehuda, and now the Gemara enters a rabbit hole. It cites a *baraita* in which this R. Yose asserts that there are situations in which a man must offer a *chatat* to expiate a sin, and there are also situations that are the same for women. It then goes on to assert that, just as in the case of men, an offering is required for the doubtful commission of a sin (*asham talui*), so too are women obligated in comparable circumstances. For a male, whether his sin is certain or uncertain, he is required to offer an animal sacrifice (though it can't be a bird), and so too for a woman the offering would be the same in both instances (though it must be a bird). The Gemara is almost finished with the exposition of the views of R. Yose, son of R. Yehuda. One might go further and argue that, just as a man's *asham talui* can be consumed by a Kohen, a woman's sacrifice (bird *chatat*) brought for an uncertain sin can also be consumed by a Kohen.

But, the argument here might just run into trouble.

29b

The *baraita* says such reasoning is overstepping, as the empowerment of a man and a woman to offer sacrifices for an uncertain sin are not, if fact, parallel—or at least not sufficiently parallel to warrant the conclusions arrived at immediately above. But, maybe this whole rabbit hole is not alleviating the central issues. So, the Gemara returns to the basic difference of opinion between R. Yochanan and Reish Lakish and tries to understand it from another angle.

To this end, the Gemara offers a *baraita* which may help. This begins by asking until what age a father has the power to have his son become a *nazir*. R. Yehuda ha-Nasi says until that youngster grows a pair of public hairs, an indication that the lad has entered adulthood (and is age thirteen). R. Yose, son of R. Yehuda, avers that the father has until his son reaches the "age of vows" (*onat nedarim*), meaning his thirteenth year (between his twelfth and thirteenth birthdays). R. Yehuda ha-Nasi agrees with R. Yochanan that the father's power to compel his son's *nezirut* derives from a law conveyed to Moses at Mt. Sinai; thus, even if the son has reached the "age of vows," his father still holds this power over him, at least until the lad can produce the requisite number of pubic hairs. Meanwhile, R. Yose, son of R. Yehuda, insists that this power only lasts until the son reaches his thirteenth birthday, and that along with Reish Lakish it was a rabbinic sanction aimed at a father's teaching his son mitzvah observance; as soon as the son becomes thirteen, his father's duty in this regard evaporates, as the lad is an adult with all the requisite mitzvah obligations.

This understanding of the disagreement between our two prominent rabbis may have seemed quite clear, but the Gemara has several more up its sleeve. In this new rendition, the Gemara claims that both R. Yehuda ha-Nasi and R. Yose, son of R. Yehuda, accept the notion that a father's right to compel his son's *nezirut* is a law taught to Moses at Mt. Sinai. The difference of opinion between them is their respective take on how a minor, who is about to enter adulthood, is attuned to what a vow entails. R. Yehuda ha-Nasi argues that a vow by such a youngster takes effect on the rabbinic plane; the father's power to compel *nezirut* (which is on a biblical plane), thus, can trump a rabbinic sanction. R. Yose, son of R. Yehuda, by contrast, understands such a vow of a precocious minor to be at the biblical level.

This one also sounds pretty good, but the Gemara wants to offer yet another explanation. Maybe, both sides in this dispute concur that a father's power to compel *nezirut* for his son, what might be dubbed *droit de père*, was rabbinic in origin and aimed at the pedagogical goal of teaching his son mitzvah observance. So, where's the beef? R. Yehuda ha-Nasi avers that the rabbinic ruling to educate one's son transcends the rabbinic ruling concerning a minor who understands vows and is about to enter adulthood. Meanwhile, R. Yose, son of R. Yehuda, does not believe this supersession applicable.

At this point, the Gemara interjects a *baraita* related to this discussion. It concerns the oldest a son can be when a father is within rights to compel *nezirut*. The Gemara introduces this *baraita* by suggesting that the debate we have seen developing parallels another one between equally well-established rabbis. R. Chanina's father imposed *nezirut* on him when he was a minor and on the same day took him to see Rabban Gamliel to check on the boy's development of pubic hairs, which the esteemed rabbi did. One must assume in this version that R. Chanina was over thirteen at the time, but it is a bit unclear why his father could not discern his son's pubic growth. R. Yose has a dissimilar report of the case at hand; he understands the visit to be aimed at establishing if the young R. Chanina had attained the "age of vows," which must mean that the lad was between twelve and thirteen and the visit was aimed at determining his capacity to comprehend the essence of a vow. The former variant affirms a father's ability to compel *nezirut* on a son until adulthood in all its ramifications has been attained (à la R. Yehuda la-Nasi), while the latter affirms such a paternal right last only until the son arrives as the "age of vows" (à la R. Yose, son of R. Yehuda).

The *baraita* picks up with R. Chanina (of course, long before he was ordained) telling Rabban Gamliel that he needn't have both check his pubic growth, because whatever the case, he plans to be a *nazir*: either (if he's still adjudged a minor) out of paternal imposition, or (if he's an adult) out of personal desire. The great rabbi listened to this young prodigy's words, rose, and kissed him on the head. He then said that the boy was soon to be a ruling rabbi himself, and the *baraita* concludes by conforming this prediction.

The Gemara, though, wants to take a closer look at R. Chanina's words. The way he stated before Rabban Gamliel his use of the terms for minor and adult abides by the "age of vows" criteria, not his actual adulthood. This works perfectly well according to R. Yose, son of R. Yehuda, but R. Yehuda ha-Nasi had claimed that the father's power in this domain lasts until those two pubic hairs have emerged. So, if R. Chanina meant by "adult" the "age of vows," then he might not have passed the point at which his father's powers ceased.

30a

That would mean, as R. Yehuda ha-Nasi has consistently argued, that the lad remains under his father's control, and R. Chanina does not yet have the power to render such a decision. The Gemara dodges this conundrum by asserting that R. Chanina really meant the terms "minor" and "adult" literally, unconnected to his comprehension of vows.

One more roadblock (about the timing of R. Chanina's growth experience) is thrown R. Yehuda ha-Nasi's way vis-à-vis R. Chanina's declaration before Rabban Gamliel, as this Gemara comes to a close, but it is dismissed with alacrity. And, Chapter Four proceeds to its final Mishna, and it's a meaty one.

It begins with another male-female difference regarding final *nezirut* rituals. When a man is preparing his final ritual sacrifices (dubbed here and later "shaving his head"), he is permitted to make use of unassigned money that his deceased father left before he could conclude his own sacrificial rites. A woman may not take advantage of her late father's funds in this way. Why should this be the case? The case is that of a father and son who have both vowed individually to be *nezirim*, and in overlapping periods. Then, the father passed away with an undesignated pot of cash left over. In the opinion of R. Yose, the money is to be spent on voluntary offerings, and the son is not allowed to make use of his father's leftover *nezirut* money—because he was already enjoying his own *nezirut* at the time of his father's passing. So, what was the Mishna talking about just a couple of sentences above? It was referring to a case in which only the father was a *nazir* at the time of his death, not the son. Thus, if the father dies before completing his *nezirut* and leaves some unexpended and undesignated money, and the son later declared that he would forthwith be a *nazir* reliant on making use of his father's money, he is allowed to do so, as the Mishna initially indicated.

We encountered a précis of this Mishna's rulings back on 27b. How is it that a son may make use of his father's unused funds when we are speaking of *nezirut* but not in other situations? R. Yochanan, as we have now seen several times, takes refuge in the claim that it is a law transmitted to Moses at Mt. Sinai. By the same token, why may a daughter not have access to leftover paternal funds in the same way as a son? The Gemara claims it's simply because sons inherit from their fathers while daughter do not—the system is rigged, gender inequality baked in. But, as always, it's more complicated than that, for the father consecrated his funds prior to his passing, and that would mean they fall outside the rules of inheritance. An interesting twist is inserted here—namely, because the distinctive laws of *nezirut* are products of *halacha* to Moses at Mt. Sinai, they accord with the son's rights to his father's excess *nezirut* funds. So, this is not ordinary inheritance, but the special rules of *nezirut* inheritance. Now, we turn to daughters. If a father in the above situation has no sons, but he does have a daughter, she is certainly the recipient of his inheritance. However, this is not an ordinary situation.

30b

We are now in the realm of the special *halacha* for *nezirut* which privileges the son but not the daughter, and it does not cover her.

The Gemara now launches a discussion of the Mishna by posing two related questions. Is the opinion attributed to R. Yose held by all the authorities? And, if the answer is no, what part of that opinion forms the crux of their disagreement: (a) that a son's *nezirut*, if even only partially, is temporally coterminous with that of his father, then he may not make use of any leftover funds from his father; or (b) that a son's vow of *nezirut*, if declared after his father's passing, empowers him to make use of those funds.

We start with a *baraita* which asks the question with which our Mishna began, albeit in declarative fashion. It makes clear what the Mishna was rather vaguer about: A son can use his late father's leftover *nezirut* money when he himself is readying his concluding sacrificial offerings—as long as he makes that a condition when he vows to become a *nazir*. If the son was already a *nazir* when his *nazir* father dies, then any leftover money that his father allocated to his own end-of-vows rituals must be spent on voluntary sacrifices. If this isn't clearly explanatory of what the Mishna intended, we are told that it's what R. Yose himself stated. The *baraita* concludes by asserting that R. Eliezer, R. Meir, and R. Yehuda disagree with the last of these rulings and allow the son who was a *nazir* in a period overlapping his father's *nezirut* before the latter died to inherit the latter's leftover funds. And, in one fell swoop, we learn that, yes, there is no unanimity on this question, and the realm of disagreement is (b).

The Gemara now addresses another area of inheritance that *nezirut* may affect. Rabbah asks what would be the case if a father had two *nazir* sons. Does the son who took his vow first get all his late father's leftover funds, or does the one who finishes first get to do so? Or, maybe, this is an area in which the law taught to Moses at Mt. Sinai about *nezirut* is the same as ordinary inheritance law, meaning that the two sons split their father's surplus money. The way traditional *halacha* dealt with inheritance was to allot the eldest son a double portion, and Rava asks if our *nezirut* case would mete out a father's leftover funds in this way or split them evenly. Rava adds, as if this was not already complicated enough, that it may be the case that, because the father's money was sanctified when he allotted it for his own concluding rituals, it may not be subject to traditional inheritance law, meaning that the eldest son would not be authorized to receive a double portion. On the other hand, maybe this makes no difference.

One final area where complications may intrude: What about a situation in which father and son have vowed different kinds of *nezirut*, the sorts outlined in earlier Mishnayot of this tractate. Suppose the father had vowed to be a permanent *nazir*, while the son was a regular one—or vice versa. Is there a difference in how the law is applied in such instances? In other words, does the category of *nezirut* adopted affect the son's capacity to make use of his late father's leftover funds? Rav Ashi gets the last word in this Gemara, and he opens up a huge kettle of worms. What happens if the father became *tamei* during his *nezirut* and allocated money for his requisite offerings of purification but then died; does this money become available to a *nazir* son who remains *tahor*? Or, vice versa?

All of these fascinating cases are only posed but not conclusively resolved, as our chapter comes to a close.

NOTES

1. "Nesia" is the Aramaic for Hebrew "Nasi" or "Prince."
2. See my *(Sacrifices) Left at the Altar: Reading Tractate Zevachim of the Babylonian Talmud* (Lanham, MD: Hamilton Books, 2014), p. 1.

Chapter 5

Mistakes and Misunderstandings

30b (CONTINUED)

Only one line from our new chapter appears at the very bottom of the *amud*, but no space is to be wasted in the Talmudic folio. This short chapter looks at vows of *nezirut* committed on the basis of mistaken ideas. How are we to deal with sanctified animals set to be offered if there was some sort of flawed information involved?

Bet Shammai get the ball rolling by stating starkly that a mistaken sanctification is nonetheless a sanctification.

31a

Bet Hillel unsurprisingly disagree. What's the crux of their discrepant views? Three cases ensue. If someone were to say that the black ox about to emerge from his house first will be consecrated, and then a white ox actually emerged first, Bet Shammai claim the white one is sanctified; Bet Hillel disagree. If someone should say that the gold coin about to emerge in his hand first will be sanctified, and then a silver one emerged first, Bet Shammai claim the silver coin is consecrated; Bet Hillel disagree. Finally, if someone were to state that the barrel of wine about to appear in his hands is to be sanctified, and a barrel of oil appeared first, Bet Shammai claim the oil consecrated; Bet Hillel (for the third time) disagree. Perhaps we shall see why the Mishna felt the need to relay three cases which, on the surface, seem to teach the same lesson.

The Mishna begins appropriately with its first ruling, a view which governs in its way the subsequent three specific cases as well—namely, when a sanctification is rendered mistakenly, it still qualifies as a sanctification. This would seem to indicate that Bet Shammai were affirming the sanctification of the white ox, the silver coin, and the barrel of oil, because they appeared first. In other words, the vow of consecration was erroneous in that the vower expected the black ox, gold coin, and barrel of wine to appear first. Why, asks the Gemara, do Bet Shammai rule in this way? It replies that a ruling of initial consecration is a function of the complex laws of substitution found in *Leviticus* (27.10): If someone mistakenly offers one animal for another to serve as a sacrifice, the Torah rules here that, despite the offerer's error, the substitute is sanctified.

Bet Hillel respond that what Bet Shammai state may be true for substitution, but that's not the situation here. The case here is the mistaken sanctification of an offering, and this does not take effect. The Gemara now takes a closer look at Bet Shammai's reasoning and wonders if the link with the rules of substitution is sustainable. The person in the Mishna's initial example fully expected to be sanctifying a black ox, but a white one first emerged, and Bet Shammai claim it is sacred because it appeared first. Substitution, however, is an error of speech, which would seem to differ widely from Bet Shammai's reasoning.

Perhaps we have misconstrued Bet Shammai's thinking, as Rav Pappa explains. When the person in the Mishna stated "first" in the case of the oxen, he actually meant the first *black* one to appear from among the black oxen would be consecrated, and he was not referring to oxen of different colors. Bet Shammai intended merely to consecrate the first black one to emerge. Seen in this way, Rav Pappa has enabled Bet Shammai's to evade comparison with substitution, for they are not consecrating a white ox but just waiting for the "first" black ox to emerge and be consecrated. The problem is that the person spoke of a single "black ox" (*shor shachor*); if he only had one, why would he ever have said the "first" one to appear? So, Rav Pappa's reasoning then would only work is the speaker had more than one black ox. Bet Hillel rebut that, if this was what was implied in the speaker's statement, his wording would seem to indicate not the first black ox (of his black oxen) but the first black ox of all his oxen, colorblind.

Rava of Barnish, addressing Rav Ashi, claims that what we have here is not a mistaken sanctification but an intentional one. Rav Pappa's reasoning rules out the mistaken quality of the person's statement, and gone then is any ambiguity. As he argued, the speaker meant the first of his black oxen to emerge would be consecrated, and that's what transpired. The Gemara excuses the use of mistaken to characterize the consecration, claiming that the error came with our initial understanding of what was meant.

Following up on this query, the Gemara asks if Rav Pappa's explanation is appropriate. By his reasoning, Bet Shammai would believe that mistaken sanctification does not qualify as sanctification, and now the Gemara cites a Mishna we shall come to momentarily, which incidentally will remind us that this tractate is about the *nazir*. If one took a vow of *nezirut*, then thought better of it and went before a sage who let him off the hook, but he had already allocated an animal to be offered at his final *nezirut* rituals, the animal is released into the flock and from sanctity. The Mishna continues that Bet Hillel confront Bet Shammai, asking if this is indeed a situation of mistaken sanctification which is the reason the animal is released to rejoin its mates. The assumption here, not stated explicitly, is that Bet Hillel knew that Bet Shammai believed mistaken sanctification to constitute the real thing and thus posed this question as a confrontation. Or, maybe it is Bet Hillel who have misconstrued things. Bet Shammai never explicitly construed mistaken sanctification as genuine sanctification, but what they were referring to by "mistaken" was how the first statement of the Mishna was misleading.

The Gemara is incorrigible, however, and will try once again to demonstrate that what that first line of our Mishna stated is to be taken at face value: Bet Shammai believe that mistaken sanctification constitutes sanctification. To this end, it cites a Mishna we shall come to tomorrow (32b). Six people are walking along the roadway,

31b

and another person is walking toward them, although still at a distance and not completely recognizable, and one of the six vows forthwith to be a *nazir* if that distant person turns out to be X. At this moment, a second member of the party of six vows to be a *nazir* if the approaching person is not X. Just as the first person was convinced the person in the distance was X, the second person is equally convinced he is not X. Then, a third person in the group vows a period of *nezirut* if either the first or second person is forthwith a *nazir*; that seems to mean that the third person will be a *nazir*, as the first and second persons have staked out mutually exclusive, binary grounds. To complicate matters further, a fourth member of the group takes the opposite tack and vows a period of *nezirut* if either the first or second person does not become a *nazir*, the obverse of the third person's vow. So, what's left? A fifth member of the group vows an unlikely prospect, namely that he will forthwith be a *nazir* if both persons one and two are *nezirim*, a vow which on the surface appears highly unlikely to be realized, but just wait. And, not to be left out in the cold, the sixth person then states that he, too, will forthwith be a *nazir* if all five of his party are *nezirim*, a vow that, like the fifth person's vow, appears highly unlikely to materialize, but (again) just wait.

In all these cases, the Mishna (30b) says that Bet Shammai rule them all *nezirim*. How can this be, if several are mutually exclusive and the vows made on the basis of mistaken understanding? It can only be so if a mistaken sanctification, just as a well-understood one, qualifies as a genuine sanctification, à la Bet Shammai. So, what could Rav Pappa have been thinking by the way he construed Bet Shammai's reasoning? He nonetheless remains firm. So, the Gemara tries another approach to getting at Bet Shammai's statement.

This time we hear from Abaye who offers a novel though very interesting reading of the Mishna, one that introduces another realm of possible complexity in other Talmudic texts as well. Inasmuch as the text with which we are dealing—indeed, the entire Mishna and Gemara—was originally unpointed, it is entirely possible that the verb translated above for "emerge" is not in the future tense but actually in the past tense. Thus, Abaye read it as the person stating, later in the day, that the black ox which *emerged* from his house first is to be sanctified. Upon learning that actually a white one came out first, he replies: Well, if I had known that, I'd not have said black. Somehow, he thought it was a black one.

The Gemara does not like this grammatical argument. In the passage about a gold coin emerging, it was clearly stated in the future tense, and because all the various cases (oxen, coins, and barrels) should be in the same tense for comparability, Abaye's argument would seem not to hold water. Simple answer: Abaye would argue that the subsequent cases need to be emended and read in the past tense, just like that of the oxen.

The Gemara now turns in an unexpected direction, as Rav Chisda notes that one black ox in a group of white oxen would lower the value of the herd, as the latter colored oxen are prized animals; furthermore, a black ox bearing a white spot is a potential sign of a disease. The argument goes on to cite the Mishna's reference to a black ox appearing first—which, despite basically agreeing with Abaye's reading of the text, it still cites it as a future tense pronouncement. The Gemara assumes that most people don't just give up their best, most valued animals for sacrifice, but save them for themselves. Nonetheless, in this instance, Bet Shammai say that the white ox is sanctified. If white oxen are more prized, as Rav Chisda asserts, then his claim would seem to have been defeated.

Maybe we should assume that people aren't so parsimonious about their sacrificial offerings; maybe that's what was behind Bet Shammai's willingness to consecrate a white ox, despite a black one to appear first. But, in that case, why when a gold coin was expected and a silver one emerged first, Bet Shammai consecrated it pronto—a person can't be both charitable and parsimonious at the same time. If ungenerous, then silver works, sure, but how about the third case? Oil is more costly than wine, so if Bet Shammai are in an uncharitable frame of mind, why sanctify the barrel of oil?

The Gemara cops out on the wine-oil discrepancy by stating that it was thinking of the Galilee region where wine is more costly than oil. The greater number of olive trees in that region of the Holy Land decrease the cost of oil. Therefore, the ungenerous line of reasoning is uncontested. We're still stuck with that first case in which Bet Shammai still consecrate a white ox, and Rav Chisda uses a similar ploy and claims that he was referring to oxen from Kerman Province (now in Iran) where the black variety are actually more valuable. We are moving ever farther from the discussion of *nezirut*, not necessarily a problem, as the Gemara here comes to an end and a new Mishna opens up, a précis of a portion of which we have seen above.

Should a person take a vow of *nezirut* and then transgress by drinking wine, either intentionally or unintentionally (not realizing his vow had begun), and he then went to ask a sage to excuse him from his commitment, but he was turned down—what's a body to do? He assesses the number of days from the time he initially vowed until his transgression—we shall see in the Gemara what this enumeration counts for. Now, if the sage actually freed him of his vow, meaning that there was something untoward in his vow that could enable the sage to retroactively declare it null and void, and he had already allocated an animal for his final *nezirut* sacrifices, that animal is set free as well and returns to its fellows.

Bet Hillel and Bet Shammai, as we already know and would in any case surely surmise, disagree on what to make of the released animal. The former ask the latter (figuratively speaking) if this is a case of mistaken sanctification. In the previous Mishna, it certainly seems as though that is precisely what Bet Shammai would say. Still, now our new Mishna effectively states that no sanctification ever took place, and the animal is free to go. Bet Shammai would reply with a ruling about animal tithing each year (dealt with in tractate *Bechorot* [First-borns]). All of one's sheep and cows born in the year run through a narrow gate and are counted off, so that every tenth animal is declared sacred; sometimes, however, one may get confused in the count and misname the ninth or the eleventh cow or sheep as the tenth. They are all nonetheless consecrated, as *Bechorot* 60a states and Bet Shammai aver: Take that, Bet Hillel! But, Bet Hillel are not so easily shunted aside. They retort that *Bechorot* rules that only tagging the ninth or eleventh animal incorrectly as the tenth constitutes grounds for sanctity; had the counter tagged the eighth or twelfth animal, for example, nothing would have taken place. It is thus the same scriptural verse (*Leviticus* 27.32) consecrating the tenth has an equivalent impact on the ninth animal

32a

or eleventh—but not the eight or twelfth.

Inasmuch as we have no rebuttal here from Bet Shammai, perhaps we should assume they have none, but we have already seen, when some of this Mishna was argued above, they will continue to dispute Bet Hillel on the issue of substitution. Ordinarily, the Talmud is much more favorable to Bet Hillel's rulings than Bet Shammai. We shall see if that trend holds up here. Also, for such a lengthy Mishna, the Gemara that follows is relatively brief, but that is surely because we have, indeed, considered a number of these issues above.

As it frequently does, the Gemara begins by asking whose opinion the Mishna is expressing, because it was not explicit. It rules out both R. Yose and the rabbis, because their opinions are explicitly mentioned in a *baraita*. That text tells us that, if a person took a vow of *nezirut* and proceeded to have a glass of wine, we are to do nothing to help him at that point until he follows the abstinences of *nezirut* for the same number of days as he transgressed and then completes however many days remain in the period he vowed. R. Yose is more lenient and compels the transgressing *nazir* to compensate a maximum of thirty days. Our Mishna only required a drinking *nazir* to count the number of days from when he made his initial vow, with no requirement to compensate with additional days. Neither of the views represented in this *baraita* accords with that of the Mishna. The Gemara nonetheless makes a valiant, almost Quixotic effort to understand the Mishna according to R. Yose and to the rabbis.

The next piece of the Mishna is the capacity of a sage to withdraw a person's *nezirut* vow. R. Yirmeya begins with Bet Shammai's ruling in the previous Mishna that a mistaken sanctification is still a sanctification. That said, they also rule that, despite that person's erroneous vow, the sanctified animal readied for his final rituals is simply released to his confrères of the flock, which would seem to indicate that that animal wasn't actually sanctified. By the same token, Bet Hillel regarded mistaken substitution as substitution nonetheless and hence sanctification of an animal offering. If, however, a sage or group of laymen withdrew the sacredness of the original animal (before substitution), the substitute loses its sacredness as well. The point of R. Yirmeya's argument is to demonstrate how Bet Shammai's perspective on mistaken sanctification can help us understand Bet Hillel's perspective on mistaken substitution.

The Gemara next addresses the question of counting newborns for a given year to offer every tenth sheep or cow as *bechorot* and what happens when one mistakenly counts the ninth animal as the tenth one. Rav Nachman claims that such an error does indeed sanctify the ninth, but only if it is in error, not a deliberate move. Rav Chisda and Rabba bar Rav Huna claim that both a mistaken count as well as a purposeful one renders the ninth sacred. In an effort to dispute Rav Nachman, Rava rehearses a piece of the Mishna and asks why Bet Hillel did not articulate a position that should have been stated; this form of argumentation from what was not said is exceedingly difficult to explicate. In other words, put simply, if Rav Nachman's view is correct, why did Bet Hillel not make a certain case?

Rav Shimi bar Ashi thinks he knows why Bet Hillel remained mum here, and he then goes on to explain what Bet Shammai would have replied to counter Bet Hillel—all of it suppositional. He concludes, though, that Bet Shammai's concocted response would not have held water, and thus Bet Hillel's lack of a rebuttal is attributed to a desire to tamp down unnecessary debate.

A new Mishna at this point addresses the case of an unfortunate person who vows a period of *nezirut*, believing full well that he has readied his sacrificial animal for the final rituals, and when he set off to bring his animal in, he discovered (to his horror) that the animal has been stolen. If he had vowed to be a *nazir* prior to the animal's theft, he is indeed still a *nazir*. In other words, the animal's disappearance in this way does not rise to a level whereby a sage might legitimately relieve him of his vow.

32b

The converse situation, declaration of his *nezirut* vow after the theft of the animal, does enable him to be released from his vow. The Mishna continues with a case study. Nachum the Mede, a well-known sage in the era of the destruction of the Second Temple (70 C.E.), made just this mistake. What happened was that people who had taken vows of *nezirut* came from places outside the Land of Israel to bring their final sacrificial offerings to the Temple in Jerusalem, and there they found the Temple in ruins. Because there was now no place to conduct their final rituals, they potentially would be *nezirim* for a very long time and thus sought to be freed of their commitments. Nachum asked them if they would have taken their vows if they would have known that the Temple would be in ruins, and of course they all replied in the negative. So, Nachum relieved them of their vows of *nezirut*. The sages later confronted this issue and declared that any vow of *nezirut* made prior to the Temple's destruction remained in place; similarly, they declared that any vow of *nezirut* made after the Temple was in ruins was open to being annulled.

Rabbah gets the ball rolling by citing a Mishna close to the very end of our tractate (64a) in which the rabbis overturn a ruling of R. Eliezer. The latter stated that a vow can be annulled by virtue of an unanticipated circumstance, but the rabbis ruled this out. Just what did the rabbis have in mind? Rava claims that, while the rabbis did make this argument that unanticipated circumstances do not enable annulment of *nezirut* vows, they do accept that a claim built on the grounds of an unanticipated circumstance could be grounds for annulment. Sounds very much like a contradiction in terms, but the Gemara goes on. Essentially, it is an effort to understand what the individual *nezirim* were thinking when they committed to their vows. If, at the time of their vows, someone had asked them if they wanted to continue knowing that the Temple would be in ruins. No one would likely have responded in the affirmative, unless they were OK with an indefinite and probably very lengthy period as a *nazir*.

Rav Yosef is not so sure. He claims (with 20–20 hindsight) that, had he been present when the rabbis found Nachum's ruling faulty, he'd have cited a verse from the book of the prophet Jeremiah (7.4), which mentions three times in succession "God's Temple." This, the Gemara explains, according to the sages, is a reference to the fact that, although the first two Temples were destroyed, there will be a Third Temple. The Gemara doesn't give up so easily and, while accepting that the *nezirim* may have known that the Second Temple would end in ruins, how could they know when this would transpire? Abaye reminds us of a prophetic vision from the book of *Daniel* which pretty much names the year of this great disaster, and the Gemara's last breath here is to respond: Yes, but how could anyone know which day. Our unfortunate *nezirim* might still have believed, even if they knew of the Temple's coming destruction, that they would complete their period of *nezirut* before that disaster.

Now for another substantial Mishna that we have seen the initial part of above. A group of six persons are walking along the roadway, and in the distance they see someone walking in their direction, but that person is still too distant for immediate recognition. Nonetheless, one of the party of six states that he is forthwith a *nazir* if that person turns out to be X, who he is certain it is, followed by a second person stating that he will be a *nazir* if that person turns out not to be X, a stance of which he is just as sure. A third member of the group declares himself a *nazir* if either the first or second person becomes a *nazir*, and a fourth person makes the obverse claim to be a *nazir* if either of the first two is not a *nazir*. Then, the fifth member of the group declares himself a *nazir* if both persons one and two are *nezirim*, while the sixth and final member of the party declares himself a *nazir* if all five of his associates are *nezirim*. As we noted earlier, Bet Shammai claim they are all *nezirim*, while Bet Hillel make a strange claim—namely, that only the one whose declaration is unsatisfied will be a *nazir*. R. Tarfon piles on and says none of the six qualifies for *nezirut*. What happens if the person walking toward our party of six were to turn and walk away before a positive ID could be made? No one becomes a *nazir*. R. Shimon for his part offers a verdict he came to on 13a. With the approaching person's identity not thoroughly clear, the first member of the group of six becomes a possible *nazir*; inasmuch as the terms of his declared vow remain in limbo, he may opt for a voluntary *nezirut* and may go on to complete his final ritual observances.

The Gemara immediately focuses on Bet Hillel's bizarre statement that it is those whose projections are unsatisfied who qualify for *nezirim*. Rav Yehuda answers simply that the text was incorrectly worded. It should be referring to those whose language *is* satisfied.

33a

Abaye now attempts to make sense of Bet Hillel's odd claim without suggesting a corrupted text, and it's more than a bit of a stretch. The Gemara does not linger on this piece of the Mishna but looks ahead to its final portion.

There the Mishna addressed the issue of the approaching individual turning around abruptly before a positive ID could be made, with a verdict that none of the six vowers become a *nazir*. In such an instance, it is the mystery person's decision to disappear, identity unknown, that results in this ruling, but, asks the Gemara now, if he had continued approaching and his identity become clear, the vower whose guess turned out to be correct would indeed have been a *nazir*. Whose claim would that mirror?

33b

[There is no Gemara text on this amud, as it is completely covered with commentary in the standard Vilna page layout of the text. I believe this is unique in this entire edition of the Talmud.]

34a

Could it be R. Tarfon? To help untangle this conundrum, the Gemara cites a *baraita* in which R. Yehuda claims, in the name of R. Tarfon, that none of the six members of that group would be a *nazir*, just as in the Mishna itself. The notion succinctly articulated in the *baraita* is that *nezirut* only takes effect if there is no uncertainty in the vower's statement. All six of the statements made by the group were shrouded in doubt, because no one knew the approaching person's identity for certain at the time they vowed, meaning none of their vows could hold.

We learn now that the Tanna, the voice behind this Mishna, is R. Yehuda, and the Gemara at this point repeats a *baraita* introduced on 8a. Back there we learned that, if a person committed to a vow of *nezirut* on the condition that a given pile of produce was 100 *kors* and when he returned to his pile it was gone, R. Shimon says his vow and its proscriptions remain intact. However, R. Yehuda says that the doubts are sufficiently strong to outweigh other concerns, and the vower is no *nazir*. R. Shimon takes into consideration the possibility that the stack, had it not disappeared, would have measured 100 *kors*, and that would clearly have meant the vow of *nezirut* would have gone into effect. Similarly, in the Mishna before us, R. Shimon argues that, if the mystery man or woman had not disappeared, his or her identity would have become known, and the vower(s) with the correct guess would have meant a proper vow of *nezirut*.

Last Mishna of chapter 5, one of the shortest in this tractate, follows, this one with nine persons involved. Somebody caught sight of a *koy* (an unidentified species of kosher animal with characteristics of both domesticated and undomesticated animals) and declared he would forthwith be a *nazir* if this creature is a wild animal. A second person then made the obverse declaration that he would forthwith be a *nazir* if it was not a wild animal. A third person makes the parallel declaration forthwith to be a *nazir* if the animal is a domestic one, while a fourth person makes a comparable declaration if it is not a domestic animal. (Maybe you can see where this is going.) A fifth person declares he shall forthwith be a *nazir* if the animal is both a wild and a domesticated animal, and a sixth person makes the obverse declaration of *nezirut* if the creature is neither wild nor domesticated. Now, a seventh person looks at the conditional vows of the six preceding him and declares he will forthwith be a *nazir* if any one of them is a *nazir*, and an eighth person makes the parallel declaration that he will forthwith be a *nazir* if any one of the first six is not a *nazir*. Finally, the ninth person vows to be a *nazir* if all of the first six are *nezirim*. The Mishna's conclusion: All their vows take effect, a position consistent with Bet Shammai's ruling back on 31b, though it might also reflect R. Shimon's ruling just above.

The Gemara is actually fairly short, given the breadth of the Mishna. It begins with snippets of two *baraitot* as a way to analyze the Mishna: (a) "nine *nezirim*"—meaning nine people's vows of *nezirut* (having something to do with a *koy* sighting) may take effect; and (b) "nine periods of *nezirut*"—meaning an instance of one person vowing to be a *nazir* (again involving a *koy*) and having to carry out nine periods of *nezirut*. So, (a) seems like a reasonable reading of the Mishna, as there are nine distinct takes on the nature of the *koy* in the Mishna. Meanwhile, (b) is a bit harder to understand, and we shall leave it at that.

Chapter 6

The Three Proscriptions of *Nezirut*

34a (CONTINUED)

The first Mishna in this chapter only gets started at the bottom of this *amud*. It begins with the three proscriptions incumbent on a *nazir*: no corpse *tumah*, no products of the grape (in particular, wine), and no shaving or cutting one's hair. None of the products of the grapevine (grapes, wine, etc.) stands alone when calculating the minimum amount required for transgressing this proscription; they all combine and must not rise to the prescribed volume of an olive. Once that threshold is reached or passed, the *nazir* is a candidate for a flogging.

34b

The Mishna now cites an early text, by which it means a ruling that long preceded the editing of the Mishna as we now have it by R. Yehuda ha-Nasi, the redaction usually dated to ca. 200 C.E. It states that the minimum volume for drinking wine that would constitute a transgression of this *nezirut* abstention is one-quarter *log* (roughly equal to a volume of 1.5 eggs). R. Akiva sticks with the olive volume and states that, even if a *nazir* merely dipped his bread into his wine and consumed it in this (odd) manner, he has sufficiently violated the law and due for a flogging if bread and wine combine to more than that minimum.

The *nazir* becomes halachically accountable if he drinks wine or consumes grapes, grape seeds, or grape skins alone—all products of the vine. R. Elazar ben Azarya has a slightly different take here: The transgressing *nazir* must consume two grape seeds and a grape skin before he reaches halachic accountability—that is, the *halacha* requires a combination of grape

111

products before rising to a transgression. The Gemara will have more to say on this front.

Finally, our Mishna asks for clarification on what we have translated as grape seeds and grape skins. One authority, R. Yehuda, translates the two Hebrew terms in the order we have them as grape skins and seeds, while another authority, R. Yose, prefers the translation in the order presented here. More to come in the Gemara.

The Gemara will keep us busy for a long time and will introduce some new explanatory techniques common in the Talmud but as yet not utilized in this tractate. The initial ruling of the Mishna about three proscriptions incumbent on a *nazir* includes, of course, no consumption of products of the grapevine, but the vine itself (namely, elements not part of the fruit itself, like the shoots and leaves) should be OK. This rather simple explanation clashes with a ruling of R. Elazar who explicitly understands the Mishna to be ruling out anything connected to the grapevine; *Numbers* 6.4 plainly prohibits a *nazir* from consuming "anything made from the grapevine" (Alter, p. 710), and R. Elazar understands leaves and shoots within this.

The Gemara goes on to say that, yes, R. Elazar has a problem with this Mishna, but it is not this part but a later piece that requires consumption to reach the volume of an olive before the *nazir* has violated the terms he vowed. So, the Gemara takes a closer look at the text. Consumption of an olive's volume of grapes themselves is a clear and present violation, but no liability attaches for consuming the grapevine. This is where R. Elazar's including of leaves and shoots of the vine comes into play, as the Mishna has specified the fruit.

The Gemara turns to look at the essence of the quarrel between R. Elazar and the sages (who follow that the Mishna's proscription is on the fruit itself). And, it turns out that the two parties are each using different hermeneutic instruments to make their cases. R. Elazar explains the verses in question by means of a technique known as amplifications and limitations (or restrictions); the sages explain the same pieces of text with a method known as general and particular. Briefly, let's try to lay out what these tools entail.

Starting with the latter terms (H. *klal ufrat*), the Torah will sometimes make a general statement which is followed by a particular, more restricted case within the rubric of the general. The reverse is also found on occasion. Ordinarily, the particular case is regarded as an explanation of the intent of the general one and restricts its use accordingly. The range of the general statement has now been clearly curtailed. This is what the Gemara states as the rabbis' approach to the issue at hand. The less frequently encountered hermeneutical method of amplification and limitation is similar, except that the limitation (as its name indicates) does not definitively explain the generalization but merely restricts its range. This topic is much more complex than this simple description, and as the text follows we shall add coloring as needed. Interestingly, the thirteen rules of biblical exposition which encompass these tools are recited every morning during the morning prayers (*shacharit*) of observant Jews.

It would probably be instructive at this point to lay out the relevant passages of the Torah (*Numbers* 6.3–4) which the Gemara will use to explicate the dispute. In Robert Alter's translation (pp. 710–11):

> from both wine and liquor he shall keep himself apart, neither wine vinegar nor liquor vinegar shall he drink, no grape steepings shall he drink, and grapes, whether wet or dry he shall not eat. All the days of his naziritehood [*nezirut*], of anything made from the grapevine, from seeds to skin, he shall not eat.

Some renditions of this piece of Torah have "aged-wine" instead of "liquor" in the two places the latter term appears here.

The Gemara starts with R. Elazar's take on the first phrase of the text under scrutiny: "from both wine and liquor he shall keep himself apart." This is one of the Torah's limitations. Later it reads: "from anything made from the gravevine." This would be an amplification of the proscription. So, the Torah starts with a restriction and then amplifies that restriction to include everything within the category being analyzed ("anything made from the grapevine") which would now include leaves and shoots. What would be excluded from this exegesis would then be the branches of the vine, which resemble wood and are inedible.

So, let's turn to how the sages would expound the passage, using their methodology. They look at the same first phrase R. Elazar addressed and deem it a specification of the Torah. The second phrase raised immediately above, they mark as a generalization, but they go one step further and take the phrase "from seeds to skin" as another specification. So, what we have here is not simply *klal ufrat*, which is a generic term for this approach to exegesis, but *prat uchlal ufrat* (specification-generalization-specification). In such a case, the generalization expands the first specification, but when it is in turn subject to a specification, the Torah is seen as restricting the generalization to items resembling the specification. So, in this case, the second specification restricts items proscribed for a *nazir* to fruit and the waste of the fruit (here meaning grapes and vinegar), and that means anything resembling those items is also off limits. The Gemara at this juncture asks an interesting question: If the second specification is as restrictive as it appears at first glance, only to include the fruit itself, what's the point of this whole *prat uchlal ufrat* method? In response, it may not just be ripe grapes themselves, but also dried ones (raisins) as well. But, both fresh and dried grapes are unambiguously mentioned in the biblical verse. OK, how about wine and vinegar? Same deal, both are there. Thus, reasoning on the basis that ripe fruit does not work, meaning that just fruit is what distinguishes the specification.

As the Gemara explains, the specification of "fruit" explicitly means the grapes and "waste of fruit" means vinegar, but what does it means by items resembling those items which are also proscribed for the *nazir*? One view for that which is considered similar to fruit here is unripe grapes; for waste of fruit, Rav Kahana suggests wormy grapes. And, that last little piece of the biblical text, "from seeds to skin," what does the "to" serve to encompass? Everything between the grape's seeds and its skin—namely, its pulp.

35a

The last piece of the schema of specification-generalization-specification was "from seeds to skin." At this point, R. Elazar ben Azarya claims that a *nazir* has not transgressed his vow unless he consumes at a minimum two grape seeds and a grape skin. The Gemara wonders where he came up with that understanding. The Gemara now struggles with whether this phrase must be used solely to complete the specification-generalization-specification or if it might be an exegetical reading all its own. Perhaps, it can serve two functions, and this last understanding is the one upon which the Gemara ultimately decides.

The Gemara now launches into an extended discussion of the two hermeneutic approaches to scripture, drawing on this wording of this case. As we saw above, R. Elazar explained this Torah verse using the method of amplifications and limitations. The Gemara asks a seemingly odd question about where he makes use of the specification-generalization-specification approach. Odd, because we just learned that he was not using this approach. The expounders over the century, while they differ in their explanations of this conundrum, have largely come to understand the issue of where in scripture R. Elazar found a specification-generalization-specification progression. R. Abahu answers the call by pointing us to *Exodus* 22.9: "Should a man give to his fellow a donkey or an ox or a sheep or any beast for safekeeping." (Alter, p. 444) This clause has three parts: "Should a man give a donkey or an ox or a sheep" (specification); "or any beast" (generalization); and "for safekeeping" (specification).

While R. Abahu's derivation would seem to work well in understanding R. Elazar's approach, Rava points us to a different scriptural verse, *Leviticus* 1.10: "And if his offering is from the flock, from the sheep or from the goats." (Alter, p. 548) Again, we have the tripartite sequence: "if his offering" (specification); "the flock" (generalization); and "sheep or . . . goats" (specification).

In this as well as R. Abahu's explication, the final specification thoroughly delimits matters to that which resembles the latter specification.

Rav Yehuda of Diskarta offers a third possibility, *Leviticus* 1.2: "Should any person from you bring forward to the Lord an offering, of beasts from herd and from flock." (Alter, p. 547) Same deal: "of" (specification); "beasts" (generalization); and "heard and . . . flock" (specification). Rava doesn't buy it, and he enjoins Rav Yehuda of Diskarta in a debate over whether the term for "beast" (*behema*) encompasses undomesticated animals or not, but the Gemara leaves this issue open.

35b

Rather than trace this debate down any further rabbit holes, the Gemara turns to the much bigger question of where in scripture the similar exegetical approach of generalization-specification-generalization may be found. It points us to *Deuteronomy* 14.26: "And you may give the silver for anything your appetite craves—cattle and sheep and wine and strong drink [or aged wine] and whatever your appetite may prompt you to ask." (Alter, p. 953) How does the Gemara take this phrase apart? Similarly: "you may give the silver for anything your appetite craves" (generalization); "cattle and sheep and wine and strong drink" (specification); and "whatever your appetite may prompt you to ask" (generalization). Although this progression concludes with a generalization, it cannot, we are instructed, exceed the boundaries set by the specification.

So, despite this sequence concluding with a generalization, we remain limited by the specification. What, then, is the point of that second generalization? Wouldn't we come to same conclusion without it? The answer is that this second generalization brings into consideration everything resembling what has just been specified. Without it, we would be limited solely to the distinct items of the specification. The Gemara goes on to compare this approach with the specification-generalization-specification sequence and the role there of the second specification. In this case, we find that without that second specification, the generalization would have wildly enlarged the field of possibilities covered.

It would seem thus far that these two approaches of (a) specification-generalization-specification and (b) generalization-specification-generalization yield the same result. What's the difference? Not much, it turns out, though (b) tends to be somewhat more comprehensive. The Gemara continues by comparing a specification followed by a generalization to the earlier method (apparently supported by R. Elazar) of amplifications and limitations, but let's move on before we get entirely lost in this labyrinth.

One *daf* back on 34b, the celebrated R. Akiva suggested that produce from grapes could be mixed with other allowable foods to rise to a volume which, when consumed by a *nazir*, would lead to his being flogged. This issue needs elaboration. R. Abahu, citing R. Yochanan, states explicitly that mixing allowable food with proscribed items does not mean that the total entity is the measure for whether or not he has transgressed the law—save for the case of a *nazir* (e.g., one-half an olive's volume of grapes and a similar amount of bread). How does he support that conclusion? He points to the term (*Numbers* 6.3) *mishrat* (translated above as "steepings") which would seem to include anything into which a grape product has been absorbed.

36a

Zeiri throws in another complicating factor—namely, this business about mixing together to form a critical mass (e.g., an olive's volume) pertains to *chametz* in an offering that is burned on the Altar—and burning *chametz* on the Altar is strictly forbidden (*Leviticus* 2.11). So, for example, if a certain amount of *chametz* mixed with enough matzah to constitute an olive's volume was then offered on the Altar, a flogging is in store for the offerer. Where did he come up with that, asks the Gemara. This line of reasoning is consonant with R. Elazar's approach, and he focuses on the words "for all leaven" from that passage in *Leviticus* which he takes to include even mixtures.[1] The Gemara adds that Zeiri could just as easily have applied his notion to the eating of *chametz* in a mixture of a minimum olive's volume, so why did he choose the case of burning on the Altar? True, concedes the Gemara, but he made his point to counter Abaye's ruling that even less than an olive's volume of *chametz* burned on the Altar (even an itsy-bitsy bit of it) is punishable by a flogging; that would mean for Abaye that there would be no point articulating this idea of mixing with respect to burning.

Other sages opined on this issue. Rav Dimi was explaining R. Yochanan's view that this mixing ruling pertains solely to the proscriptions incumbent on a *nazir*. Abaye isn't buying. He introduces an elaborate "proof" from the case of a *tevul yom* (one who has submerged in a *mikveh* on that very day to expunge some impurity) who touches a bowl of porridge (or some dense soup) mixed with garlic and oil—and the porridge is *teruma* (meaning only for a Kohen's consumption)—and a Levi or Israelite eats an olive's volume of this mixed dish—didn't R. Yochanan rule him subject to a flogging? And, isn't this a case other than the prohibitions of a *nazir*?

36b

Rav Dimi promptly comes to R. Yochanan's defense and tries to explain what the latter really had in mind. As he sees it, Abaye misunderstood R. Yochanan whose point was that a non-Kohen needs to consume an olive's volume of *teruma* itself (with nothing added in), within the time it takes to consume half a loaf of wheat bread, before his transgression rises to the level deemed worthy of a flogging. In other words, he said nothing in this context about mixtures.

Abaye does not give up so easily, however, and he asks if this ruling follows biblical *halacha*, for otherwise a flogging could not be the result of a transgression. Rav Dimi avers that, indeed, the olive's volume consumption in this context is biblical. This give-and-take exchange continues for one more round before Abaye turns to another direction concerning the Bible's role in accountability for a flogging. In two further challenges, Abaye cites *baraitot* describing cases in which containers (mortars and pots in one case and boxes of two sorts in the other) filled, one with *teruma* spices (and later with grain) and the other with the same conventional items, fell in together with one another. Abaye's point, which I have only barely sketched in outline, is to dismantle Rav Dimi's defense of R. Yochanan's argument re: mixtures rising to culpability. Rav Dimi, of course, will not let this go unanswered, but we shall have to wait until tomorrow for his response.

37a

Rav Dimi dismisses this approach with barely a sentence. Although I'm sure there's depth there, it seems highly arcane, and Abaye doesn't pursue it. He turns to a new area of reasoning. He points to that word we saw at the end of 35b, *mishrat* ("steepings"); there we saw that R. Yochanan focused on this word (also translated "infused" or "soaked") to come up with his ruling on consuming a mixture of forbidden and allowed foods for a *nazir*. Abaye wonders if that was what the term is designed to instruct. Maybe, he suggests, its point is to equate taste with essence, such as a dish of non-kosher meat and potatoes cooked together; if the meat is taken from the pot and the potatoes retain its flavor, the potatoes may not be consumed. One olive's volume eaten leads to a flogging.

The Gemara at this point seems almost to be expressing exasperation. Abaye has gone to great lengths to demonstrate that consumption of an olive's volume of a mixture of forbidden and permitted dish constitutes a transgression far beyond the limited case of a *nazir*, but now he seems to be arguing an altogether new ruling from R. Yochanan's prooftext. The answer is that Abaye had come around to Rav Dimi's line of argument and acknowledged it; indeed, his last point about taste equals essence was a stab at why the mixture idea even adheres for a *nazir*.

The Gemara now extracts Abaye and Rav Dimi from the discussion as it settles in with a definitive ruling, one that Abaye actually interjected, and cites a *baraita*. The thrust of the term *mishrat* is to equate taste and essence, such that if a *nazir* saturated grapes in water, affording the later the taste of the former, then he would be asking for a flogging if he drank that water. Because the proscriptions incumbent on a *nazir* are temporary (dependent on the length of his vowed period of *nezirut*), not directed at his earning any profit, and can be abrogated at any point if so adjudged by a sage or group of laymen, then how much more severe is the prohibition on *kilei hakerem* (planting a mixture of a species of grain or vegetables with a grapevine) which is perpetual, may not be a source of profit, and can never be abrogated. The point of this exercise is to stress that the Torah uses the term *mishrat* to demonstrate the taste-equals-essence principle and not the idea of mixtures (which R. Abahu back on 35b cited in R. Yochanan's name).

Maybe I spoke too soon, as an unnamed rabbi claims that R. Abahu was actually citing a position held by R. Akiva who disagreed with this very *baraita* and held to the mixture ruling based on the same, much-used term *mishrat*. Where did R. Akiva render such a judgment such that R. Abahu would be citing him. Well, back on 34b, R. Akiva stated that bread dunked in wine, if a minimum of an olive's volume and consumed by a *nazir*, renders the *nazir* primed for a flogging. But, importantly, he did not mention anything explicit about mixing the volume of the bread with the wine, so he may just have been referring to the quantity of wine. Now, if that was his aim, it would seem to be utterly unnecessary, as that point has been made. Maybe R. Akiva's aim was to alter the quantity needed to rise to liability from one-quarter *log* to an olive's volume, with the bread extraneous to the whole equation. The Gemara extracts itself now from this problem by citing yet another *baraita* in which R. Akiva declares with crystal clarity that the entire mixture of bread and wine, if minimally an olive's volume, will lead the *nazir* (when consumed) to a flogging.

Now that we have finally settled on what R. Akiva argued in this instance, what does this mean for his views in other arenas? If, as we now have concluded, he argues the prohibited mixture idea from the term *mishrat*, how does he derive the taste-equals-essence principle which has much wider application than just for *nezirut*? For this, according to Rav Acha, son of Rav Avya, R. Akiva would cite the well-known scriptural ban on meat cooked in milk which serves to proscribe both. That seemed almost too easy, but it still leaves the unnamed rabbi of the *baraita* in question hanging, as he used *mishrat* in the taste-equals-essence sense. What's wrong with the milk-and-meat prohibition as a source? Apparently, this Torah law is considered a "novelty" (*chidush*), something characterized by its uniqueness and thus not productive in any wider application. Several efforts to puncture this notion are raised—apparently to rule them out—before we learn the novelty of milk and meat is that one can immerse meat in milk all day long (with the tastes transferred both ways), and nothing is ruined, but it's cooking the meat in milk that is proscribed.[2]

Wouldn't R. Akiva have no choice but to agree with the novelty of the meat-milk law, meaning that he would then be unable to use it to buttress his position on taste equals essence in all cases? Back to the drawing board, as the Gemara seeks a new source for R. Akiva.

37b

How about *Numbers* 31.23: "everything that can come into fire you shall pass through fire and it will be clean"? (Alter, p. 844) In other words, as the Gemara interprets this, a pot absorbs whatever is cooked in it; if that pot was owned by a non-Jew, then whatever a Jew puts in that pot to cook becomes a banned substance, unless the pot undergoes a thorough cleaning by fire (burning any possible residue from the non-Jew's past meals). Any taste imparted from a banned substance bans the whole thing (one bad apple spoils the whole bunch).

Again, this law is declared a novelty. It compares the taste conveyed to the pot by idolaters' cooking to that of a spoiled food, but the taste of spoiled food isn't banned in the Torah. The ruling on non-Jews' cooking devices is then unique, by this reasoning, because it bans the use of any such device until purged by fire. Something here is not right. Be that at it may, R. Akiva still needs a source for taste equals essence. Rav Huna bar Chiyya suggests that the ban on a non-Jews' cooking device only lasts for the day of use, and there is nothing extraordinary involved. The sages of the Mishna might also agree, but it is at this point that I have lost the train of Talmudic reasoning here.

The Gemara abandons this approach for a moment and looks back to R. Abahu's report on R. Yochanan's restriction of the mixture idea to *nezirut*. On the previous *amud*, the rabbis claimed that the force of *mishrat* vis-à-vis a *nazir* was to equate taste with essence, and then via a *kal vachomer* argument it applies to all such scriptural proscriptions. R. Akiva agrees that the *kal vachomer* based on the term *mishrat* had depth and breadth applicability in the Torah. Hence the question: Why did R. Yochanan limit it to *nezirut*?

Rav Acha, son of Rav Avya, was the one who posed this question to his colleague Rav Ashi, and the latter sage replied in such a way as to make this line of reasoning even more complicated. He claims, as we shall see momentarily, that the Torah laws on the *nazir* and regarding *chatat* comprise "two passages that come as one"—meaning that they cannot instruct us in contexts other than the ones addressed, a common principle of the Talmud. The underlying idea is that one specified item in the Torah would have had potentially a much wide applicability, but when a second item is identified as being restricted similarly, we are to understand that, without that identification, we would not have made the link solely from the first specification. Thus, we conclude that this combo only applies to the two contexts. But, we still don't know what the Gemara means by "come as one" regarding a *nazir* and a *chatat*.

The issue regarding the *nazir* is, of course, *mishrat*. That of *chatat* necessitates citation of a *baraita* which begins with reference to *Leviticus* 6.20 concerning a *chatat* offering: "Whatever touches its flesh shall become holy." (Alter, p. 566) The Hebrew of this citation includes the preposition "in" (*bi*), and the *baraita* takes this to mean that touching alone doesn't do the trick; there needs to be some absorption of the *chatat* "into" the other item, and then the sanctity of the *chatat* passes into that other item. If the *chatat* is for whatever reason ruled out or deemed unacceptable (such as waiting too long after slaughter to consume it), then the other item similarly must be ruled out. If the *chatat* passes muster, then the other meat that has become sanctified by contact with the *chatat* must be consumed according to the more stringent rules regarding *chatat* consumption.

The next question is tossed back at the rabbis and wonders why they applied *mishrat* to taste equals essence in all cases, which leaves the scriptural phrase regarding *chatat* to teach the separate case of mixtures. The answer here, other than simply to agree to disagree or concede, is that the rabbis are of the belief that we need both of these two scriptural passages to substantiate the taste-equals-essence position. The thrust here is that using this line to argue only one of these two, then the other would be left high and dry. Conclusion: the taste-equals-essence rule simply can't originate in *nezirut* by itself.

This back-and-forth has gone on so long now that the Gemara just says either "and the rabbis" or "and R. Akiva" with a presumed question mark after. So, how would R. Akiva respond to this reading of the rabbis? He earlier noted that the mixture notion applied to both *nezirut* and to *chatat*: two verses teaching one law. The rabbis, though, just argued that both verses teach essential and independent rulings. R. Akiva doesn't buy the idea that the proscription adopted with a vow of *nezirut* regarding grape seeds is any harsher than others mandated by the Torah, and thus it can provide a paradigm for wider application.

The debate goes one more round, before turning to another sage. Rav Ashi asks Rav Kahana what on the surface appears to be an odd question. A *baraita* teaches that the *Numbers* verse we have seen cited several times— "anything made from the grapevine"—means that two grape-related products can be mixed into an olive's volume to reach transgressional levels. R. Akiva, though, ruled that it was a mixture of the allowable with the prohibited that was forbidden, so does this pose a problem? Rav Kahana replies that the mixture of the allowable and the prohibited only becomes a problem when consumed together—as in the case of bread immersed in wine—but two items prohibited to a *nazir* can mix if consumed seriatim. The *daf* ends as it re-introduces R Shimon.

38a

Back on 4a, you may recall, R. Shimon rejected all this talk of mixtures, for as far as he was concerned, the least consumption of a grape product was enough for a flogging. The Gemara asks how this position, differing as it does from that of the rabbis, would handle "anything made from the grapevine," the phrase used above by those debating various views about mixtures of prohibited substances for the *nazir*. On 3b, R. Shimon noted that, if someone wants to take a vow of *nezirut* and fails to mention all three of the essential abstentions—cutting of the hair, corpse *tumah*, and wine—then he is not a *nazir*, and that is where he would use this phrase.

Channeling the words of R. Elazar, R. Abahu now suggests that, of the several times in the Torah that the volume measure of one-quarter *log* is mentioned, the only time that allowable and proscribed portions mix to constitute a quarter *log* is in the case of the *nazir*. Why? That is the instance in which *mishrat* is stated. The Gemara then inquires how R. Elazar's view differs from that of R. Yochanan. Simple: R. Elazar is only speaking of liquids, while R. Yochanan would include solid food as well, like bread.

The Gemara immediately above noted that the Torah includes several mentions of the one-quarter *log* measurement, and it now lists laws for which it is essential. It is not central to the debate we have been tracking, but oftentimes the Talmud will include such ancillary information perhaps out of a sense of completion. So, R. Elazar points to ten instances of such, and Rav Kahana provides an organizing principle to remember them. Five cases are concerned with red liquids, and five with white liquid. Rav Kahana has a mnemonic device to remember the five red ones: "A *nazir* [1] and a person offering the pascal sacrifice [2] who made a ruling [3] in the Temple [4] and died [5]." [1] is easy, a *nazir* who drinks one-quarter *log* of wine is liable for a flogging (I guess white and rosé, at least in this context, were not options at the time); [2] refers in its way to the Passover seder and the obligatory four cups of wine, each of which must contain one-quarter *log*; [3] refers, again in its way, to the law that anyone who has consumed one-quarter *log* of wine may make no legal rulings until he returns to sobriety; [4] is linked here to a ruling elsewhere in the Talmud that anyone who consumes a quarter *log* of wine and then enters the Temple precincts before regaining sobriety is liable to death at the hands of heaven; and [5] is derived from a law (*Leviticus* 21.11) about that volume of blood from a corpse and the need for the High Priest staying away from the dead.

For the five white liquids, we have this mnemonic: "A loaf [1] of a *nazir* [2] and a *metzora* [3] who were disqualified [4] on Shabbat [5]." [1] obliquely refers to the quarter *log* of oil that accompanied certain of the various breads that are part of the *todah* or thanksgiving offering (see tractate *Menachot* 88a)[3]; [2] concerns the quantity of oil which a *nazir* is required to bring with the final rituals at the end of his *nezirut*; [3] evokes the one-quarter *log* of water that is part of the purification ritual of a *metzora* (see 14b above); [4] has something to do with mixtures of impure liquids that minimally contain a quarter *log* in volume which, if consumed, disqualifies a person from consuming *teruma*; and [5] concerns carrying this volume of certain liquids on Shabbat as a serious no-no.

The Gemara protests that there are several other instances in which the quarter *log* is cited as crucial to a given situation and wonders why they weren't included in either mnemonic. Three are mentioned and each brushed aside in the same manner: They weren't included because the two lists did not contain items in dispute, only accepted law. Unperturbed, the Gemara throws back the case of a *mikveh* for purifying utensils which, biblically, may be purified in minimally one-quarter *log* of water. It turns out that the rabbis abolished that law in favor of everything attaining purification in the regular sized *mikveh*, and (like disputed cases) rabbinically annulled cases are not listed in the mnemonics.

38b

The Gemara now turns to the phrase in our Mishna (34a) about consumption of an olive's volume being the minimal amount leading to a flogging. There apparently was an earlier text of the Mishna which stated that the minimal amount was one-quarter *log* of wine, but R. Akiva cites a rabbinic ruling that changed this to an olive's volume. The original Tanna had different measures for liquid and solid consumption, but R. Akiva wants the olive volume to be the standard for all the proscriptions incumbent on a *nazir*; the "and" in the scriptural passage, "and grapes, whether wet or dry he shall not eat," links the two forms of food.

The Mishna goes on to individually proscribe wine, grapes, seeds, and skins. A *baraita* is now invoked to emphasize that "grapes, wet or dry" means that consumption by a *nazir* of one or the other, and should he consume the minimal amount of both, he's in for two floggings. The *baraita* then pulls a neat trick. Just as in this instance of two items dubbed, at least in part, with the same name—"grapes, wet or dry"—so, too, wherever else in the Torah, any two items with similar names may rise to sustain two liabilities.

Now that two possible sets of floggings are a conceivable (if painful) possibility, the Gemara wonders about other ways in which manifold punishments for a *nazir* might emerge. Abaye gets the first bite at the apple by suggesting that, should a *nazir* consume just a minimally liable quantity of grape seeds, he gets two floggings—same for a like amount of grape skins; and consumption of that same quantity of both seeds and skins would lead to three floggings. In each instance, as Abaye sees it, one flogging comes for the violation of the general proscription and one for either consuming the seeds or skins—or, in the third case, both. Rava disagrees, as he sees no grounds for punishment due to violation of the general proscription.

Rav Pappa offers another rebuttal to Abaye. He cites a *baraita* in which R. Eliezer rules a *nazir* who was consuming wine all day long, no matter how many times he exceeded the minimum punishable volume overall, incurs only one flogging. If he is warned to cut it out, then he incurs a separate flogging for every time he ignores the warning and continued drinking. The *baraita* goes on to put together a cluster of seeds, skins, grapes, and grape juice consumed which rise to a liability of five floggings. R. Eliezer asks then why there is no sixth flogging for Abaye's principle of a separate one for violating the general proscription. The answer from the Gemara is that the *baraita* here isn't indicating everything, for on occasion it skips over some with comprehensiveness not to be assumed.

OK, then, what else did the *baraita* skip, asks the Gemara. The answer is interesting: The vower made a vow to follow the rules of *nezirut*, and he broke his word. This appears to have been stated in support of Abaye's stance. This response it dismissed because it is not an item specific to a *nazir* that has been skipped over. All vowers must face the music, not just *nezirim*. Well, Ravina of Parzakya adds, the *baraita* mentioned many parts of the grapevine, but it did skip grape pulp (see 34b), and consumption of it in a minimally punishable amount should mean a flogging.

Actually, we now learn, Rav Pappa didn't really mean to say that the *baraita* he quoted explicitly pointed to "five." What this is all about picks up on the next *daf.*

39a

It was he, Rav Pappa, who claimed the number "five," not the *baraita*, but he raised it as a challenge to Abaye, which goes nowhere.

This lengthy Gemara concludes by addressing the question raised in the Mishna. It concerns the identification of the terms for grape skins and seeds; R. Yehuda reads their meaning in this order, while R. Yose argues their meanings should be reversed. Rav Yosef examines the celebrated Aramaic translation of scripture by Onkelos and determines R. Yose to be correct.

A new Mishna now takes us back to an issue concerned with shaving. We have long ago established that a regular term of *nezirut* is for thirty days. If a *nazir* shaves or if he is forcibly shaved against his will (by outlaws), he can lose as many as thirty days. This means that if at any point during his period of *nezirut* he shaves, he must start his count over so that he has a full head of hair, thirty days' worth, when carrying out his final rituals. One final note: If a *nazir* cuts his hair with a pair of scissors or shaves with a razor, or even pulls out the tiniest quantity of hair by hand, he is cruising for a flogging.

The Gemara begins with what appears to be a bizarre question: Where do we point to when examining where hair grows? In other words, it goes on to explain, does it grow from the roots or from the ends? The reason for this question is that, should an outlaw just cut off (presumably with scissors) some hair, but not all the way to the skin, of a poor *nazir*, that would still leave a certain amount of growth emanating from the skin. The first response, which is quickly discarded, directs our attention to a louse that attaches itself to a hair's base. If hair grows from the base, at the skin line, then the louse should eventually emerge as the hair grows, but it doesn't. The rejection is swift— any energetic louse could repeatedly move down toward the scalp.

The Gemara is not giving up so quickly on an explanation involving lice. How about a dead louse attached to the base of a hair? Would it not eventually grow out with the hair? If hair grows from the free end, our dead louse should remain at the root, further and further from hair's end. Again dismissed with alacrity, the Gemara notes that a deceased louse has no control over its fate and will slowly be compelled to grow out toward the hair's end.

A third and final effort comes from another realm. Look at the way the Kushites, an ancient people inhabiting Ethiopia, braid their hair. With the passage of time, as the hair grows, we observe the braid intact, but the hair at the scalp becomes looser and looser, indicating that that is the place of growth. The Gemara isn't convinced any more that it was living or dead lice. In dismissing this attempt at an explanation, it states simply that the looseness of the hair by the roots is not a result of growth but a person's lying on it while sleeping.

Finally, a proof is suggested and accepted by the Gemara. When sheep are marked with red paint or dye, that part of their wool becomes more knotted and inflexible. With growth, the wool at the root retains its softness, and this must be the new stuff. Interesting that the Gemara never questions if sheep and human beings might have different hair-growing patterns or experiences. It then adds a better proof: Older men who color their graying beards black find that, the whiteness

39b

returns as the beard grows out. It grows from the base!

The Gemara now points to a possible problem. It cites a *baraita* which states that, if outlaws cut a poor *nazir*'s hair not all the way to the skin line but sufficiently that the hair can be bent over to touch its our base, then this *nazir* will not have lost any days in his count. If hair indeed does grow from the base, wouldn't that mean that he would lose days from his *nezirut* count? No, rebuts the Gemara, this *baraita* is referring someone who was shaved by others after he finished his full period of *nezirut* but prior to his final rites. The Gemara then asks and answers that the *baraita* is articulating a position taken by R. Eliezer. He has made the claim that, whatever something nefarious (including an improper or prohibited haircut or shave) transpires after the *nazir* finishes his period but before the final rituals, he only loses seven days.

Where did R. Eliezer come up with this seven-day business? Ordinarily, a *nazir* concludes his period of *nezirut* with a growth of at least thirty days. His reasoning involves invoking questions of *tahara* and *tumah*, but they remain fuzzy at best. It is interesting that, if the outlaws minimally left seven days' worth of growth, then no days at all are lost, and he proceeds with the final rituals. What is special about a period of seven days? The sages know, somehow, that hair grows enough every seven days to bend it over to touch the scalp.

The Gemara turns now to the passage in our Mishna in which various means of removing hair—scissors, razor, one's own hands—are discussed, and irrespective of means, even the tiniest quantity of removal rises to liability for a flogging. It cites a *baraita* to help clarify things, because the "razor" part is specifically mentioned in the Torah, but what about removing hair by hand? So, the *baraita* asks (rhetorically) what the scriptural basis for this would be. It then quotes from *Numbers* 6.5: "[That which he sets apart for the Lord] shall be holy, to grow loose the hair on his head." (Alter, p. 711) In other words, removing one's hair in any way means that a *nazir*, who vowed not to cut or shave for his period of *nezirut*, has violated his vow.

The *baraita* concludes by assigning this argument to R. Yoshiya. R. Yonatan takes a more literal approach, saying essentially that a razor is only a razor, while hair removal by hand is not scripturally proscribed. The Gemara apparently thinks that R. Yonatan has missed something, as it reiterates the phrase about the *nazir* growing his hair out: "[It] shall be holy." Isn't the method of removing the hair ultimately irrelevant? R. Yonatan would respond that shaving with a razor is distinctive, because doing this would involve violation of a positive and a negative commandment.

The Gemara now takes a step back and addresses this verse from *Numbers* with another *baraita*. It begins with the same phrasing from the previous *baraita*, asking for a scriptural basis for claiming that removal of hair by hand incurs liability for a flogging. The answer, though, is different, albeit from the same verse: "no razor shall pass over his head." (Alter, p. 711) Although the verse mentions the razor, the *baraita* indicates that it refers to the proscription of any means of hair removal. But, then why is "razor" explicitly stated? Scripture surely didn't have to be so specific if it sought a more general prohibition. The "razor" is mentioned here with regard to the final shaving that is to be done, because the Torah mentions that final shaving, of course, but does not specify use of a razor. Now, we could possibly, it might be argued, acquire this knowledge from the laws governing the purification of a *metzora*, as all body hair is shaved off a *metzora* in the process of completing his purification, but that is immediately ruled out.

40a

Why? You can't use a stringency as the basis for ruling on something less stringent so as to make the latter just as rigorous—the *nazir* only shaves the hair of his head as part of his final rituals, while the *metzora* shaves his entire body of all hair.

The Gemara proceeds to lay out three laws that can only have been derived as having been given to Moses at Sinai. Rav Chisda states that it takes only a single hair's removal to incur a flogging. To annul the validity of the final head shaving, minimum two hairs must be missed (one hair missed is OK). To lose days in a *nazir*'s count, he has to remove most of his hair. In each of these cases, use of a razor to remove the hair is required. On this last law, the Gemara agrees that razor removal, of course, incurs a flogging, but wouldn't other ways of removal deserve the same punishment? So, it refines that last statement to mean that all forms of haircutting in which a razor or something similar is used—meaning that the hairs is removed down to the skin line. To confirm the point, the Gemara cites a *baraita* which states clearly that any *nazir* who removes any of his hair by hand, even a tiny amount, will be subject to a flogging, but he does not lose any days of his count until a majority of his hair is gone and that the result of a razor. R. Shimon ben Yehuda cites his namesake R. Shimon to say that all it takes is cutting two hairs for a *nazir* to lose days.

While we're on the subject of shaving, the Gemara cites a Mishna from another Talmudic tractate. Three groups are mandated by the Torah to shave: the *nazir* as part of his final rituals, the *metzora* as part of his purification process, and the Levis as part of their purification (as God commanded Moses). These shavings must be done with a razor and cannot leave two hairs standing. Why did the Mishna have to specifically say that they must shave? The Torah could not be more explicit. Perhaps it was to spell out that other forms of hair removal might be seen as acceptable, which they are not.

What was that source in Torah upon which the Mishna based its ruling? The latter stated that, if any of these three groups should shave without a razor, they have not performed the ritual at all. The scriptural bases for a *nazir* we have dealt with many times ("no razor shall pass over his head"); and for the Levis it's *Numbers* 8.7: "pass a razor over all their flesh" (Alter, p. 722). The problem is that the *metzora* is commanded (*Leviticus* 14.9) as follows: "he shall shave all the hair of his head" (Alter, p. 600). Inasmuch as there is no mention here of a razor, how do we know a razor must in fact be used? One might analogize with the Levis who similarly were required to shave their entire bodies and with a razor, but this idea is quickly rejected, because the Levis had other requirements altogether different from those of a *metzora*. Maybe through comparison with the *nazir* who similarly must shave and with a razor? No, this too is promptly ruled out, because the final rituals incumbent on a *nazir* are altogether different from the laws surrounding a *metzora*—the Gemara mentions the breads a *nazir* must bring with his offerings.

We still need a source. The Gemara does something interesting at this point, something we have not seen thus far in our tractate. Individually, the cases of the *nazir* and the Levis don't help here, but maybe together they can complement one another to provide a source. This style of exegesis allows the expounder to use the strengths of each of the two individual cases to compensate for their weaknesses. So, for example, the case of the *nazir* was rejected as a derivation for the *metzora*, because the *nazir* brings breads which plays no role in the *metzora*'s purification. But, maybe the breads aren't that important, because the Levis have no bread requirement. Similarly, the *nazir* has none of the distinctive requirements incumbent upon the Levis. Putting aside their distinctive obligations, what the Levis and the *nazir* do have in common is the requisite shaving which must be accomplished with a razor. The *metzora* also must shave, just like the *nazir* and the Levis, so it only makes sense that he must also employ a razor.

Ingenious, yes, but Rava of Barnish argues before Rav Ashi that this form of reasoning by analogy based on a common trait simply doesn't work for him.

40b

The basis of his rejection is that in the case neither of a *nazir* nor of the Levis does their wealth or poverty play any role in the offerings they are required to bring, but that is not the case of a *metzora* whose relative financial standing can determine the cost of his final sacrificial offering. This argument apparently is sufficient to disembowel what seemed to be a solid approach to the problem.

So, the Gemara goes in search of a source for a *metzora*'s use of a razor elsewhere. In yet another tractate, we find a law, attributed to the rabbis, requiring the observant Jewish male to be careful not to cut off the edges of his beard with a razor, and R. Eliezer extends the prohibition to the use of other instruments. How does the rabbis' view of things help with explaining why a *metzora* must use a razor? A *baraita* teaches that scripturally a *metzora* is required to shave "his beard" as part of his purification. Why explicitly the beard? Elsewhere in the Torah, the Kohanim are forbidden to cut the edges of their beards, meaning that the injunction for a *metzora* to remove "his beard" overrides this proscription. Confusing though this reasoning may be, the argument concludes that this proves a *metzora* must employ a razor.

The rabbis' argument is premised on the notion that the ban on cutting the edges of one's beard refers to removal by a razor. Through some comparative analysis of Torah citations, a *baraita* demonstrates that the ban on Kohanim cutting the edges of their beards refers to all Jewish men and that the only way this can make sense is if it is done with a razor. The wording of the citations also confirms the rabbis' analysis that the *metzora*'s shaving must be done with a razor. The Gemara isn't quite ready for the latter part and questions the way the rabbis used "his beard" to come to their conclusion. The Gemara makes quick work of this response and then proceeds on the next *daf* to make the rabbis' argument even stronger.

41a

Because use of a razor is not specifically mentioned in the requirement to shave a *metzora*, one might think that use of such things as a plane, which can cut the hair right at the skin's surface, might satisfy this obligation. Structured this way, we have a positive commandment confronting a negative one—ideally, we would like to satisfy both, but if that is impossible, then the positive one takes the cake. Nice try, replies the Gemara (in so many words), for "his beard" does not make using a razor an elective choice; it makes it compulsory.

What did R. Eliezer have in mind as his basis for necessitating a razor? Back on 40b, we cited the verse from *Leviticus* (14.9) concerning "all the hair of his head." R. Eliezer focuses on the word for "his head" which he sees as unnecessary to make the point—but, of course, nothing is unnecessary in Torah from an exegetical point of view. Through an intricate association with same word regarding the proscription of a razor during *nezirut*, he comes to the conclusion that a *metzora* has no choice but to use a razor at the appointed time.

If indeed "his head" is superfluous, then the rabbis must account for it as well. They can't explain the central theme here of using only a razor, because they have already accounted for that by the term "his beard." They use it in conjunction with another proscription in *Leviticus* (19.27): "You shall not round off the edge-growth of your head." (Alter, p. 629) Ordinarily, one wouldn't expect that a *metzora* would be required to shave the edges of his head—the positive commandment overrules the negative one here. Yet, as we saw in the *baraita* cited on 40b, "his beard" should be sufficient to satisfy the necessity of shaving in this otherwise proscribed manner. Basically, the rabbis are asking what need there is for "his head," if "his beard" does the trick just as well.

Rather than defend one side or the other, the Gemara takes the interesting tack of arguing that both explicit terms are needed. Had scripture only stated "his beard" (and not "his head"), one might think that cutting all of one's hair would not constitute a proper cutting of the edges of one's beard and so make it allowed; inclusion of "his head" informs us that, no, ordinarily cutting all of one's hair is proscribed.

41b

A similarly confusing mix of logic affords the Gemara the rationale to argue that, had scripture only included "his head" (and not "his beard"), its reasoning would have run aground. But, with both terms complementing one another, we learn that a *metzora* has got to be shaved with a razor.

How does R. Eliezer know that a positive commandment supersedes a negative one, reasoning he applied above? He bases it on a proscription against wearing *sha'atnez*, a mixture of wool and linen in one's garments.

42a

And, then, in the very next phrase of the same verse (*Deuteronomy* 22.12), we read: "You shall make yourself tassels on the four corners of your garment." (Alter, p. 987) These "tassels" are a twisted mixture of wool and linen, and thus here a positive commandment supersedes a negative one.

Back on 40a, we cited a stray Mishna which linked the three figures who scripturally were required to shave with a razor and right down to a single hair: *nazir*, *metzora*, and the Levis. Rav Acha, son of Rav Ika, states a position he takes to be scriptural: The preponderance of something is equal to its entirety. On this basis, he argues that, only in the case of the verse about a *nazir* shaving to purify himself as a consequence of contracting corpse *tumah*, do we find the shaving requirement mentioned twice. Once would have been enough, unless there was another reason stressing the need to shave the entire head—not just most of it. Thus, only with the *nazir* do we learn that removal of a majority of one's hair does not fulfill the obligation. Without that extra verse, generally speaking, a majority would do the trick.

R. Yose, son of R. Chanina, will have none of this. The verse Rav Acha cites refers to a *nazir* who contracts *tumah*. What does this have to do with the obligation for a *nazir* to shave right down to a single hair during the final rituals concluding *nezirut*? The Gemara trumps the entire discussion at this point by stating that "in the West" (meaning the Land of Israel) the sages laughed at R. Yose, son of R. Chanina, and supported Rav Acha's most-equals-all principle under ordinary circumstances. Clearly, one needed to have a thick skin in those times, but this phrasing also indicates the sense of superiority attributed to the Land of Israel and its sages both by those sages themselves and by their fellows in Babylonia.

As this lengthy Gemara is beginning to wind down, it seemingly wants to tie up some loose ends. Abaye raises a point heretofore not addressed. Suppose a *nazir* shaves leaving two hairs (meaning that the shaving is incomplete and does not fulfill the requirement); when his hair grew back a bit, he shaved only those two remaining hairs from the initial shave. What happens? Has the shaving requirement been successfully met? Rava now asks an even more refined question: Suppose a *nazir* shaved but left two hairs standing, waited a bit, and then before the shaved hair could grow back, he shaved one of those two initial hairs (and left the other in place). What happens?

Rav Acha of Difti asks Ravina if Rava's query concerns the cogency of shaving one hair under these circumstances. Surely, this cannot be questioning if the shaving of one hair when there are only two fulfills the obligation, because this is obvious. Ravina explains that Rava is referring to a situation in which one of those two hairs fell out by itself and then the final one was shaved. Ravina then concludes that this does not constitute a proper shaving. The Gemara, though, thinks that, *au contraire*, what could be a better instance of a proper shaving; Ravina must have meant that, despite the appearance of no hair, the shaving mitzvah has not been properly met.

We now move to a short Mishna, followed by a short Gemara. While a *nazir* may remove absolutely no hair from his head during his period of *nezirut*, he is allowed to wash and shampoo his hair, even if inadvertently some hair may fall out. That would be unintentional and would be allowable. He may also separate the hairs on his head, but combing is definitely out.

The Gemara begins by ascertaining that it is R. Shimon's view represented in the Mishna—unintended is allowable—that permits washing and separating one's hair. The objective is clean hair, not removal of it. The proscription on combing, though, accords with a position of the rabbis—namely, that what is unintentional, though possibly foreseeable, is definitely out. So, how can this one-sentence Mishna begin by adhering to R. Shimon and end by adhering to the rabbis? Rabbah makes it very simple by averring that both halves of the Mishna follow R. Shimon, because the use of a comb is (at least in part) intended to remove orphan hairs.

R. Yishmael now articulates another short Mishna which segues nicely with the previous one. He claims that a *nazir* is forbidden from shampooing his hair with earth, which that previous Mishna allowed. He reasons that such a shampoo concoction unavoidably causes hair to fall out. He would agree that the unintentional is allowable, but just what is clearly inevitable should be foreseen.

The Gemara starts with a question about the earth mentioned in the Mishna. Is shampooing with it prohibited because a certain kind of earth causes hair removal, or is it that any kind of earth leads to hair removal? This question would only matter if there was, in fact, a kind of earth that did not have the effect of reducing one's follicle volume. If one knows that a certain kind of earth is safe, then maybe R. Yishmael would positively sanction its use. However, maybe he was outlawing any and all kinds of earth. The Gemara invokes a frequently invoked non-resolution here: *teiku* 'let it stand' unresolved.

Now for a long Mishna. We have seen that a *nazir* incurs the sentence of a flogging if he intentionally contravenes the terms to which he committed in vowing his *nezirut*. Also, he should have been warned, shortly before he broke his vows, what he was about to do and what the sentence would be. This Mishna concerns what constitutes a legal warning, and it does so via the circumstances surrounding the three primary vows to which a *nazir* commits.

First up is a *nazir* who, for whatever reason, is drinking wine throughout the day. If he is given a single warning, he is accountable for a flogging (one set of strikes with the whip). If, though, he was warned more than once not to continue drinking and what the consequences would be for such a violation, and he ignored the warnings, he incurs a flogging for each time he consumes wine after having been warned.

Second, we have a *nazir* who, again for whatever reason, keeps shaving his head throughout the day. If he is given a single warning, he is accountable for a flogging. If, though, he was warned more than once not to continue shaving and what the consequences would be for such a violation, and he ignored the warnings, he incurs a flogging for each time he shaves after having been warned.

Third, we have a *nazir* who keeps contracting corpse *tumah* throughout the day. If he is given a single warning, he is accountable for a flogging. If, though, he was warned more than once not to continue polluting himself and what the consequences would be for such a violation, and he ignored the warnings, he incurs a flogging for each time he pollutes himself with corpse *tumah* after having been warned.

42b

The Gemara starts with corpse *tumah* which anyone, not only a *nazir*, can contract in one of three manners: by touching a dead body, by carrying a dead body, and by one's presence under the same roof as that of a dead body. These will all be dealt with in greater detail in Chapter Seven. Citing words from Rav Huna, Rabbah gets the ball rolling by declaring that the verse from *Numbers* 6.7, which begins *lo yitama* (he shall not be defiled), covers all three cases. Thus, when in verse 6.6 we read "he shall not come to a dead person" (such as in a roofed structure), this previous verse qualifies as a warning, as it is not specific to any form of contracting corpse *tumah*. So, if a *nazir* does become *tamei* by any means and then is thusly warned, should he additionally expose himself to corpse *tumah*, he has twice violated his vow and is accountable twice. Rabbah concludes that, should a *nazir* become *tamei* from a dead body (by any of the three ways) and then did it again, the second incidence is not counted as a separate transgression, even if the *nazir* was warned. Hmm, this seems to contradict the Mishna.

Rav Yosef, also apparently privy to Rav Huna's views here, claims that Rav Huna did, in fact, argue that two incidents of contracting corpse *tumah* would lead to two violations. He gives an example, also taken from Rav Huna, of a *nazir* who finds himself in a graveyard. While there, he touches the corpse of either a relative or another person. He is, of course, accountable for a flogging. But, inasmuch as he was already present in a graveyard, he was already *tamei* simply by virtue of being there. That would mean a double case of corpse *tumah* and two floggings.

Abaye is unsatisfied with Rav Yosef's rendering of Rav Huna's views, and he invokes a *baraita* to make his case. It should be noted that the same prohibitions with respect to corpse *tumah* that apply to a *nazir* also apply to the High Priest (*Kohen gadol*); namely, no contact with a dead body, relative or otherwise, is acceptable. The *baraita* posits a Kohen (actually, the High Priest) carrying a dead body and then having others present him with another dead body or a relative's which he touches. One would think him accountable for two floggings, but actually the prior pollution is not taken into account.

Rav Yosef responds by referring Abaye back to the Mishna. One who is warned not to pollute himself gets a flogging for every time he continues to violate the law and pollute himself with corpse *tumah* after such a warning. Prior *tumah* counts every bit as much as the subsequently incurred violations, where a warning was issued. If Abaye (or anyone else) claims that the Mishna and the *baraita* contradict one another, Rav Yosef has a solution. The second case, the one raised by Abaye, concerns someone carrying a dead body when another is brought forth and he touches it; the first case refers back to a Mishna, and it concerns someone who let loose the corpse he was holding before he touched the other one. In order to reach a higher degree of contamination, one must have contact with a corpse, release it, and then touch it (or another corpse); if he is still holding a dead body and makes contact with another, he retains his same degree of *tumah*. In the Mishna's case, the *nazir* severed contact with the corpse before going on to touch it again; verdict: two transgressions. The *baraita* has our *nazir* still in contact with a dead body when he touches another corpse; verdict: one transgression.

Underlying Rav Yosef's exposition is the idea that the *baraita*'s form of "*tumah* while in contact" is a biblical violation, but is it? If one touches a *tamei* person, he himself remains *tamei* until nightfall, but if he touches someone who is presently in contact with a corpse, he remains *tamei* for a full seven days. Rav Yitzchak bar Yosef, however, notes that this law does not apply in the case of a *nazir*. It may be true at the rabbinical level that he is *tamei* for seven days, but scripturally "*tumah* while in contact" does not apply. In actuality, Rav Yosef's case is that of someone who had contact with a *tamei* person and also with a corpse, and that leads to a seven-day "sentence" of *tamei*—at the scriptural level.

The Gemara returns at this point to Rabbah's understanding that one who becomes *tamei* from a corpse and then does so again by his being within a roofed structure in which a corpse is present has incurred two violations of *halacha*. However, should the second *tumah* violation be for something other than roof *tumah*, it's only one violation. Is something inherently wrong here? Perhaps he is not accountable a second time, because he was already *tamei*, but shouldn't that eventuality also hold when he serially becomes *tamei* from a corpse and then enters a roofed edifice in which a corpse is present.

Back to the drawing board with respect to what Rabbah actually said. He didn't mean contracting *tumah* in two instances seriatim, but simultaneously. R. Yochanan clarifies that the two violations mentioned are entering the structure containing a corpse and making contact—the polluting acts take place at the same time, despite being considered separate. Two violations lead to two floggings. When a *nazir* contracts corpse *tumah* in a field—namely, no roof over his head (or that of a corpse)—even if he touches the dead body twice, he has only violated the *halacha* once.

43a

A possible problem ensues. Actually entering a structure is defined from the point that a majority of one's body is inside, but one can contract *tumah* by just sticking one's hand inside a roofed site containing a corpse. In other words, these two events do not occur simultaneously. R. Elazar doesn't disagree, but suggests that a *nazir* who walks in with his hands firmly by his sides would, practically speaking, accomplish both together. Too simple, responds the Gemara, for one's nose will always precede him, polluting him from there on down. Rava has a better idea, again not disagreeing with the foregoing. If one walked in with his head bent backward, pollution would occur at the moment of entrance. No, says the Gemara, for one's toes would always precede the rest of the body, even with one's head inclined to the rear.

Rav Pappa offers a solution. If a *nazir* went into a box or trunk which was partly inside a contaminated house, this would protect the *nazir* from pollution. Then, someone else came and helped him open the box or trunk. In such a situation the two events, entering and becoming polluted, would transpire at the same time. Mar bar Rav Ashi suggests another scenario: The *nazir* enters the house while someone inside is taking his last breaths, and while the *nazir* is present that person then dies. Same resolution.

Implicit in the way Mar bar Rav Ashi set up the case is the idea that someone on the verge of death does not actually become a source of corpse *tumah* until passing. The Gemara cites a *baraita* from the rabbis which interprets *Leviticus* 21.4, a Kohen "shall not defile himself . . . to profane himself" (Alter, p. 635), to mean that one does not convey *tumah* before actual death. R. Yehuda ha-Nasi, however, focuses instead on a verse (*Numbers* 6.7: "when they die" [Alter, p. 711]) concerning the *nazir* which he interprets in much the same way. So, what is the difference of opinion between them? R. Yochanan states that they are making the same point—only in death does corpse *tumah* commence to be transmitted; they differ only in ascribing a derivation for this ruling. Reish Lakish offers his own explanation.

The Gemara turns at this point to a frequently observed tack. When two derivations for something both seem acceptable, it asks how each explains the competing scriptural citation. The rabbis based their reading on the verse "to profane himself"; so what will they do with "when they die"? Similarly, R. Yehuda ha-Nasi based his interpretation on the verse "when they die"; what does he make of "to profane himself?" Through some fancy Talmudic footwork, the Gemara demonstrates how each party focuses on a single word—"they" for the rabbis and "himself" for R. Yehuda ha-Nasi—to teach that their phrase of explanatory choice serves a dual purpose.

43b

The issue of self-profanation will now consume the Gemara on into the next *daf*. The text has been effectively comparing the case of a Kohen and a *nazir* with regard to the proscription of contaminating oneself with corpse *tumah*. Unlike a *nazir* who is banned from contact with the dead under any circumstances, an exemption is afforded a Kohen when it comes to a member of his family who has died and also a corpse who has no one present to inter it (*met mitzvah*). Channeling Rav, Rav Chisda notes that, if a Kohen's father's head is severed from his body, the Kohen is not permitted to participate in the burial. Why? Isn't this precisely what the exemption was all about? No, because the verse in question here, *Leviticus* 21.2, exempts the Kohen "for his father," and that would imply a whole body (albeit deceased) and not one missing some part thereof. In other words, without his head, it's not really his father.

Rav Hamnuna responds that, if the Kohen's father were to be murdered and decapitated far from home in barren, desolate terrain, who would bury him if not his son? Rav Chisda concedes a bit, replying that if Rav Hamnuna was speaking of a *met mitzvah*, then of course the Kohen would be permitted to self-contaminate, even if that corpse was headless and once belonged to his own father. The Gemara, however, thinks Rav Chisda may have conceded too much too quickly. It asks if the case at hand actually qualifies as a *met mitzvah* and cites a *baraita* which specifies that a *met mitzvah* must have no one who can inter the corpse, but if the Kohen can call on others to do so, then we are not speaking of a *met mitzvah*. The Gemara rebuts simply: We're talking of a Kohen making his way along the road when no one else is around to help him—clearly, a *met mitzvah*.

There is now another possible problem with Rav Chisda's position. A *baraita* begins by citing *Leviticus* 21.3: "and for his virgin sister who is close to him, as she has not become a man's, for her he may be defiled." (Alter, p. 635) Yes, but not for severed body parts of her, from which one can contract *tumah*. Inasmuch as he is forbidden to have contact with a body part of his closest relative, his own father, a body part of his sister is certainly proscribed from contact. He may, though, go back to the site of his father's internment to place a missing bone at the same site, if he has already contracted *tumah*.

This would seem to contradict the ruling that a Kohen may not contract *tumah* from his own father's corpse if it was not whole. The Gemara now introduces the position of R. Yehuda who, contrary to Rav Chisda, explicitly does allow a Kohen to bury his father, even if the latter's body is missing one or more parts. What is R. Yehuda's position and where is it to be found? That's usually pretty easy, as there would seem to be a *baraita* for just about everything. R. Yehuda expounds *Leviticus* 21.3 to mean that a Kohen may self-pollute for his sister but not for one of her body parts, because even he is prohibited from self-contamination from a body part severed from his father when the latter was alive. When it comes to a body part from his late father, he is permitted to self-pollute, if he was already *tamei* from his father's dead body.

At this point, the Gemara offers a *baraita* in the name of R. Eliezer ben Yaakov, as laid out by Rav Kahana. Yes, a Kohen may self-pollute for his sister, though not for her detached body parts. But, wait, there's more, a complicated set of body parts which are exempted from the ban: spinal column, skull, and more. We shall deal with them a bit more on tomorrow's *daf*.

44a

The thrust of Rav Kahana's rebuttal is that, while the ruling used for analysis here was related to one's sister, it holds for other relatives as well; also, where Rav Chisda stated that a Kohen cannot self-pollute with the dead body of a relative missing body parts, Rav Kahana's ruling makes that possible.

A new Mishna at this point returns to matters involving a *nazir*. As we have now seen spelled out numerous times, there are three principal proscriptions facing a *nazir*: corpse *tumah*, shaving the head, and consumption of grapevine products. Violation of the first two of these are treated more rigorously in one way than that involving the grapevine. One loses days toward completion of his period of *nezirut* by contracting *tumah* or cutting off a majority of his hair, while grapevine violations do not lead to this sort of loss. By the same token, there is one way in which consumption of grapevine products is dealt with more rigorously than the other two: No exemptions at all are allowed for grapevine transgressions, while there are for *tumah* and head-shaving. A *nazir* may contract *tumah* in an instance involving a *met mitzvah*, and he is actually required to shave if afflicted with *tzaraat*. In one way, *tumah* is dealt with more harshly that shaving of the head; it results in the *nazir*'s loss of all accrued days and the requirement to offer a sacrifice. The *nazir* who shaves off the majority of his hair loses a maximum of thirty days, and there are no requisite offerings resulting from his transgression.

The Gemara proceeds by shoring up all challenges to the rulings of this Mishna. First up, it questions if there can be any exemption to a *nazir* acquiring corpse *tumah*. Using the *kal vachomer* line of reasoning, it notes that wine consumption brings about no loss in one's count of days accumulated (and hence is lenient or *kal*) and there are no exemptions; shouldn't *tumah* which does lead to loss of days (hence stringent or *chomer*) have no exemptions as well? The Gemara identifies a "superfluous" verse in the *Numbers* (6.6–7) passage by which a *nazir* is allowed to attend to a *met mitzvah*.

The Gemara now turns this *kal vachomer* around. If there is an exemption for a *nazir* to contract corpse *tumah* (the *chomer*), which incurs loss of days, in the case of a *met mitzvah*, shouldn't the more lenient (the *kal*) prohibition of wine consumption, no loss of days, be exempt when it comes to drinking wine in otherwise obligatory situations? Again, the Gemara cites a passage from a slightly earlier verse from *Numbers* (6.3), which it deems superfluous, as evidence that wine is not an option for a *nazir*.

The Gemara now takes a slightly different approach, still using the *kal vachomer* tool, and argues that (contrary to the Mishna) consumption of wine should lead to a loss of accrued days. While *tumah*, which is relatively *kal* in that it does provide for an exemption and does lead to loss of days, shouldn't wine, which is relatively *chomer* in that it provides for no exemptions, also lead to loss of days? And, once again, the Gemara identifies a portion of a verse in *Numbers* (6.12) as superfluous to emphasize that corpse *tumah* leads to loss of days, but wine consumption does not.

What about a *nazir*'s prematurely shaving his head? Shouldn't he lose all his accrued days? One who brings a *nazir* into contact with a source of *tumah* suffers no consequences, while the *nazir* himself is subject to a flogging, and *tumah* leads to a loss of all accumulated days. Meanwhile, anyone caught shaving a *nazir* is subject to a flogging, just like the *nazir* himself, making this more harshly treated that the *tumah* case. The Gemara then cites a verse to justify the apparent imbalance here.

Wait a minute, though. What about this notion that one who brings a *nazir* into contact with *tumah* gets off scot-free? Shouldn't he suffer the same fate as the transgressing *nazir*? Shaving the head can lead to loss of a maximum of thirty days, while contracting corpse *tumah* leads to a loss of all one's days. Shouldn't one who causes a *nazir* to become polluted be subject to the same punishment as a *nazir* who pollutes himself (by shaving)? Nope, the verse in question from *Numbers* (6.9) about the fate awaiting a head-shaver is only meant for one who shaves his own head. Flipping the reasoning here, the Gemara next asks why we must treat the shaver of heads just as harshly as we do the *nazir* whose head is shaved. The verse cited here from *Numbers* (6.5)—"no razor shall pass over his head" (Alter, p. 711)—actually covers both one who shaves his own head and one who shaves another's.

The Mishna provided for one exemption regarding a *nazir*'s shaving, instances when he is afflicted with *tzaraat*. Why the exemption? Wine consumption which leads to no loss of accrued days has no exemptions to its proscription to a *nazir*, so shouldn't head-shaving which does lead to a loss of days also have no exemptions to its proscription? In this instance, the verse from *Leviticus* (14.9) trumps the prohibition incumbent on a *nazir*, something discussed at length back on *daf* 41, and shaving for a *metzora* must proceed irrespective of a *nazir*'s obligations.

Several more of these arguments by *kal vachomer* are raised and, of course, shot down to help us understand some of the intricacies of the Mishna. The laws articulated in the Mishna here are not so obvious from a reasoning perspective and they are also not simple injunctions (as in cases of *halacha* taught to Moses at Sinai). By taking them apart as the Gemara has just done, we are given a first-class lesson in Talmudic reasoning.

44b

The next Mishna turns to practice over theory and describes how an actual head-shaving, when required, takes place. A *nazir* has become *tamei* from contact with a corpse and requires a head-shaving, the Mishna's shorthand term for all the purification rituals he must undergo. During the seven-day period of his "decontamination," he must be sprinkled on days three and seven with water into which has been mixed ashes from a red cow (*parah adumah*), and then on that last day he shaves his head. The following day (eight) he brings his sacrificial offerings to the Temple. If the *nazir* waited and shaved on day eight, he is permitted, according to R. Akiva, to bring his offerings then. R. Tarfon poses a question to R. Akiva: How does a *nazir*'s final rituals differ from those of a *metzora*? In fact, a *metzora* (who also undergoes a seven-day purification) is obligated to shave off all his body hair on day seven and bring his offering on day eight, but if for whatever reason he waited to shave until day eight, he may not bring his offering on that same day. He has to wait until the next day. So, the thrust of R. Tarfon's query is what makes the *nazir*'s case different. R. Akiva explains that the head-shaving incumbent on a *nazir* is not the crucial point of his reaching purity—after the two sprinklings, followed by *mikveh* submersion, the *nazir* waits until sunset and he's good to go, even before shaving. He can then wait a day, shave, and proceed to bring his sacrifices. Purification of a *metzora*, by contrast, is structured around the head-shaving. He is not permitted to bring his offering until he has shaved and the sun has set.

The Gemara begins by asking if R. Tarfon buys R. Akiva's explanation. To answer it he turns to a *baraita* of Hillel (not the famed one from many, many generations earlier) who put it very simply: If a *nazir* shaves on day eight, he brings his sacrifices on day nine. Had R. Tarfon agreed with his colleague's reply, the *baraita* would surely have stated that the *nazir* brings his sacrifices on day eight. So, R. Tarfon probably disagreed. Wait, though, as Rava is not quite ready to come to this conclusion, he sees a way to jibe the *baraita* with R. Akiva. The Mishna's judgment that a *nazir* who shaved on day eight can bring his offerings that very day; after his visit to the *mikveh* on day seven, he is no longer *tamei* on day eight. The claim in the *baraita* that the offerings can wait till day nine involves a case of one who waited to go to the *mikveh* until day eight and would thus still be *tamei* until sunset that day; he must wait until day nine to bring his sacrificial offerings.

The Gemara segues at this point to a topic not directly addressed in the Mishna: the ways in which those afflicted with *tumah* may be constrained from entering the Temple grounds. Before settling in Jerusalem, the Jews who were wandering in the desert for four decades formed their periodic settlements in three concentric circles: the camp of the Shechinah (divine presence) at the center, the holiest; surrounding it the camp of the Levites, less holy; and surrounding them the camp of the Israelites, less holy still. These three camps were later replicated in Jerusalem (in the same order): the Temple and Inner Courtyard; Temple Mount including the Nikanor Gate; and the wider city of Jerusalem. Entrance restrictions on *tamei* persons depended on which sections of the city and which type of *tumah*.

Abaye tells of encountering a colleague studying the complexities of the law via a *baraita* which asks when a *tamei* person is permitted to enter the camp of the Levites and bring his offerings to a Kohen. It answers its own question that such a person must submerge in a *mikveh*, wait till sunset, and then permission is granted. As Abaye understands this, a *nazir* who has become *tamei* cannot come to the Nikanor Gate until after he has submerged and waited for sunset, but he finds such logic unacceptable.

45a

In fact, he proceeds to eviscerate it and demonstrates that such an afflicted *nazir* may enter the Levites' camp. He resorts to a *baraita* which states explicitly that a *nazir* who has become *tamei* from a corpse may, indeed, enter there—and in fact a corpse itself may be transported into the camp. How can he have reached such a conclusion? Well, just turn to *Exodus* 13.19: "And Moses took the bones of Joseph with him." (Alter, p. 389) He focuses on "with him" (*imo*), noting that, as a Levi, Moses lived in the Levites' camp.

A new Mishna now addresses issues relating to the final rituals a *nazir* must undergo when he has completed his period of *nezirut*. These involve three sacrificial offerings and shaving of the head. The latter serves as a synecdoche for all the rituals, but the Torah (*Numbers* 6.18) does not explicitly tell us when the *nazir*'s head must be shaved. The Mishna thus begins the exegesis with the view of R. Yehuda. So, subject brings three animals to be offered—a *chatat* (a female lamb), an *olah* (a male lamb), and a *shelamim* (a ram); he slaughters the *shelamim* and then proceeds to shave his head. R. Elazar differs slightly and states that the shaving takes place after slaughtering the *chatat*, as the *chatat* always takes precedence as the first animal to be sacrificed. Rather than leave the result of this debate to chance, the Mishna just asserts that the subject has fulfilled his duty on this front no matter which animal he first sacrifices and then shaves.

Our Mishna then addresses another issue. Rabban Shimon ben Gamliel states that, if a *nazir* brought his three animals as sacrifices to the Temple but failed to identify which animal was for which sacrifice, each of the animals appropriate to each sacrifice—fixed in scripture by gender and species are to be sacrificed accordingly.

The Gemara here begins with a *baraita* that elucidates R. Yehuda's notion that the head-shaving comes after the *shelamim* is sacrificed. The Torah states: "the nazirite shall shave his . . . head at the entrance of the Tent of Meeting." (Alter, p. 713) This passage, according to the *baraita*, is a reference to the *shelamim* which is to be offered before he shaves. How so? Well, back in *Leviticus* (3.2), we read: "and [he] shall slaughter it at the entrance to the Tent of Meeting." (Alter, p. 553) That doesn't exactly shore it up, but apparently the common expression, "the entrance to the Tent of Meeting," is an indication not so much as a place for the head-shaving but the proper sequence that the shaving follows the sacrifice.

The *baraita* continues by asserting that, to the contrary, maybe the phrase indeed means just what it says—it names the place where the *nazir* shaves. However, it replies rhetorically, wouldn't that be rather demeaning to the Temple? Of course it would, so the literal meaning won't fly. There just so happens to be a ruling by R. Yoshiya claiming that one need not build proof for the ban on shaving in that particular spot on the basis of these Torah passages. He cites *Exodus* 20.26: "And you shall not go up by steps upon My altar, that you may not expose your nakedness upon it." (Alter, p. 434) This may still be somewhat unclear, but the idea is that one ascends the Altar on a ramp, not stairs, because climbing stairs necessitates separation of the legs in a way deemed disrespectful and which is avoided by walking up a ramp. If something like this is demeaning to God's Temple, then surely shaving right there would have to be outlawed.

R. Yitzchak goes this proof one further by claiming that even R. Yoshiya's derivation is unnecessary. (BTW, we're still in the same *baraita*.) He directs our attention to the continuation of *Numbers* 6.18: "and he shall take the hair of his nazirite head and put it on the fire." (Alter, p. 713) The action verbs required of the *nazir* are "to take" his hair and "to put" it on the fire—nothing mentioned about "to shave." Therefore, the best case scenario is for the shaving to take place at the same place as the required actions of "taking" and "placing," and that would be the site of "the fire" cooking the *shelamim*, far from the Temple entrance.

The Gemara suggests yet another way we might explain the verse in question. Citing the view of R. Eliezer, Abba Chanan argued that we need learn from *Numbers* 6.18—"the nazirite shall shave . . . at the entrance of the Tent of Meeting"—that, if the door to the Tent of Meeting is closed, the *nazir* mustn't shave. R. Eliezer has interpreted "entrance" literally as "opening," and from there he insists that the doors be open before the *nazir* shaves. It would appear that he follows R. Elazar's view stated in the Mishna.

One more explication ensues, that of R. Shimon Shezuri who avers that the same verse points only at the head-shaving of a male *nazir*, not a *nezira*.

45b

It would be potentially seductive for a woman to expose her hair before the throngs of young Kohanim at the Temple gates. If that be so, what about the *sotah* whose hair a Kohen explicitly exposes before the Temple—let the titillated young Kohanim be damned. So, a *nezira*'s uncovering her hair should present no problem. R. Shimon Shezuri responds that a *nezira* is wearing make-up which may be alluring, while the *sotah* is not. And, the *baraita* comes to end here.

The next Mishna takes up more of the final rituals of a *nazir*. We touched on what the *nazir* was supposed to do with his hair post-shaving. The Mishna tells us that he places that hair severed from his head and dumps it in the fire on which his *shelamim* is cooking in a pot. As pointed out above, this head-shaving doesn't have to be done in any specific place, so if the *nazir* shaved outside Jerusalem, he does not place his hair in the fire under the pot. There cannot be anything that intercedes between shaving and offering his *shelamim*, and actually transporting the hair to Jerusalem qualifies, so no placing the hair under the pot.

The foregoing, as the Mishna clarifies, refers to a *nazir* who was *tahor*, but what happens when the *nazir* is *tamei*? The Torah specified that burning the hair in the fire is incumbent only for a *nazir* who is *tahor*, which would indicate that one who is *tamei* does not do this. R. Meir argues that it is incumbent on all *nezirim*, polluted or purified, but he singles out a *nazir* who is *tamei* and performing his shaving outside Jerusalem.

The Gemara looks to a *baraita* to help sort out some of the specifics for handling the head shavings. Once the *nazir*'s head has been shaved, the *shelamim* slaughtered and cooked, the subject removes some gravy from the pot, places it on the shavings, and then tosses it all in the fire under the pot. This works just as well if our subject tosses it under a pot cooking a *chatat* or even an *asham*. The Gemara innocently asks if there is an *asham* sacrifice associated with a *nazir*'s final rituals (a *tahor nazir*, that is), although it must know the answer is a definite NO. Then, what was the *baraita* talking about? Rava clarifies that this is appropriate in the case of *tamei nazir*, because he is required to bring an *asham*, but not a *shelamim*.

And, what's up with this business about gravy? The Gemara, as we have seen so often, finds a superfluity in *Numbers* 6.18 and uses to explain as follows. The redundancy might point to tossing some of the *shelamim* itself in the fire, but we know that, if an offering is edible, then it can't be burned. So, it must be implying gravy. Similar language rigamarole is used to expound how we can use gravy from other sacrificial offerings in this manner.

We noted above that all *nezirim* were to toss their hair shavings in the fire with the lone exclusion of a *tamei nazir* who did his head shaving outside Jerusalem—according to R. Meir. The latter is supposed to bury his hair, but we get no explication of this ruling. R. Yehuda rules that all *nezirim* who were in a *tahor* state, whether they shave in Jerusalem or elsewhere, toss their shavings under the pot; if they are *tamei*, wherever they shave, no hair goes under the pot. The sages conclude this *baraita* by complicating things; they state that only a *nazir* who is *tahor* and shaves in the Temple has properly executed the final ritual in the way it was scripturally supposed to be carried out, so only he tosses his hair in the fire.

More on the *nazir*'s final rituals in the next Mishna, with something resembling a recipe: The *nazir* can cook his *shelamim*—he may even cook it to excess. Then, the officiating Kohen takes the now cooked foreleg of the *shelamim* ram together with a loaf of unleavened bread and an unleavened wafer. He puts them all into the palms of the *nazir* and then waves them, all in accordance with *Numbers* 6.19–20. This marks the point after which the *nazir* is allowed to consume wine and come into contact with *tumah* from a corpse. (The Mishna finishes up on the next *daf*.)

46a

R. Shimon identifies the moment when the *nazir* can consume wine a bit earlier. As soon as the blood from one of the *nazir*'s sacrifices is thrown (in the appropriate manner) on the Altar, he may partake of wine and contract corpse *tumah.*

The Gemara starts by citing a *baraita* with similar views. It asserts that the *nazir* is free to consume wine as soon as he has completed all the final rituals, a position in line with R. Eliezer. The sages, however, claim that all that is necessary is for him to have carried out one piece of those rituals, a view consistent with R. Shimon's. How did the sages come to such a position? They focus on the term *achar* (after) which appears twice in *Numbers* 6.19–20. In one of those instances, "after" refers to a single event (head-shaving); the other instance is less specific, so reasoning by means of a *gezera shava*, the sages also adjudge it to indicate one event.

The Gemara responds that, because the shaving of the head follows the bringing of sacrificial offerings and waving, a *nazir* remains under his formal abstentions until both have been completed. If that is true, we have left hanging a *gezera shava* with an object for it to demonstrate to us. This will require some more investigation.

Rav turns our attention to the waving practice and claims that, before it has been performed, all the *nazir*'s abstentions remain in force. Where, asks the Gemara, did Rav acquire this ruling? Can't be the sages, because they focused on the centrality of the head-shaving as necessary before the *nazir* can consume wine. Maybe R. Eliezer? Yet, he required all the final rituals to be completed before wine might be consumed, so Rav's statement would be too evident to require articulation if he was filiating with R. Eliezer. Elsewhere in Torah-based ceremonies, one finds waving of sacrificial parts, and it never reduces the efficacy of the sacrifice; maybe it isn't as central to the *nazir*'s final fulfillment of his vows. And, that was Rav's point: The case of a *nazir* is different, for here it is utterly indispensable to the entire process.

46b

Perhaps that was just too easy, as the Gemara immediately starts to question Rav's placing the waving ceremony front and center in ending a *nazir*'s proscriptions. It questions whether R. Eliezer himself saw the absence of waving as tantamount to an incomplete relinquishment of *nezirut* bans. It then cites what must be only a snippet of an odd *baraita* which avers that the laws regarding the entire *nezirut* process hold whether or not the *nazir* has palms in which to hold and wave the offering pieces. This conclusion is based on the final verse (*Numbers* 6.21) regarding the rules governing a *nazir*: "This is the teaching for the nazirite." (Alter, p. 713) The point is that one, singular "teaching," not a multiplicity of them; all are treated in the same manner. The *nazir*'s hair might be treated similarly to his palms, then, and would a bald *nazir* then not have to shave his head? And, would failure to shave, despite the absence of hair, eviscerate his final rituals? Or, might the head-shaving not be as central to this process?

This line of reasoning is going nowhere fast. So, the Gemara scuttles itself by citing another *baraita* which looks at what a bald *nazir* should do. Bet Shammai assert that he can skip the use of a razor on his head in his final rituals, while Bet Hillel (not unexpectedly) claim the opposite, that he must go through the motions of running the razor over his head. Ravina explains that Bet Shammai are not excusing the *nazir* from this requirement, but claiming that such a *nazir* will never be able to end his commitment to the requirements of *nezirut*. By contrast, Bet Hillel, according to Ravina, afford our bald *nazir* a way out. Either way, the head-shaving is an essential step in the process, and thus "hair" cannot be equated with "palms." Ravina then goes on to cite a teaching from R. Pedat which looks suspiciously close to that of Bet Shammai and to R. Eliezer who was a disciple of Bet Shammai.

The Gemara then, almost *Rashōmon*-like, rehearses this entire discussion regarding Rav's initial assertion but from a different perspective. So, Rav claimed that waving was the critical part of the *nazir*'s final rituals, before which all the *nezirut* proscriptions remain in force and after which consumption of wine is permitted. It then runs through the same arguments, but a different conclusion. After recounting the views regarding the centrality of the head-shaving of Bet Shammai and Bet Hillel, as we just saw them laid out, a certain R. Avina states that Bet Hillel's requirement that the bald *nazir* run a razor over his bald head means that head-shaving is indispensable to a *nazir*'s fulfilling his final rituals. Such a *nazir* is really out of luck, and the central import of head-shaving is re-affirmed. Meanwhile, R. Avina understands that Bet Shammai afford the bald *nazir* a way out, and that in turn means that R. Pedat's statement that R. Eliezer and Bet Shammai are in agreement would be incorrect.

Time for a new Mishna, still concerned with final rituals and potential problems lying in wait. If the *nazir* proceeds to shave his head after making his first sacrifice and then discovering that that offering was nullified for one of a number of possible reasons, the head-shaving is also nullified; in addition, the other animals he brought as offerings to follow upon the head-shaving are judged ineligible as such. If the *nazir* performed the shaving after offering his *chatat*, but the sacrifice was carried out with improper intent, and he then went on to bring his other sacrificial offerings with proper intent, the head-shaving is deemed null and void, and those offerings are judged ineligible. Suppose he shaved after sacrificing either his *olah* or his *shelamim* without proper intent, and then he went on to bring the other sacrificial offerings with proper intent, all is similarly lost. R. Shimon is easier on him, claiming that the sacrifice offered with improper intent is nullified, but the others are still valid. Finally, if our *nazir* were to shave after making all three of his sacrifices, only one of which was acceptable, the shaving passes muster but he has to replace the invalidated sacrifices.

As potentially meaty as this Mishna is, the Gemara is considerably less so. It focuses entirely on R. Shimon's exceptions to the overall rules. Rav Ada bar Ahavah explains R. Shimon's view a bit. If a *nazir* shaves after sacrificing a voluntary *shelamim*, according to R. Shimon, he has fulfilled his commitment. How did he get to this? The oft-cited verse from *Numbers* (6.18) tells us, if properly understood, that the *nazir* places his shorn hair on the fire cooking the *shelamim* offering. It pointedly does not refer to his (the *nazir*'s) *shelamim*, which Rav Ada (and thus R. Shimon before him) take to mean that the head-shaving can come after any *shelamim* offering.

47a

The last Mishna in this lengthy chapter concerns yet another possible misstep in the final rituals a *nazir* undergoes to complete his purification. If he throws the blood of one of his sacrificial offerings on the Altar and then contracts *tumah*, R. Eliezer rules that his whole final procedure is for naught, and he must start his period of *nezirut* all over again. The sages cut him much more slack; all he must do is bring the other(s) of his offerings and go through his own purification process. The sages rebut R. Eliezer's rather harsh prescription by telling of the case of Miriam of Tarmud (or Tarmod, which should be the city of Tadmor). A *nezira*, she had the blood of one of his sacrifices thrown on the Altar. Just at that point, she was notified that her daughter was deadly ill. So, she went to her child, but by the time she arrived her daughter had died. Miriam thus had contact with a corpse, making her a *nezira* who had become *tamei* in the middle of her final ritual sacrifices. The sagely authorities in her case declared that she should go ahead with the remainder of her sacrifices and proceed with her own purification.

The Gemara starts with R. Eliezer's statement that in such a case the *nazir* loses everything. In an earlier Mishna back on 16a, he stated that a *nazir* in a situation such as this would lose only seven days, during which he purified himself and then got back on track. Have we caught him in a contradiction? Rav explains that in the present Mishna, when R. Eliezer states that a *nazir* loses everything, he means all his sacrificial offerings. All the animals are forfeit, and after purification he must bring three new ones, but he needn't redo the entire period of *nezirut* to which he was committed. The sages differ insofar as they claim that the *nazir* must offer the remainder of his offerings following his purification, while R. Eliezer apparently disqualifies the one he already brought.

The last point of the Gemara here rehearses the Mishna's statement concerning Miriam of Tadmor to clarify the difference between the sages and R. Eliezer. The focus of their disagreement is not over whether or not she must redo her entire period of *nezirut* from scratch but rather whether or not her sacrifices are legit.

NOTES

1. A very similar discussion takes place in tractate *Menachot* 58a; see my *Grains of Truth: Reading Tractate* Menachot *of the Babylonian Talmud* (Lanham, MD: Hamilton Books, 2014), p. 191.

2. We're talking of Torah law here, for the rabbis ruled both cooked and uncooked milk-and-meat combos prohibited.

3. See my *Grains of Truth*, pp. 299–301.

Chapter 7

Corpse Contamination

47a (CONTINUED)

This chapter will be primarily concerned with the proscription incumbent on a *nazir* not to contract corpse *tumah*. We have already confronted much discussion and many rulings on this subject, and more will emerge in the ensuing pages. Back on 42b, the text touched on the topic with which our first Mishna here begins. Kohanim are prohibited from contact with the dead, except if they are among a group of close relatives. The High Priest is the exception, as he can't even attend the funeral or in any way contract *tumah* even from a relative—and in this case, the *nazir* resembles him. The one exception for both the High Priest and the *nazir* is that of a *met mitzvah* or unattended corpse, as the rule for burying a corpse, when no one else is present to do so, overrides the prohibition here of corpse *tumah*. This much we have seen in preceding *dapim*.

So, then, what happens if the High Priest and a *nazir* were walking along the road and came upon a dead body with no one around to bury it. Should they do it together or should one of them step back? R. Eliezer rules that the High Priest must do the honors and the *nazir* not become *tamei*. The sages, by contrast, opt for the *nazir*, as they think even a regular, old Kohen shouldn't contract *tumah* (let alone the High Priest). We see immediately the relative levels of holiness these two judging parties hold the Kohanim and the *nazir*.

R. Eliezer reasons that the Kohen should be the one to contaminate himself, as he need bring no offerings as part of his purification, while the *nazir* ought not because sacrifices are required of him for contracting *tumah*. The sages reply that it is the *nazir* who should bury the corpse and contract *tumah*, because his period of *nezirut* during which he is considered sanctified is temporary (with a few exceptions), while that of a Kohen is inherently

147

permanent. Defiling the *nazir*'s sanctity is thus the better choice under the circumstances.

The Gemara commences by stating what it takes to be obvious; namely, what the sages argue and what R. Eliezer argues. It will soon turn to a series of instances of two people walking along and coming upon an unattended dead body, and the question of the two persons' relative sanctity is addressed to assess the two opposing views of the Mishna. First, though, it directly addresses the issue of relative sanctity itself. Comparing a High Priest who has been properly anointed and adorned with the eight vestments reserved for the High Priest

47b

to a High Priest who has only been dressed in those vestments (anointment manqué), clearly the former enjoys a higher degree of sanctity. So, should these two fellows be walking along the road and come upon a corpse, the unanointed High Priest must perform the difficult work. Not addressed in the Gemara is what possible situation would compel the presence of an anointed High Priest and an unanointed one at the same time. The rabbis over the ages have worked this out, and no stone can ever be left unturned. The superiority of the anointed High Priest in the scenario is assured by the Gemara, because of an offering he must bring in a given situation (the bull *chatat*) which is not required of the unanointed High Priest.

The Gemara notes that there are circumstances in which the sanctity of an unanointed High Priest may supersede that of an anointed High Priest. If the latter has stepped down from office and the former is presently serving as High Priest, the anointed High Priest should be the one to self-contaminate for a *met mitzvah*. The presently serving High Priest enjoys superior sanctity, because he is responsible for performance of the Temple rituals, something the anointed High Priest is no longer qualified to do.

What about two High Priests, neither of whom is presently serving, one of whom left office because of *tumah* contracted from a seminal emission and the other due to the eruption of a bodily blemish. The former is exempted from burying the *met mitzvah*, because he may soon (as early as the following day) be back in the High Priest's seat, while the latter is out until his blemish disappears.

Now we move into a slightly different realm of sanctity comparisons. If the option is either the Kohen anointed for war or the Deputy High Priest, perhaps the former enjoys a higher degree of sanctity because he must lead troops into battle and defend the population, or maybe it's the latter who is ready, as necessary, to step into the High Priest's role on Yom Kippur. To answer this question, the Gemara tells us (for the twenty-ninth time in this tractate) to "Come [and] listen" (*ta shma*), and it then answers with a *baraita*, which records that in many ways these two important personages are at similar levels, but if they just happened to be walking together along the road and came upon an unattended dead body, it would be the Kohen anointed for war who would be responsible for its burial.

Just a second, inquires the Gemara, for it seems there's a possibly competing *baraita* which privileges the Kohen anointed for war over the Deputy High Priest. Mar Zutra offers some assistance in making sense of this. He claims that the Kohen anointed for war enjoys primacy if the issue is nourishment (such as when the two men find them in a serious quandary), because he is the lead defender of the people. When the issue is the contracting of *tumah*, then the Deputy comes first. Why? R. Chanina ben Antignos claims in another *baraita* that the very rationale for the creation of the post of Deputy was to step into the High Priest's place, as necessary, for the all-important Yom Kippur service. This is something the Kohen anointed for war cannot do, so it's up to him to self-pollute should they confront a *met mitzvah*.

We have seen in the Mishna that R. Eliezer and the sages disagreed about who, the High Priest or the *nazir*, when walking along together, was obligated to become contaminated by corpse *tumah*—though they agreed that, traveling along, either would be so obligated. How do we know any of this? A *baraita* to the rescue, citing *Leviticus* 21.11: "And near any dead people he [the High Priest] shall not come in, for his father or for his mother he shall not be defiled." (Alter, p. 637) Why, wonders the *baraita* rhetorically, does the verse start by disallowing self-contamination for "any dead people" and then say no defilement for a parent? Why the "extra" stipulation? Adding "for his father" is not there to rule out self-pollution for the father—that's already been stated just one clause before—but it implies that he *is* allowed to contract corpse *tumah* from a *met mitzvah*.

If this appears rather obscure, that's because it is. Inasmuch as we know that the High Priest may not self-defile even for his father (or any other relative), and we of course know the same for any non-relatives, by adding "for his father" we are to learn that this is meant to teach that the High Priest may indeed self-defile for a non-relative *met mitzvah*. I think I should leave this as is.

48a

The Gemara goes on to try similarly to explain why "for his mother" is there, as it too should be unnecessary. The Gemara links this with the allowance of a *nazir* to make physical contact with someone suffering from *tzaraat* or *zivah*. The reaction is swift, because we know (and have seen mention of it numerous times) that the only *tumah* prohibited to a *nazir* is that of a corpse. How do we know that this is similarly the case for a High Priest? This leads to an elaborate manipulation of verses, at one point using a *kal vachomer* argument and at another using a *gezera shava* (with the term "his mother").

On the previous *daf*, we saw that a High Priest may become defiled to handle a *met mitzvah*. What proof do we have that a *nazir* may do the same? The verse it focuses on (*Numbers* 6.6), via a *baraita*, reads: "All the days of his setting apart for the Lord [as a *nazir*], he shall not come to a dead person." (Alter, p. 711) The two words of the term employed for "dead person" (*nefesh met*) reinforce our understanding that we are referring to a *nefesh* (literally, soul) of a human being, not an animal. R. Yishmael argues that this reasoning is excessive, because the verb "come" in the scriptural passage concerning dead bodies only refers to human beings.

Now, we're still faced with the next verse about the *nazir* not self-polluting for a parent but being allowed to do so for a *met mitzvah*. Before the Gemara addresses this phrase by addressing it as redundant, as we just did for a High Priest, however, perhaps we can handle this issue by noting (via a *kal vachomer*) the following. A High Priest enjoys permanent sacredness and yet may attend to a *met mitzvah*, so a *nazir* who does not enjoy such ongoing sanctity should surely be allowed to do the same should he confront a *met mitzvah*. The Gemara doesn't buy it. The law governing a *nazir* and pollution is stricter than that for a High Priest. Should the latter become *tamei*, he goes through purification but is not required to bring any sacrifices, while a *nazir* of course does. Given such strictness regulating a *nazir* and corpse *tumah*, maybe in the case of a *met mitzvah* he is also more strictly controlled than a High Priest. The argument concludes that, while a *nazir* is prohibited from contracting *tumah* from a parent, he is permitted to contract from an unattended corpse.

Again, the Gemara suggests that the specificity of ruling out defilement for a parent may signal that the *nazir* is actually permitted to self-defile for other dead persons to whom he is not related. The Gemara doesn't like this derivation for a *nazir*'s allowance to bury a *met mitzvah* and become *tamei* from a corpse.

48b

Bottom line: The aim of specifying that a *nazir* may not become defiled by the *tumah* generated by the corpse of one of his parents is to emphasize that he may become so defiled for a *met mitzvah*.

At this point, the Gemara appears to want to explain where we have arrived, and so it reiterates how the statements regarding proscription on pollution with the dead for a High Priest and a *nazir* reinforce and indeed help explain one another. And, they lead us to the conclusion stated from the outset of allowing both to self-pollute with a *met mitzvah*. But, even that the Gemara won't let pass, noting that the same sort of reasoning might be used for a regular Kohen. The *baraita* then comes to an abrupt conclusion, stating that the apparent redundancy of singling out the *nazir*'s proscription on *tumah* from a dead parent is meant to imply allowance to contract *tumah* from a *met mitzvah*. The Gemara wonders about the sharp ending of an otherwise lengthy *baraita*, and it does with a sibling a similar exercise as we saw for a parent.

But, R. Akiva has another idea about how we should understand *Numbers* 6.6–7. He sees the term "dead person" (*nefesh met*) differently: *nefesh* signifies one's distant relatives, while *met* points to one's close relatives. The phrase about not allowing self-defilement for a parent is, indeed, redundant, because *met* implies (and has already been stated in the scriptural verse) a relative, and its impact is to allow defilement on behalf of an unattended corpse. He goes on to make a similar point about the inclusion of the passage disallowing corpse *tumah* for a brother. The ruling disallowing self-pollution for a sister is then derived from another source which is meant to demonstrate that permission to bury a *met mitzvah* transcends other rulings.

R. Akiva actually introduces the hypothetical case of a High Priest who is simultaneously a *nazir*—is that even allowed? In such an instance, how would we know that such a person was allowed to deal with a *met mitzvah*? R. Yishmael (again) has a simple answer. Scripture makes allowance for burying an unattended corpse—for a *nazir* and for a High Priest. Do we need two special allowances? The Gemara then rushes back into the seemingly superfluous cases of siblings to substantiate (once again) that self-defilement overrides all other prohibitions about corpse *tumah*.

49a

R. Akiva observed that the allowance accorded a High Priest to self-defile for a *met mitzvah* also works for a High Priest who is simultaneously a *nazir*, a position he drew from one of the "extraneous" references to a sibling in the much-used verse from *Numbers*. This also, though, is ascribed to the super-fluity of mention of the father, and the question is raised about why both are necessary. The answer jumps all over the place for which a Talmudic map would have been helpful, but the conclusion is clear that there can be no defilement for the corpse of a parent, father or mother.

As this extensive ride begins to wind down, the Gemara offers one last point about the purpose for a verse from *Leviticus* (21.11) which was cited (see above) on 47b (and mentioned on 38a). Have we not learned this else-where in the Torah?

49b

This time we get an extremely close reading of the verse in question. The term "come in" is understood to dismiss non-relatives from those for whom a High Priest is permitted to defile himself. The word "dead" here works to eliminate any relatives in the same manner. Finally, "people" (*nafshot*) is plural and thus refers to the proscription incumbent on a High Priest from pollution with one-quarter *log* of blood from two dead bodies combined. And, this is said to make the case.

A new Mishna arrives in the nick of time. We noted earlier that a *nazir* can not only become *tamei* from an intact corpse but also from detached body parts. This Mishna looks specifically at which parts incur corpse *tumah* and thus necessitate that the *nazir* go through the special purification incumbent upon him, closing with the head-shaving and then the reinstatement of his period of *nezirut*. These are those items which cause a *nazir* to start the process: a corpse itself, as little as an olive's volume of a corpse, an olive's volume of corpse fluid from decomposition that has coagulated (*netzel*), a ladleful of decomposed corpse dust, a corpse's spinal column and skull, a corpse's arm or leg or such from a live human being (on which there is enough flesh to rejuvenate, if that body was whole and alive, and less than an olive's volume), one-half *kav* (one *kav* = 1.5–2.65 quarts, according to the experts) of bones from a corpse, and one-half *log* of blood. Becoming *tamei* by contact with any of these, carrying them, or finding oneself under a roof with any, and the *nazir* must shave (meaning that he must undergo the entire ritual purification process). One more detailed ruling: Carrying or touching a bone as big as a grain of barley, the *nazir* must shave; implied is that there is no roof *tumah* for bones unless they rise to a quantity of one-quarter *kav*.

The Mishna then tells us what the purification process entails: After having purifying waters sprinkled on him on days three and seven of the process, the *nazir* shaves. He loses accrued days from his period of committed *nezirut* and then recommences such once he regains *tahara* and has brought his sacrificial offerings. Many of these rulings have been presaged in earlier *dapim*.

The Gemara starts with a *baraita* which gets to its point with a story. R. Meir died, and R. Yehuda made it explicitly clear to his students that none of the late R. Meir's own students were to be allowed into his dwelling or yeshiva. Why? Because their only purpose would be to attack him, R. Yehuda, and use their presumed acuity to disrupt his teaching, not to learn from him. Somehow, one of R. Meir's disciples, Sumchos, forced his way in and blurted out that R. Meir had taught him that a *nazir* must undergo purification concluding with a head-shave for contracting *tumah* from a corpse or even just an olive's volume of a corpse. The assumption must be that R. Yehuda had not included the term "for a corpse" when he was instructing his pupils in this Mishna. R. Yehuda was not amused and indignantly berated his students for letting this annoying individual from the camp of R. Meir inside. Of course, if a *nazir* must shave due to defilement for as little as an olive's volume of a corpse, what need is there to mention an entire corpse?

50a

R. Yose pipes in that, with R. Meir no longer around to defend his position, he feels it necessary to state that an entire corpse must be mentioned so as to include a full corpse missing only an olive's volume of flesh, an entity deemed full enough to transmit *tumah*.

One might shoot back, in defense of R. Yehuda, that an arm or leg of a corpse could have less than an olive's volume of flesh, and it would still cause a *nazir* to become *tamei*. That fact alone should indicate that such a ruling ought cover an entire corpse. A defense of R. Yose's stance is now presented in a teaching of R. Yochanan who claims that mention of a full corpse is necessary to cover an aborted fetus whose limbs are not completely developed and whose volume might be less than that of an olive. Thus, "for a corpse" is intended to include an aborted fetus, whose limbs alone wouldn't qualify as bearers of *tumah*. Rava has another idea. We need to have mention of a full corpse to cover cases in which there is a majority of a body's skeleton or its bones, but those bones do not add up to one-quarter *kav*. The idea is that these are cases which might otherwise not have been considered significant enough for *tumah* contraction.

The Gemara moves now to consider another portion of the Mishna. One can contract *tumah* from as little as an olive's volume of a corpse or an olive's volume of corpse fluid from congealed decomposed matter. Identifying the latter, called *netzel* in our text, can be difficult, and indeed can be confused with other substances in appearance such as mucus or saliva. R. Yirmeya states that if such a substance has coagulated, it is deemed *netzel*, but if it hasn't coagulated, it might still be mucus or saliva which do not convey corpse *tumah* and thus do not necessitate that a *nazir* shave.

Abaye at this point asks Rabbah what the law for animal *netzel* is. Does it convey *tumah*, as it does for human beings, or is it qualitatively different? At this point, the Gemara distinguishes between greater and lesser *tumah*, though only the former is of concern here. Any animal not properly slaughtered may not, of course, be consumed by a Jew; its carcass is dubbed *neveilah* and is a source of a more stringent *tumah*. Non-Jews are permitted scripturally to eat the meat of animals not ritually slaughtered. It ceases to be a source of *tumah* when it is no longer edible even for a dog, and animal *netzel* then does not convey *tumah*.

To help understand these distinctions, the Gemara introduces a short *baraita*. Imagine a kosher bird that has died without proper slaughtering; even if its fat is melted over fire and hence no longer congealed, it still conveys *tumah* (as a *neveilah*) when consumed though not by simple contact. If that same fat were exposed to a hot sun and melted, it is actually deemed *tahor*, because it putrefies and is thus effectively *netzel*. The *baraita* apparently indicates that the rulings above concerning *netzel* don't concern *neveilah*. However, we know that melted fat in the sun has putrefied such that it is like dust, and even a dog wouldn't touch it. Nothing new here.

The Gemara now segues to a peripherally related topic, that of melted food and *tumah* conveyance. It begins with a citation from a Mishna in tractate *Machshirin* (Preliminaries to the Preparation of Food, 5.9) which concerns how certain liquids predispose certain foods to become sources of *tumah*. It states that a liquid poured into a container (including the connective stream) remains *tahor*, even if that container is *tamei*, with the exception of two very thick items. In the latter case, even when the flow is broken in pouring, the link is understood to remain in existence. Should one break the flow, the viscous liquid in the source is drawn back into it.

50b

For this last reason, Bet Shammai adds a few items to the list of viscous liquids deemed exceptions to the rule.

Rami bar Chama asks if a melted item poured between the source and object containers constitutes a stream per se. In other words, was the original exception of two very thick substances a consequence of those substances being drawn back when the stream is broken, while for melted items when poured would not serve to link the *tumah* of the object container with the source? Or, maybe it's due to the viscosity of those two items, something they share with melted food? A *baraita* is now introduced which helps a bit. If one took a piece of fat with the volume of an olive from a dead body and melted it, it remains a source of *tumah*. If, however, it was sliced up into pieces, each smaller than an olive in volume, it ceases to be *tamei*. If such an olive's volume of corpse fat was melted and poured, it would very likely have lost some of its volume during the melting process and thus not convey *tumah*.

The Gemara goes through another round of rejections and further attempts to make sense of all this, though it never asks why anyone would be heating up an olive's volume (or any amount) of fat from a human corpse. This is one of those rabbit holes that the Talmud loves to explore to satisfy every ramification imaginable to a ruling—as a reminder, we're dealing with an extrapolation of the laws governing corpse *tumah* and how contact with it for a *nazir* can throw his whole *nezirut* into chaos.

Back to our own Mishna and the issue of a ladleful of decomposed corpse dust. The Gemara here starts by asking how big a ladle we're dealing with. Chizkiya opines that it is comparable to the human ladle: a palm. R. Yochanan states that it is what would fill a hand. They apparently differ inasmuch as the former would constitute the amount that would fill a palm without enclosing one's fingers around it, while the latter includes the fingers and presumably can hold more. A *baraita* (is there one for everything?), as stated by R. Meir, defines a ladleful of decomposed corpse dust as including the entirety of a hand's fingers, which would seem to dispute Chizkiya's definition. The sages, however, aver that a ladleful equals a handful. That puts R. Yochanan's words in line with the sages, while Chizkiya's views seems to accord with no one. Still, another anonymous view is that measuring to fill a palm does indeed include from the knuckles to the ends of one's fingers, the measurement which was used by R. Meir and which would fit with Chizkiya's opinion. There is some lack of certainty with how R. Meir actually defined his measurements, but the Gemara has had enough of this back and forth, and it resolves to leave this one unresolved.

51a

Under what circumstances does that ladleful of decomposed corpse dust convey *tumah* necessitating a *nazir* who comes in contact with it undergo the special purification rituals before he may resume his *nezirut*? To answer this question, the Gemara turns to a *baraita* which indicates that the corpse had to have been interred naked in a coffin made of marble or on a stone floor—the reasoning is that, unlike clothing or other coffin material, neither marble nor stone decays into something that might mix with a corpse. Thus, in the case of a clothed corpse or one interred in a coffin made of wood or one laid to rest on a floor made of brick, the ruling on corpse dust does not adhere. In other words, the corpse dust must be free of any alien particles.

Ulla now adds a further prerequisite. The corpse dust must be the decayed residue from flesh, sinews, and bones for it to qualify as a conveyor of *tumah*. Rava responds from a *baraita* insisting that corpse dust solely from decayed flesh is actually *tahor*, and he takes that to mean that such decayed residue solely from bones would be *tamei*. So, Ulla's phrasing is slightly rejigged to say that, yes, corpse dust from flesh is *tahor* except if there is bone within, implying that the resultant decayed dust includes bone matter. Well, then, what about the sinews? Answer: If you have flesh and bone in a human body, there necessarily will be connective sinew.

Rav Shmuel bar Abba, channeling R. Yochanan, adds yet another element to this law. If two corpses were interred together and decomposed to dust, each intermixes with the other and does not qualify as a potential conveyor of *tumah*. Rav Natan immediately quotes yet another *baraita* stating explicitly that corpse dust from two bodies is indeed *tamei*. Rava to the rescue. The case involving the two corpses mentioned in the *baraita*, he claims, was one in which the two bodies were interred separately and decomposed on their own. The total corpse dust between them came to a ladleful, and together this ladleful can transmit *tumah*. Rav Shmuel was referring to two corpses interred together and decomposed in a mixture.

Rabba bar bar Chana, also channeling R. Yochanan, adds an odd piece of information. If someone were to cut some or all of the hair of a corpse and then had it interred with the body, the hair is considered alien to the corpse and thus forms a mixture that does not convey *tumah* when it all decays to dust.

Before it can discuss this point, the Gemara segues to a Mishna from another tractate to delineate the body parts that can convey *tumah*. Actually, teeth, hair, and nails aside, the entire rest of a corpse transmits *tumah*. What's more, if those three entities are still connected to the corpse, they too convey *tumah*. Chizkiya at this juncture asks a question that returns us to Rabba bar bar Chana's point. If the corpse's hair or nails, at the time of death, reached a point at which they would have been cut, is contact with them defiling? In other words, if hair or nails were set for cutting, do we treat them as if they were actually cut or does contact with them convey *tumah*? Now, we learn something of the background to Rabba bar bar Chana's otherwise strange intervention: He witnessed or learned second-hand of someone cutting the hair of a dead body and interring it with the corpse. Decomposed dust from hair that was connected to the body is not deemed a mixture, and hence it has the capacity to defile. What he did not address was hair that had reached a length ready for cutting (but had not been before death), because he must have been uncertain about its status.

R. Yirmeya has a couple of questions. First: What's the story with corpse dust from a decomposed heel? As it contained several layers of dead skin while the person was living, it was already dead when the person passed and would not on its own convey *tumah*; or, maybe it's just like the rest of the corpse and does transmit pollution. On the one hand, dust from the heel is likely part of an entire corpse's dust; on the other, the Gemara clarifies R. Yirmeya's question, he accepts that dust from the heel certainly combines with dust from the rest of the decayed body, but he was referring to dust from a heel beside a single limb, the only body part thus far decomposed. The Gemara passes on this one.

Second: What about a woman interred while she was pregnant? Does the unborn fetus constitute a mixture? R. Yirmeya goes on to note that elsewhere in the law we know that a fetus is considered as its mother's limb, meaning that it is a part of her body, and meaning further that when it decays, its dust is not deemed a mixture to the dust of its mother. Together they can convey *tumah*. On the other hand, though, the fetus was going to be born and become an entity unto itself, meaning that it was not a permanent part of its mother's body. In this sense, its dust perhaps would be deemed a mixture.

51b

That being the case, what about corpse dust as residue from any possible semen left from the interred corpse of a woman? While it had not become an embryo at the time of its mother's death, it might not be regarded as a mixture, but by the same token its source was external to her body which would technically make it a mixture.

The list of questions of this sort is only getting started, as Rav Pappa then asks about any excrement inside the intestines of a woman's corpse. She had to eat and digest while alive, but perhaps the excrement is to be regarded as a product of something (like semen) initially not part of her body. Rav Acha, son of Rav Ika, asks about dust from the decayed skin of a corpse, and Rav Huna bar Manoach asks about saliva and mucus. Are these considered extrinsic to the corpse? Rav Shmuel bar Acha responds in a way that seems most rational. All these items asked about—hair, nails, mucus, saliva, excrement—are going to be found in almost every corpse. The Gemara concocts an almost silly response of a way in which a dying and then dead person might be freed of all such entities.

Abaye adds an interesting twist to our discussion of corpse dust. If a dead body was ground into dust, that does not constitute the kind of corpse dust we have been discussing and is not regulated by the corresponding laws. What if the corpse was ground and then decayed into dust—does that qualify? Again, the Gemara cannot come to a conclusion on this one.

But, it's not done with the issue of corpse dust. A corpse missing a body part is not regulated according to the laws of corpse dust that we have been discussing, according to *baraita* noted by Ulla bar Chanina. Nor is regulated by other laws concerning corpses, but they are not the concern of what follows. Despite a challenge thrown its way, this ruling remains intact.

Rava, who has had much to say on the topic, asks about someone whose limb fell off or was severed and decayed while he was still living, and said person then passed away. What is the status of his corpse dust? The dust residue from a live human being does not pollute is because that person is still alive, meaning that, were he dead, that limb severed from his body prior to his passing should now be governed by corpse dust law. But, no, a whole corpse reduced to dust is subject to the laws we have been outlining, but no piece of a living human being is.

If you thought the preceding discussion wasn't ghoulish enough, what follows ups the ante a bit and should probably come with a warning. Rava asks about the case of someone who consumes (somehow) an ant that is one limb short of whole. As background, from elsewhere in the Talmud we know that consuming a complete creature earns one a flogging, irrespective of its size. Rava wonders if one consumed such a creature, a five-legged ant, what would be the law. The question boils down to whether the fullness or completeness of the ant is the criterion here or the fact of its creature-hood (alive in spite of the loss of a leg).

52a

We now hear from Rav Yehuda from Diskarta a proposed solution based on a *baraita*. He notes that *Leviticus* (11.31) spells out a series of eight *sheratzim* (creeping creatures; "swarming creatures" according to Alter, p. 586; sing. *sheratz*), and "with them" causes one to become *tamei*. It would seem that "them" here indicates a full creeper. However, the very next verse speaks of "from them," and this might be understood as meaning just a portion of one of them. Had scripture mentioned only the latter ("from them"), then *tumah* would be the result of even the smallest bit of a creeping creature. So, the former verse ("with them") trumps this and makes such minimal contact not productive of *tumah*. So, let's combine the implications of the two phrases and suggest that, while contact with a tiny bit of a *sheratz* may not be enough to contract *tumah*, touching a significant portion of one (even if less than its entirety) must transpire for *tumah* to result. What constitutes this significant amount? The rabbis decreed that the size should be comparable to a lentil, because that is the size of one of the creatures mentioned in *Leviticus*.

Rav Shemaya rejects this approach to measuring what constitutes a creature. He suggests that a better measurement is the living capacity of such a creature, and even among those tiny creepers mentioned in *Leviticus*, it is possible that they may be smaller than a lentil and still be living, breathing entities. An ant can be alive even minus a leg.

The Gemara now proceeds to consider the Mishna's piece about a corpse's spinal column and skull, and it asks if the preposition should be understood as "and" or "or" (in Hebrew, it can mean either). Rava refers us to a *baraita* which indicates that a spinal column missing the majority of its ribs would be *tahor*, as it would have changed so much as to no longer be regarded definitionally as a spinal column. Interred, however, a spinal column whose ribs have been separated from it for whatever reason would be *tamei*, because the grave itself functions to bring all the bones together, figuratively speaking. If a spinal column whose ribs have been cut off is *tahor*, then implicit (according to Rava) is the fact that with all the ribs intact the spinal column would be *tamei*, with or without a skull. Thus, "or" wins the day.

Not so quick, rebuts the Gemara. There was no mention of a skull in the *baraita*. It dealt with a spinal column and rib cage. The case of a spinal column with a skull has yet to be discussed.

The Gemara moves to another *baraita* at this point in which R. Yehuda notes that six items were deemed *tamei* by R. Akiva and *tahor* by the sages—and R. Akiva later withdrew his judgment here. We'll get to these in a moment, but first a story with a moral. A box full of bones was on one occasion brought, for some reason, to the smiths' synagogue and left outside so as not to envelope anyone with corpse *tumah*. A doctor named Todos (or Todus), accompanied by medical colleagues, went to work studying the bones and concluded that the bones did not constitute a complete spinal column from a single corpse; hence, no *tumah* defilement. Again, by negative implication, it is assumed that, had there been bones of a spinal column or skull from the same one corpse, that would have sufficed to force a *nazir* to shave. Again, "or" wins the day.

Hold on a second, warns the Gemara. The wording of what has been derived from Todos's statement about the bones does not suffice to reach such a conclusion. We still need more analysis before concluding the Mishna's intent here.

Back to that *baraita* and the six points of disagreement between what R. Akiva deemed *tamei* and the sages *tahor*: (1) a single arm or leg put together from two corpses; (2) the same from two living persons; (3) one-half *kav* of bones drawn from two corpses; (4) one-quarter *log* of blood from two corpses; (5) a bone no bigger than a barley grain broken in half; and (6) a spinal column and skull drawn from two corpses.

52b

As is often the case, just when you think a number is hard and fast, there is always just one more. So, the Gemara notes that, if you believe that "or" (and not "and") is how (6) should be read, then there is a seventh point of disagreement. Actually, though, the Gemara also suggests that that seventh one should be counted but (5) about the bone the size of a barley grain was a disagreement between R. Akiva and only one sage, R. Yochanan ben Nuri, so it might be dropped from the list, leaving the number of six intact.

Maybe, though, we should stick with six, not seven, by cutting (2) or rather combining (1) and (2). Or, maybe six refers to those cases in which a *nazir* would contract corpse *tumah* from shared enclosure under a roof—which would exclude (5); back on 49b it was ruled that a bone the size of a barley grain can convey *tumah* only by contact or carrying, not via a roof. There is yet another way to come to six: exclude the one case, (4), wherein R. Akiva did not concede to the sages and withdraw his view. Evidence that he none-theless did not cease teaching (4) is provided by R. Yehuda ha-Nasi, and R. Shimon concurs.

And, so, for the thirty-first time in our tractate, the Gemara begins its lengthy discussion of the unresolved issue of "and" vs. "or" with *ta shma* (Come, listen). Can either a skull or spinal column separately defile, or must they be together? A dispute between Bet Shammai and Bet Hillel over how many bones may come together to constitute the requisite measure for roof *tumah* and even an effort posed by R. Yehoshua to bring the two schools together and resolve their differences appear at this point. As it turns out, though, it is Shammai himself (and not just his school, meaning his students) who had argued that all it takes is a single bone from a corpse's skull *or* spinal column to convey *tumah*. Inasmuch as he requires a single bone, the assumption is that the rabbis require either an entire skull or an entire spinal column. Shammai is respected but his view here is dismissed as extremely severe.

The Gemara then tries to turn this attempted proof on its head and use it to substantiate the "and" option. It all hinges on how the Hebrew language subtly distinguishes "and" from "or," but before the Gemara can get very far along this line of argument, it notes that the only point of dispute between the rabbis and Shammai is over the single bone business. They accept a whole skull or spinal column as pollution-inducing.

We now enter what is thought by many to be one of the most reason-defying sections of the entire Talmud. It concerns the volume of bone which cause a *nazir* to contract corpse *tumah* and the parts of the dead body from which those bones come. It concludes (as our *daf* comes to a close) that bones drawn from the skull or spinal column are just like other bones from a corpse. Only when they reach a measure of one-quarter *kav* do they defile a *nazir* sufficiently to force him to shave, meaning he has been afflicted with corpse *tumah*.

53a

We soon, however, learn that, following the acquaintance with a teaching of R. Akiva, Rava withdrew his "proof" and went back to the drawing board. This time, a *baraita* is cited to attempt a resolution. Shammai himself is quoted to the effect that any one bone from a spinal column or skull is sufficient to convey *tumah* via a roof. By implication, then, those rabbis who disagree with this ruling would argue that it takes either a full spinal column or skull to convey defilement, or it would mean that their ruling on defilement requires a smaller quantity of bone, e.g., one-quarter of a *kav*. This last position is almost rejected out of hand, with the claim that Shammai's ruling about a single bone is exceedingly rigid.

So, the Gemara takes a different approach and suggests that Shammai's ruling of a single bone from the spinal column or skull is actually less rigid, requiring far less than others who demand an entire skull or spinal column. Before this reverse argumentation can so much as get off the ground, the Gemara tosses it out, and again we find ourselves back at the drawing board.

Much of the foregoing debate has centered around whether it requires one-quarter or one-half *kav* of bone (or one-quarter or one-half *log* of blood) from a corpse to convey roof *tumah*. The Gemara takes us now back to a much earlier time when the small amount (and hence greater stringency) was in effect. Those measures gave way in later times to the larger amount, while the smaller amount was used not as a measure of what would bring about defilement but of what could prohibit consumption of certain sanctified foods. The Gemara questions where such a ruling came from, and it concludes that it was the lineal descendant of an oral tradition going back to several of the less well-known prophets.

The last phrase of the Mishna at hand sums up all that preceded it by saying that these are the things that compel a *nazir* to shave. Why bother assessing such an apparently innocuous line? Well, that was essentially how the Mishna began, and redundancy always means something—it isn't even really "redundant." The repeated words are "for these [things]," and the Gemara quickly tells us what those words in their different spots in the Mishna teach. It is exceedingly unclear how that assessment came to be.

And, just when you thought the Gemara had exhausted the various cases outlined in the Mishna, it goes back for another run at several of its rulings. This time around, it looks once more at bone quantities needed to defile a *nazir* and the circumstances in which such *tumah* pollute.

53b

Different rulings apply if the bone pieces are small or even ground to dust, and different kinds of *tumah* (touching, carrying, and/or roof) attach to them.

Another case from the Mishna for which the Gemara seeks more discussion is that of the *tumah* arising from the arm or foot of a dead body or the severed arm or leg of a living person; in the latter case, there should be enough corporeality to be revitalized should that limb still be connected to its original body. If there is insufficient corporeality in this last case, what does it take for a *nazir* to become contaminated and have to shave? R. Yochanan insists that touching or carrying such a body part does not necessitate that a *nazir* shave, while R. Yehuda ha-Nasi rules to the contrary that it does. R. Yochanan's reasoning is quite simple. The Mishna speaks of a limb with enough flesh to be revived were it connected to the living person who originally bore it; if it lacked that flesh, it lacks the capacity to contaminate. R. Shimon ben Lakish (also known as Reish Lakish), though, directs our attention to the next Mishna (54a) on which is listed a series of those items which do not cause a *nazir* to contract corpse *tumah*—and this one is not there; thus, he reasons, it must actually be a cause of pollution.

R. Yochanan isn't buying this line. He understands that his own argument was clearly implied at the start of the Mishna, and therefore there was no need for it to be repeated in that next Mishna. Its absence in the latter's list, as a result, means nothing. The Gemara bats this debate back and forth a couple of times, but it then moves on to look more closely at the arm or leg of a corpse. If it still contained the minimal amount of bone (a barley grain in size), contact via touch or carrying for a *nazir* does not spell contamination for R. Yochanan. The Mishna here is explicit that it does. Similarly, if its bone content does not rise to this minimal amount, how can Shimon ben Lakish argue that contamination nonetheless ensues? The latter sage explains himself by citing a *baraita* which states that, if someone comes upon a corpse, or a grave, or even just the bone from a corpse in the open air and touches it, he has contracted *tumah*. On the surface this explains little, but the *baraita* goes on to interpret such an instance to substantiate its case. To do so requires a whole lot of creative engineering of the language. This kind of creative manipulation of the wording is not something at all rare in the Talmud, although the case at hand it still quite extraordinary.

54a

After extensive discussion and analysis of roof *tumah*, the Gemara turns to the contraction of *tumah* via touch. R. Yehuda cites a *baraita* which quotes *Numbers* (19.18) concerning one who touches a bone or a corpse of someone cut down by a sword. The *baraita* then identifies the "bone" as the minimal (barley-grain) size and the corpse cut down by a sword as the arm or leg of a live being but without enough corporeality to be revived (were the limb reattached). Again, these associations seem somewhat far-fetched, but the *baraita* is meant to buttress the argument being put forth by Shimon ben Lakish. Both he and R. Yochanan somehow accept the notion that the reference is to a severed limb; their difference revolves around whether said limb contains a barley-grain-sized bone. In the end, both parties continue to insist on their positions outlined above.

Our Mishna laid out the procedures for a defiled *nazir* who must shave and who must also go through sprinklings on the third and seventh day of his seven-day period of decontamination and then the loss of accrued days in his term of *nezirut*. Days lost is only the beginning of things, as the *nazir* must now recommence the period of abstentions to which he earlier committed. Before doing so, though, he has to be thoroughly purified, and the Gemara wants to establish when that occurs: Does that mean sundown on the seventh day of the purification process? R. Eliezer affirms this position. The rabbis, however, insist that purification only comes on day eight, after the former *nazir* brings his sacrifices to the Temple.

The Gemara, for the forty-third time, begins its answer with *ta shma*. The new counting of days commences right after the purifying rituals on day seven, but apparently this only means cases in which no offerings are required. Where they are required, then they are brought on day eight, and the count recommences right afterward.

A new Mishna now picks right up where the last one left off. As hinted above, it presents an inventory of those things which cause *tumah* contraction, but ones that are not sufficiently severe to compel a *nazir* to shave and bring offerings, even if there is a certain level of pollution. These include (to be analyzed in detail by the Gemara to follow): overhanging tree branches or stone outcroppings, a field that once had a grave in it and has been dug up, terrain outside the Land of Israel, tomb coverings, blood of a minimal quantity of one-quarter *log*, one-quarter *kav* of bones for roof *tumah*, instruments that come into contact with a corpse, or a *metzora* who is counting out the days of his purification procedure. So, for these the *nazir* need not shave, though he does have to go through the third- and seventh-day sprinkling, and unlike the harsher forms of *tumah*,

54b

he loses no days on his count. As soon as these purifications are complete, he can pick up his count where he left off and no animal sacrifices are required of him. He does, nonetheless, lose the few days he was *tamei*. If a *nazir* experiences a seminal emission and thus becomes a *zav* (or a *nezira* experiences menstruation beyond her normal period), no days are lost from their count. Similarly, the period during which someone is restricted in movement before he is declared a *metzora* is also allowed for counting in the *nazir*'s period once purification is concluded.

To help us understand what the Mishna meant by "overhanging tree branches or stone outcroppings," the Gemara begins with a citation from the tractate *Oholot* (Tents) of the Mishna. The former refers to branches from trees that hang over the ground (as branches tend to do), and the latter are overhangings of stone that spread out from a wall. What about the terrain outside the Land of Israel? What about this land causes *tumah*? Did the sages do this to prevent people from leaving the Land of Israel, or were they fearful that graves outside the Land were not properly marked and thus an ever-present possible source of *tumah*?

The Gemara's first stab at answering this question is to note that the list of *tumah*-inducing events from our Mishna requires of all that they receive sprinklings on the third and seventh day of purification. If the ruling was to keep people from leaving the Land of Israel, that is unrelated to corpse *tumah*, so it must be for the latter reason which is directly related to graves and dead bodies and the possible contracting of *tumah* from a corpse. That would (apparently) be too easy a resolution, for the Mishna's conclusion that these various and sundry corpse *tumah* defilements lead to sprinklings may actually not be for all of them—just all the others beside the Land issue. Actually, the reference in the Mishna to instruments that come into contact with a corpse leads to only a single day of contamination with no need for sprinkling. So, it's not "all" in the listing that require a full gamut of purifications, including sprinkling on days three and seven, but "most" of them.

55a

There's a *baraita*, as it turns out, recording a disputation between rabbis of an earlier generation that appears similar to this one and goes like this. If one were to travel onto foreign terrain while on a conveyance similar to a covered sedan chair, or in a covered trunk of some sort—in any event, such that one's feet did not touch the ground—R. Yehuda ha-Nasi deems such a person *tamei*, while R. Yose bar R. Yehuda deems him *tahor*. The former would seem to have reached his ruling because this person left the Land of Israel, while the latter came to his conclusion because said person never touched the ground and hence did not become contaminated. But, no, that's not the crux of the earlier debate, according to the Gemara. There, the issue was whether a moving tent constituted an *ohel* (a tent shielding against *tumah*): R. Yehuda ha-Nasi (no), R. Yose bar R. Yehuda (yes). In fact, the Gemara dredges up another *baraita* in which R. Yose bar R. Yehuda explicitly rules that such a tent does not shield one from *tumah*.

The Gemara then tries once more to identify the basis for this disagreement. This time it argues that all parties in the earlier debate agree that *tumah* was the consequence of traveling outside the Land of Israel. What they disagreed about was traveling inside a covered sedan chair-like vehicle. As far as R. Yose bar R. Yehuda was concerned, this was so unusual that it was not to be decreed a source of *tumah*, but despite this unusual situation R. Yehuda ha-Nasi deemed it contaminating. Substantiation comes in the form of yet another *baraita* which decrees that leaving the Land of Israel for foreign terrain in an enclosed vehicle or the like does not bring about *tumah*, but in an open wagon or sea-going vessel it does.

Just when you think that the Gemara has nailed down definitive proof, it frequently tries out a different explanation. Suppose all our authorities really believe that the issue concerns fear that someone traveling abroad will be exposed to the land itself, perhaps by sticking head and arms or legs out of whatever he is being conveyed in. And, sure enough, there's a *baraita* in which R. Yose bar R. Yehuda avers that, if someone does travel outside the Land of Israel in an enclosed vehicle or the like, he will indeed remain *tahor* until such time as his pokes his head or the bulk of his body outside. So, this one either remains unresolved, or possibly we are to understand that it can be understood either way.

We next examine the Mishna's statement about the *nazir*'s taking up his counting of days right after his purification is finished. One of the items listed as not to be counted in the number of days toward completion of his *nezirut* are those of substantiated *tzaraat*. Rav Chisda claims that this only applies in a regular, thirty-day period of *nezirut*, but if someone was committed to a longer period, those days do, indeed, count. No, says Rav Sheravya, for the following reason. In order to shave (which is required of a *metzora* as part of his purification), a *nazir* must have thirty days of hair growth—that's impossible if a regular *nezirut* has been interrupted by a *tzaraat* outbreak.

55b

So, he concludes, this line from the Mishna must be referring to a longer period of *nezirut* commitment. Rav Sheravya then offers an example of how his understanding of the Mishna would play out: fifty-day total *nezirut* commitment, twenty days going along fine, contraction of *tzaraat*, purification including body-shave, and then thirty days till completion of *nezirut* with sufficient hair growth to shave.

56a

Rami bar Chama then poses another objection to Rav Chisda's position, citing a Mishna we shall come to on 59b. That Mishna, which we shall address in due course, discusses a *nazir* who may have contracted corpse *tumah* and may be a *metzora* himself. The analysis proceeds from here down an extremely long and circuitous rabbit hole, and how it gets to its conclusion that this can only work if the period of *nezirut* is three years and thirty days is complex beyond my capacities. We shall try again when we come to it in four days.

Rav Ashi now introduces a *baraita*, a very long one, that confronts Rav Chisda's position. It starts by stating something (at this point) obvious: The days that a *nazir* is contaminated by corpse *tumah* do not count for his period of *nezirut*. How do we know the same of *tzaraat* pollution, asks the *baraita* rhetorically. To answer this, it takes shelter in logic rather than scripture: purification from the corpse *tumah* requires head shaving and sacrificial offerings, while purification from *tzaraat* requires full-body shaving and offerings. Thus, since the latter seems more stringent than the former, if corpse *tumah* days don't count, certainly *tzaraat* days won't as well.

The *baraita* goes on to scrap this analysis in favor of something else to come. The reason his days spent contaminated by corpse *tumah* do not count toward his period of *nezirut* is that they compel him to lose all the accrued days prior to defilement. Meanwhile, the same can definitely not be said of his days as a *metzora*—no loss of accumulated days prior. And, then, the *baraita* itself enters another lengthy rabbit hole concerning counting of days for a *metzora* and much more.

56b

After this extensive discussion, the end product is to refute Rav Chisda's view. A *nazir* afflicted with *tzaraat* does not get to count those days toward his *nezirut* period.

A new Mishna at this point begins with R. Eliezer stating a position in the name of R. Yehoshua. Anyone who has contracted corpse *tumah* to an extent which would compel a *nazir* to shave and go through purification before he can resume his *nezirut* is forbidden to enter the Temple grounds, and the penalty is fairly severe. If the corpse *tumah* contracted did not rise to a level compelling a *nazir* to shave, he does not face serious consequences for entering the Temple grounds. R. Meir notes in the latter case that the penalty should be at a level comparable to one afflicted with *tumah* from a creepy, crawling creature, which is also quite severe.

When the Talmud mentions "R. Yehoshua" (a common name, as we shall see momentarily) without a patronymic, it is referring to R. Yehoshua ben Chananya, but here there seems to be some confusion, because we have a *baraita* which indicates otherwise. The *baraita* notes that R. Eliezer tells of visiting one R. Yehoshua ben Peter Rosh while the latter was in discussion with R. Meir. This R. Yehoshua articulated the very view we just noted in the Mishna, and R. Meir replied in the same fashion we have seen above. R. Eliezer then asked this R. Yehoshua if he knew one R. Yehoshua bar Mamal. After an affirmative response, R. Eliezer went on to state that R. Yehoshua bar Mamal had relayed to him this very position in the name of R. Yehoshua ben Chananya. So, R. Eliezer didn't hear it from R. Yehoshua ben Chananya in the flesh, but the later was the ultimate source of this teaching.

The Gemara uses this case to lay out an exegetical ruling. When a ruling is conveyed via a series of three or more sages, it is sufficient to name the first and the last participants in the series. The middle figures need not be stated by name. (This ruling is not always followed by others.) Rav Nachman bar Yitzchak cites a Mishna in support of this ruling, *Peah* (Edge) 2.6.[1] This Mishna records a long line of transmission relayed by Nachum the Scribe going all the way back to Moses when he was atop Mt. Sinai, but it fails to mention two figures in the middle of this lengthy series covering hundreds of years. Interestingly, it should be noted, the series of sages in *Peah* may not have named everyone in it, but it does mention more than two names.

On now to the last Mishna in this chapter of our tractate. Earlier it was taught that a *nazir* need not shave based on the *tumah* contracted from one-quarter *log* of blood from a corpse. Here, R. Akiva articulates his opposition to such a ruling. He stated to R. Eliezer that we know that a bone the size of a barley grain does not pollute a person via a shared roof but does compel a *nazir* to shave for pollution via touch or carrying. And, inasmuch as a quarter *log* of blood from a dead body defiles a person via a shared roof, wouldn't it make sense that a *nazir* is contaminated and need proceed to shave and bring offerings if he touched or carried it? R. Eliezer isn't buying this line of reasoning (R. Akiva used a *kal vachomer*), but he doesn't explain in the Mishna what he finds objectionable. So. R. Akiva presented his arguments to R. Yehoshua, and the latter praised his well-expressed position, but R. Yehoshua was also not convinced.

57a

Maybe the Gemara can help us understand what the problem was. So, R. Eliezer dismissed R. Akiva's analysis apparently because a *kal vachomer* here just didn't work, and R. Yehoshua explained the reasoning behind this rejection: Laws taught to Moses at Mt. Sinai and then transmitted over the generations orally cannot be used as the foundation for a *kal vachomer*. Who knew?

What was this law that dates back to Moses and the mountain? The Gemara considers two possibilities, but it concludes that compel a *nazir* to shave due to touching a barley-grain-sized piece of bone was the law taught to Moses. Reasoning based on the quarter *log* of blood from a corpse which can force a *nazir* to shave via a shared roof can, indeed, be used to argue with a *kal vachomer*. But, such is not the case with the bone fragment. And, so chapter 7 comes to a close.

NOTE

1. There is no extant Gemara for Mishnaic tractate *Peah* (Corner) in the Babylonian Talmud. There is an extensive Gemara for this tractate in the Jerusalem Talmud, but interestingly this particular Mishna has no Gemara discussing it. The text simply stops at 2.5.

Chapter 8

Doubts and Certainties

57a (CONTINUED)

This chapter will only consume four *dapim*, and it is primarily concerned with doubts that may afflict a *nazir* and how he gets himself into more certain terrain. The two big ones are: worry that he may have contracted corpse *tumah*; and worry that he may have inadvertently become a *metzora*. All sorts of problems ensue from either of these, and extrication can be both complex and difficult. This chapter promises to be a bit less ghoulish than the last one.

We begin with a beefy Mishna. Picture this scene: Two *nezirim* are standing together when they are approached by someone who says: I observed one of you contract corpse *tumah*, but I can't be sure which one it was. As a result, both are regarded as possibly contaminated. What's a body (a live body) to do? The Mishna explains that, assuming both are in the midst of a regular thirty-day period of *nezirut*, both proceed to the conclusion of their periods, shave at that time, and bring both an offering for *tumah* and one for *tahara* after undergoing their sprinklings. Then, because these two *nezirim* don't know who had contracted *tumah* and thus which sacrificial offering applied to whom, one of the two declaims that, if he was the *tamei nazir*, the *tumah* offering is his and *tahara* offering is his colleague's; and if he was the *tahor nazir*, then the *tahara* offering is his, and the *tumah* offering is his colleague's. From that point forward, both *nezirim* count another thirty days and then bring a joint *tahara* offering; one of the two declaims that, if he was the *tamei nazir*, the *tumah* offering earlier was his, the *tahara* offering was his colleague's, and the present offering is his concluding sacrifice for *tahara*. If, however, he was the *tahor nazir*, then the *tahara* offering previously offered was his, the *tumah* offering was his colleague's, and the present offering is his colleague's *tahara* offering.

169

The Gemara begins where the Mishna did, with one of two *nezirim* having contracted corpse *tumah*, but the person who observed this did not know which one of them it was. Now, if the doubt transpired in a private domain, both parties are deemed *tamei*, and the reason is based on the ruling regarding a suspected adulteress (*sotah*). Only two persons are privy to the guilt of a *sotah* (the woman herself and the suspected adulterer); similarly, dubious *tumah* in private (when only two parties are there) is ruled *tamei*. The difference in the present Mishna is that there is a third party: the observer who witnessed the contamination. That should therefore constitute a public domain, and under those circumstances dubious *tumah* is ruled *tahor*.

Rabba bar Rav Huna makes it a bit more complicated. He notes that the third person, the observer, was watching the action from a considerable separation; he saw the polluting object tossed between the two *nezirim*. And, Rav Ashi agrees with evidence from a close reading of the very Mishna at hand.

58b

The very fact that the Mishna speaks of this third wheel not knowing which of the two *nezirim* contracted corpse *tumah* indicates that he can't have been at all close to the action. Had been there and thus party to the formation of a public domain, he would surely have seen who was contaminated.

The Mishna then goes on to note that the two *nezirim* shave and bring sacrificial offerings together. Why should they both shave? One of them is bound to be *tahor*, and that one would be rounding the corners of his head—namely, shaving off his sidecurls and beard which is ordinarily forbidden. Shmuel offers a very particular reading by insisting that this individual would likely be a woman or a minor who are protected from this Torah dictate. The Gemara responds that the thorough shaving a *nazir* (or suspected *nazir*) undergoes is different.

Is it? Rav Huna avers that, shaving a minor's beard is virtually a non-sequitur, cutting the corners of a minor's head is a clear breach of this proscription on the part of the shaver. Rav Ada bar Ahavah delivers a warning of sorts to Rav Huna, asking who does the shaving of his children in his house. After Rav Huna points to his wife, Rav Ada bar Ahavah suggests that her doing so is effectively issuing a severe sentence on their children. And, sure enough, in one of the Talmud's frequent tales of woe for violations of laws, scriptural and rabbinic, Rav Huna is said to have lost all of his children.

What was the actual difference of positions between these two men? They agree that rounding of the head by a thorough shaving contravenes a Torah proscription. The verse in question is *Leviticus* 19.27: "You shall not round off the edge-growth of your head nor ruin the edge of your beard." (Alter, p.

629) Rav Huna reads these two proscriptions as one, meaning that a woman, not being subject to the beard part, is also not subject to the rounding part, either personally or when doing it to others. Rav Ada bar Ahavah, on the other hand, sees both shaver and shaved as complicit in transgressing a proscription. The minor may not yet be old enough to incur retribution for a violation, but the person who shaved him most certainly is.

The two rabbis in debate here date back to the Amoraic period (ca. 200–500 CE), but prior to this in the Tannaitic (ca. 10–200 CE) era, a similar debate may have transpired.

58a

A *baraita* (which we encountered back on 41a) raises the Torah injunction that a *metzora* must, as part of his purification ritual, shave every last hair off "his head." This would then mean that there are cases in which the rounding proscription is held in abeyance. As we saw on 41a, the explicit mention of "his head" is now interpreted to mean that a *nazir* who is also a *metzora* must shave completely.

A vigorous debate ensues about the distinction (or lack thereof) between rounding the head and shaving the entire head. Some make the distinction, while others see the latter encompassing the former. What we have, though, is a familiar and interesting conundrum. A negative commandment about rounding confronting a positive commandment about shaving. Which supersedes the other? As Reish Lakish points out, the best policy is to try to satisfy them both, but if that proves impossible, the positive commandment overrules the negative one.

Yet, how do we know that a positive commandment can overrule a negative and thus be used as a means of explaining the case at hand? This time the Gemara points to verses in *Deuteronomy* (22.11–12): "You shall not wear *sha'atnez*, wool and linen together. You shall make yourself tassels on the four corners of your garment with which you cover yourself." (Alter, p. 987) The first part instructs us in what we are not to do, while the latter proceeds to tell us where we are (literally) to "violate" this. These "tassels" (*tzitzit*) are twisted cords made of wool and linen. This positive> negative may be the prototype for subsequent contradictory propositions.

Why, the Gemara wonders, doesn't the author of the *baraita* about "his head" base his ruling on this *sha'atnez* vs. *tzitzit* case. Rava thinks he knows. It is possible, and Rava thinks it may be, that the Tanna of the *baraita* actually read those verses from *Deuteronomy* as indicating that *tzitzit* have to be made from the same material as the garment to which they are attached; or, when the verse reads "wool *and* linen," one should actually read this as "wool *or* linen." The Gemara goes further with this exposition, but Rava's position seemingly carries the day.

We're not done with these issues of positive and negative commandments in conflict—far from it. What happens when a positive commandment meets up with the combo of a positive and a negative one? The Gemara teases out such a confrontation from the *baraitot* back on 40b-41a.

58b

There it's the case of a Kohen who contracts *tzaraat*; does he shave as a *metzora* must as part of his purification? The special case involving a Kohen is prompted by the verse (*Leviticus* 21.6) directed solely at the priestly caste: "They shall be holy to their God." (Alter, p. 636) Add to that the prohibition on a Kohen's shaving and then facing a *metzora*'s necessary shave, and you have a genuine conundrum. The shaving must go on, but we are enjoined not to read a general principle from this case concerning Kohanim. The priestly caste constitutes a distinctive case.

The Gemara takes another bite at the "his beard" business we encountered earlier and the stark restriction of cutting it. It then descends back into the discussion we dealt with at length about the manner in which cutting would be accomplished and hence interdicted. It resolves things, as it did before, that only a razor would lead one into standing for a flogging, were it used to harm a beard.

We have devoted enough attention to removal (cutting, shaving, etc.) of facial hair, at least for now, and the Gemara now moves on to hair found elsewhere on a man's body. The prohibition of shaving the head is a dead certainty for a *nazir*, but Rav argues that a man is indeed allowed to shave other hair (e.g., underarms) and with a razor to boot. Some, though, argue that, because many women regularly remove bodily hair, for a man to do so transgresses the prohibition in *Deuteronomy* 22.5: "a man shall not wear a woman's garment." (Alter, p. 986) In fact, there is a *baraita* which states this explicitly that a man who shaves his armpit or pubic area is in for a flogging. So, the Gemara has to refine things a bit. The injunction against shaving armpits and pubic hair refers to use of a razor, while Rav must have been referring to cutting with a pair of scissors. But, but, Rav did unambiguously refer to a razor! The Gemara cops out: Yes, Rav said razor, but he meant scissors resembling a razor; apparently, cutting with a pair of scissors close to the skin line is comparable to use of a razor. Who knew?

We' re not done with this issue, as R. Chiyya bar Abba, channeling R. Yochanan's words, states that a man who removes (not cuts) hair from armpits or pubic area has transgressed and awaits a flogging. The Gemara rebuts this with a *baraita* stating that such removal of hair is indeed proscribed by rabbinic law but not by Torah law. So, where does R. Yochanan get the idea that a flogging is in the offing? Simple: R. Yochanan was talking about a flogging sanctioned rabbinically.

59a

Maybe, it's actually not so simple. It may just be that, when R. Yochanan invoked the verse from *Deuteronomy*, he was effectively noting that the punishment for doing this was scripturally sanctioned. So, a *baraita* is cited here to specifically note that hair removal is not proscribed by scripture but solely by rabbinic ordinance. There is actually, though, a competing *baraita* which supports R. Yochanan's original basis for his ruling. The message here is that issue remains unresolved. The verse from *Deuteronomy* is batted around for its essential meaning, and it emerges to no one's great surprise that it is not primarily about dress-up but about intermingling of the sexes and gender roles.

Perhaps shading off into the realm of gossip, some yeshiva lads reported to R. Shimon bar Abba that R. Yochanan did not himself have hair under his arms. How they could have detected as much remains unexplained, though they may have seen him in the bath house. R. Shimon bar Abba deciphered this one tout de suite: His hair had fallen out due to old age. Mystery solved.

Case in point ensues. There was a man in R. Ammi's court who was to endure the punishment of a flogging. When his top garment was taken off so that the whip could hit skin directly, it became clear that he had not used a razor on his armpits. R. Ammi had him released on the spot and declared him observant insofar as armpit-shaving was concerned.

Rav seems to want closure and queries R. Chiyya directly about shaving body hair. R. Chiyya replies simply that it verboten (*asur*). Rav wants more precision and notes that such hair can become annoying—shouldn't it be OK to alleviate irritation? In other words, it's not a matter of trying to be prettier, which might be associated with feminine behavior. R. Chiyya replies that, when it gets to the point of becoming irritating, bodily hair drops out. Rav has another question for R. Chiyya, this one on the odd side of things. Can one legally scratch his armpit or pubic hair in public to remove hair? R. Chiyya replies with the same one word: *asur*. How about, asks Rav, doing the same with one's clothing with the same end in sight? This time, R. Chiyya says it's allowed. Enough of this, as it's time for a new Mishna.

59b

Although we may have lost sight of it, the last Mishna concerned someone observing two *nezirim* and noting that one of them had contracted corpse *tumah*, but he could not discern which one. It went on to prescribe the formula for disentangling such a case and preserving their *nezirut* commitments to the end. We now confront a similar situation, only this time there is an added complication: One of the two *nezirim* dies before things are ironed out. So, R. Yehoshua states that the surviving *nazir* must find a volunteer prepared to vow a period of *nezirut* in a manner that follows so as to help extricate him from his ambiguous position. The survivor says to his prospective volunteer: If I was the *tamei* one, then you are a *nazir* right now; if I was the *tahor* one, then you will become a *nazir* thirty days from now. They then proceed to count out thirty days and bring both an offering for *tumah* and one for *tahara*. At this point, the survivor says to his volunteer: If it was I who was *tamei*, then the *tumah* offering is mine, and the *tahara* offering is yours; if it was I who was *tahor*, then the *tahara* offering is mine, and the *tumah* offering is sacrificed in doubt.

We're not done yet. The two men then count out another thirty days and offer a joint sacrifice for *tahara*. At this point, the surviving *nazir* says: If it was I who was the *tamei* one, the *tumah* offering of thirty days ago (the first one) was mine, and the *tahara* offering at the same time was yours; the *tahara* sacrifice that I am presently offering brings my *nezirut* to its end. He then continues: If it was I who was the *tahor* one, the *tahara* offering of thirty days ago was actually mine, the *tumah* offering was at that time sacrificed in doubt, and what we are now offering for *tahara* will satisfy for your *nezirut* to come to its end.

That's complicated enough, but Ben Zoma refuses to accept this solution, and the Mishna goes on to explain why. Ben Zoma doubts that the surviving *nazir* will be able to round up anyone willing to go along with R. Yehoshua's protracted scheme. So, he offers a less convoluted route to our survivor's bringing his *nezirut* to an end. When thirty days have transpired, the survivor brings a *chatat* offering (a bird) for *tumah* and an *olah* offering (an animal) for *tahara*. He then says: If it was indeed I who was *tamei*, this *chatat* constitutes a portion of my duty, and the *olah* offering is a voluntary one; if, by contrast, it was I who was the *tahor* one, then the *olah* one is a portion of my duty, and the *chatat* is a consequence of the doubt. He proceeds from this point to wait out another thirty days, offers a *tahara* offering, and says: If I was the *tamei* one, the *olah* I offered thirty days ago was actually a voluntary one, and the one being offered now is my duty; if I was *tahor*, however, that earlier *olah* was my duty, and the one now being offered is voluntary.

When you get into the weeds on sorting this all out, both schemes are much more complicated. The Mishna ends with R. Yehoshua not being terribly satisfied with Ben Zoma's approach and its timing of sacrificial offerings. Ben Zoma, though, wins the approbation of the sages, meaning that either of the schemes laid out here are acceptable. And, this is one of those relatively rare instances in which the Gemara is much shorter than the Mishna.

In the Mishna, R. Yehoshua indicated that Ben Zoma affords the surviving *nazir* the opportunity to bring the various offerings in pieces rather than all at once. The Gemara begins by asking why he should be dissatisfied by Ben Zoma's approach. Rav Yehuda suggests that R. Yehoshua only laid out his complex explanation not as dogmatic but as a way to test his students; in fact, he agrees with Ben Zoma. Rav Nachman has a complaint about R. Yehoshua's approach, but it seems he was not party to Rav Yehuda's resolution, so the Gemara comes to an end here, and a new Mishna appears.

More doubts burden a *nazir* and what he must do to extricate himself should he possibly have contracted *tzaraat* and corpse *tumah*. If a *nazir* suspects that he may have become *tamei* from a corpse and that he may be a confirmed *metzora*, he must wait sixty days before he can consume any sacred food. He must wait a full 120 days before he will be permitted to consume wine or become defiled by corpse *tumah*. In this case the shaving one must perform for the purification ritual at the conclusion of *tzaraat* transcends the proscription on head-shaving incumbent on a *nazir*, but only when there is no doubt about *tzaraat*; when doubt looms, there is no transcending. All this will be explained further on the next *daf*.

60a

The Gemara immediately begins with a *baraita* asking what case the Mishna just laid out was meant to address. Answer: a regular period of thirty days. If one committed to a period of one year, the ban on the consumption of sacred food would last two years; similarly, the ban on wine and corpse *tumah* would last a full four years. Another *baraita* then immediately lays out the head shavings and offerings incumbent on a *nazir* who becomes *tamei* as the Mishna describes. There are four shavings: (1) following the completion of thirty days (in the Mishna) or a full year (in the *baraita*'s case), he offers up a bird pair, involving the ritual sprinkling that commences the purification from *tzaraat*, and he also offers a bird *chatat* and an animal *olah*; (2) after sixty days when the second period comes to a close, he offers up a bird *chatat* and an animal *olah*, and at this point he will be purified of *tzaraat*; (3) following the ninetieth day, he again offers up a bird *chatat* and an animal *olah*; and (4) thirty more days later, he brings the final offering for *tahara*.

Remembering this is all about covering all bases due to doubts about corpse *tumah* and *tzaraat*, the Gemara now explains how the reasoning behind such an elaborate series of rituals is to be completed. We start with the first shaving. Suppose he was a *metzora* but not afflicted with corpse *tumah*, then he must undergo the sprinkling noted above, the blood of the bird *chatat* is properly applied to the Altar in the Temple, although its carcass is discarded, and the *olah* is considered voluntary. In theory he should shave after a week's time, but *Numbers* 6.5 (cited in part on 44a: "no razor shall pass over his head, until the days come to term") rules that possibility out until completion of his thirty days.

Suppose, by contrast, that he has become afflicted with corpse *tumah* but not by *tzaraat*, then it is incumbent upon him to bring the bird *chatat* as a portion of his offering for *tumah*, the sprinkling noted in the previous two paragraphs (though outside the Temple grounds), and the *olah* which is regarded as voluntary. Finally, suppose he is actually neither a *metzora* nor one who has contracted corpse *tumah*, and he is thus a *tahor nazir*. So, he goes through the sprinkling outside the Temple, brings the bird *chatat* (dealt with as if he were a *metzora* but not corpse-*tamei*), and offers his *olah* which is a portion of his final rituals as *nazir*.

Let's now move on to the rituals involved with the subsequent shavings. No birds at this point need be brought for the sprinkling, as that ritual has already been completed. Should he actually have been a *metzora*, he needs to offer a bird *chatat* at his second shave and another at the time of his third shave on the off chance that he was afflicted with corpse *tumah*. When he finally reaches the point of the fourth shaving, he offers what a *nazir* ordinarily would sacrifice to fulfill his obligations and attain *tahara*. He then states for the record (paraphrasing):

60b

If I was *tahor nazir* at the time of any of the first three shavings, then the previous animal *olah* was incumbent upon me, and the present one is voluntary; if I had contracted both corpse *tumah* and *tzaraat*, all the times I brought an *olah* should be regarded as voluntary, while this one is incumbent upon me; and the *chatat* and *shelamim* I am now offering are elemental to my concluding ritual.

At the beginning of 60a, we were outlining the various shavings and linked sacrificial offerings as detailed in a *baraita*. That was interrupted by the subsequent explanation, but the Gemara now returns to the same *baraita*. Should a *nazir* know that he was a *metzora* but have doubts about whether he had contracted corpse *tumah*, he is required to wait eight days before he may consume sacred food, and he must wait sixty-seven days before consuming wine or having contact with the dead. By contrast, should a *nazir* know that he had contracted corpse *tumah* but have doubts about whether he was afflicted with *tzaraat*, thirty-seven days must pass before he may consume sacred food and seventy-four days before he would be allowed to consume wine and have contact with the dead. In one last case, if our poor *nazir* knew for certain that he had contracted both corpse *tumah* and *tzaraat*, he is required to wait eight days before consuming sacred food and forty-four days before consuming wine and having any contact with a corpse. Why these specific numbers of days are not explained in the *baraita* or elsewhere in the Gemara, but various commentaries explain the inordinate complexities of these situations.

In discussing the various shavings that a *nazir* in doubt must undergo, it should be noted that any one shave can count for a *tamei nazir* or for a *tzaraat* affliction, but it cannot satisfy both requirements. A new *baraita* is now introduced to elucidate the rationale behind this. The famous R. Shimon ben Yochai was asked by his disciples if a *tahor nazir* who was also a *metzora* can have a single shaving fulfill both obligations. The answer was simply: No. So, they asked him why. Because the objectives of the two shaving requirements (for a *nazir* and for a *metzora*) are fundamentally distinct, each only fulfills the end goals of itself but not the other.

The disciples were quite ready to concede at this point, and they respond several times with increasingly minute and detailed queries for R. Shimon ben Yochai. And, each time their master explains where their thinking has veered off the path. He must have been a very patient man. Before this *daf* comes to a close, it rehearses one of the exchanges between master and disciples in a somewhat different rendition.

61a

As we near the end of Chapter Eight, another *baraita* is invoked, this one credited to R. Chiyya, which reasons an awful lot like R. Shimon ben Yochai, albeit in somewhat more cryptic language. It involves the order of the various rituals involved in the purification of a *metzora* and a *tamei nazir* as well as a *tahor nazir*.

At the end of the Mishna at hand (back on 59b), there was discussion of the shaving one must perform for the purification ritual at the conclusion of *tzaraat* and its relationship to a *nazir*'s final shave. This was the impetus for the Gemara to lay out the four shavings above. Rami bar Chama asks an interesting question: About those four shavings, is the objective there to carry out the ritual requirements, or is it only to remove the hair from the head of the *nazir* from when he became *tamei*? What's the difference, asks the Gemara. It comes down to whether the hair must be shaved off, or whether a chemical substance might be used to get rid of the hair. By this point in our tractate, the answer to this query should be a foregone conclusion: It's got to be shaved off. No substitute for a razor.

Chapter 9

Tumah of the Deep and Floating *Tumah*

This is the final chapter in tractate *Nazir* of the Babylonian Talmud, and it begins with a theme we have not confronted as of yet. Cuthites, identified as an ancient designation of a non-Jewish people who were idolators, have no relationship to the rituals and practices of *nezirut*. By the same token, both women and non-Jewish slaves (owned by Jews) may involve themselves in *nezirut*; an important distinction here is that, while a husband may not compel his wife to transgress the conditions of her *nezirut* (drinking wine and the like), a slave owner can compel his slave to transgress in this fashion. As an aside, slaves enter the Talmud at many junctures, and the topic is as utterly fascinating as it is soul-searching in retrospect (especially, but not exclusively, for Americans). It is not a topic to be dealt with lightly.

The Gemara starts by wanting to know how it is that Cuthites (as idolators) fall outside the ken of *nezirut*. This one seems relatively straightforward, as a *baraita* directs us to the verse from *Numbers* (6.2), wherein God tells Moses in the context of *nezirut*: "Speak to the Israelites." (Alter, p. 710) Clearly, God didn't want Moses to go out of his way to get the pagans in line. The same verse goes on to add (superfluously): "and say to them." This addition must mean something, and the Gemara takes it as an injunction to include slaves among those who are permitted to become *nezirim*.

Not so quick, cautions the Gemara, for there's no need for this additional verse to teach us something special for slaves here. Elsewhere in the Talmud, the point is sharply made that all mitzvot incumbent on women are also incumbent on slaves. If women may invoke *nezirut*, so too may slaves. Rava tries to explain. *Numbers* 30.3 teaches about vows more generally: "Should a

179

man take a vow or make an oath to the LORD, to take upon himself a binding pledge." (Alter, p. 838) Only a free man is in any position to make such a
"binding pledge"; a slave has no control over his own individual self to do so.
Thus, you would expect that a slave could never commit to become a *nazir*,
but this is where "and say to them" comes in to grandfather slaves into the
capacity to vow periods of *nezirut*.

What I just indicated as seeming awfully straightforward is now questioned. How does "Speak to the Israelites" necessarily exclude pagans? Does
Israel or Israelites in scripture automatically rule out non-Jews? Through
a highly complex and circuitous route, the Gemara suggests that idolators
might be eligible for inclusion in the arena of *nezirut*, irrespective of the
expression "Speak to the Israelites." But, we learned earlier that one who has
vowed a period of *nezirut* may not contract corpse *tumah* even for his own
parent. Now, in the context of Jewish law, pagans do not enjoy parent-child
relations, meaning that *nezirut* has no bearing on their lives. This line is
promptly refuted by insisting that in matters of inheritance, a pagan does
indeed acquire his father's legacy, as prescribed by scripture. This teaching
was articulated by R. Chiyya bar Avin in the name of R. Yochanan and supported by a verse in *Deuteronomy* (2.5): "For I have given the high country
Seir as an inheritance to Esau." (Alter, p. 886)

The Gemara tries a different run at the same parent-child distinctiveness
that scripture accords Jews. Jews are commanded, we are told, to honor their
parents, while there is no comparable commandment imposed upon pagans.
As such, vows of *nezirut* have nothing to do with idolators. Nice try, the
answer promptly responds, for there is no mention of honoring one's parents
in the passages of the Torah where the laws of *nezirut* are described.

That same verse from *Numbers* (6.7) in which a *nazir* is enjoined not to
pollute himself with corpse *tumah* even for a parent is now brought out to
prove that it can only apply to someone who can contract *tumah*.

61b

Inasmuch as pagans can't contract corpse *tumah* (or any form of it), they can't
be in any way governed by the rulings of *nezirim*. To support this assertion,
the Gemara cites a verse (*Numbers* 19.20): "a man who becomes unclean and
does not cleanse himself, that person will be cut off from the midst of the
assembly." (Alter, p. 780) The "assembly" refers to the community or con-
gregation of God and thus by definition dismisses pagans from consideration.

Maybe, suggests the Gemara in rebuttal, the pagan is indeed not part of
the assembly, but he might nonetheless contract *tumah*. The issue boils down
to the *tahara-tumah* relationship. Yes, pagans might become *tamei*, but they

cannot become *tahor*. Rav Acha bar Yaakov steps up with a different approach now that goes back to the import of inheritance and the fact that slaves do not have it, but his approach is promptly rejected as well. Rava now comes up with a proposal that can only be described as highly complicated. The words from *Numbers* 6.2 cited above mentioning "Speak to the Israelites" goes on to mention a "man." He argues that the inclusion of the latter word may be used to make *nezirut* conceivable for pagans. Several challenges are thrown in the face of Rava's argument, and one can only assume that it bites the dust.

62a

Back on the last *daf*, the Gemara cited a *baraita* which launched the invoking of *Number* 6.2 ("Speak to the Israelites"). As noted at the time, it mentioned that this might be used to differentiate that Jews can become *nezirim* but idolators cannot. It also mentioned, and we did not address it there, that idolators cannot—as Jews can—assert a vow of *erech* or assessment. The Torah delineates for their monetary value eight categories of persons differentiated by age and gender, laid out in *Leviticus* 27.2–8. There is some discussion of whether idolators can even be the object of such a valuation. This is batted around but rejected. The debate centers around the inclusion of "man" in the verse cited immediately above.

Somehow the discussion in the Gemara circles back to the declarations of *nezirut* we examined at the very start of this tractate (2a). There, our text presented a debate between those who required such a declaration to be crystal clear—e.g., "I shall forthwith become a *nazir*"—and those who accepted an assortment of partial, often oblique declarations as valid. The question comes down to the clarity with which a vow—either *nezirut* or *erech*—must be articulated. Clarity would seem to win the day.

62b

A new Mishna now picks up a theme from the Mishna on 61a. This involves the greater level of inflexibility for a slave's *nezirut* than for that of women. While a husband can withdraw his wife's *nezirut* commitment, he is not so empowered vis-à-vis his slave. True, a slave owner can order his slave to transgress one or more of the laws governing *nezirut*, but he cannot cancel it altogether. Now, once a husband has withdrawn his wife's vow to be a *nezira*, she may never again vow a term of *nezirut*—even if he dies or divorces her. If he orders his slave to transgress his vow, this does not (as we have seen) constitute a revocation of that vow, but it halts it in place. Should the slave subsequently be manumitted, he must complete his period of *nezirut* from the point of interruption.

The Gemara starts, as it often does, with a *baraita*, this one to clarify the master-slave relationship with respect to a master's ordering a transgression of his slave's vow. It states simply that a master may not overrule a slave's regular vows (laid out in detail in tractate *Nedarim*) or *erech* vows, but he can compel a slave to violate his vow of *nezirut*. Why this difference? What makes the *nezirut* vow something over which a master can exercise some control? The Gemara directs us to *Numbers* 30.2 which speaks literally of a man's commission of an oath as binding "his soul" (*nafsho*) to it. The problem is that a slave's soul does not belong to him but to his master; so, a slave may vow to be a *nazir*, but that vow is not binding, because the master can overrule him.

Now, wouldn't the same hold true for *neder* vows declared by a slave? Surely, a master could have at least the same power over a slave in this regard as he has vis-à-vis *nezirut*. Rav Sheshet attempts to differentiate the essence of a *neder* vow and one of *nezirut*, as concerns a slave and the areas in which the master can and cannot overrule such vows. This discussion also goes around in a circle. Abaye sums it up by averring that a slave's *neder* vows cannot take effect, while those of *nezirut* can—with each part of this ruling relying on a different scriptural verse.

Next up is a short Mishna. Suppose a slave takes a vow of *nezirut* and then promptly escapes. How does that effect his vow? R. Meir rules that he is forbidden from drinking wine, meaning that while he has disappeared from his master's immediate authority, he must continue to abide by his vow. R. Yose, by contrast, states that he may consume wine, meaning that the master still owns the slave and can overrule his slave while the latter is on the run.

The essence of this Mishna is the disagreement between the two rabbis. Shmuel has apparently argued that, when a master proclaims his slave no longer the property of another, that (now former) slave is given his freedom, even without a writ declaring such. What, one might ask, does this have to do with the case of the Mishna? If a master's slave escapes and the master sees no hope of recovery, that is the same as stating the slave is no longer his property. R. Meir appears to abide by Shmuel's ruling, while R. Yose appears not to. The latter does not regard a master's despair of ever getting his slave back to be the same as setting his slave free. If he is still the property of the master, then even if he is not presently in his master's service, the master retains the power to compel the slave to transgress his *nezirut* vow.

Appearances notwithstanding, the Gemara will now demonstrate that positions of both rabbis can be brought into agreement of sorts with Shmuel's ruling. There is no mention in the Mishna that the master has reached the point of despair at his slave's coming "home." R. Yose's claim that the slave may drink wine implies his belief that he will eventually return to his master. This line of reasoning would involve the master's allowance of his slave's consumption of wine as a preventive of the latter's not getting too exhausted and weak. He wants his property back, and a little wine might help. Now, R. Meir's thinking would run as follows: Cut off his consumption of wine, let the renegade slave feel some irritation or uneasiness, and that'll enhance his desire, in the end, to come back to his master's service.

63a

A new Mishna at this point moves in a different direction. First, we have the case of a *nazir* who concludes the period of his vow, shaves, performs the final ritual sacrifices, and only then discovers that while he was a *nazir* he contracted corpse *tumah*. What happens? If the cause of defilement is known, he loses the entire period of his vow, meaning he must go through the purification process and then redo his full *nezirut*. By contrast, if the source of defilement was hidden from sight and unknown at the time to anyone, only to be discovered at a later date, then he does not lose his completed *nezirut*. If, however, the source of his defilement, whether known or unknown, is discovered just before he shaves, he does in fact lose his accrued *nezirut*. In explanation, the Mishna presents as a case of known (or knowable) *tumah* a *nazir* who enters a cave and submerges in a pool of water as part of his purification from *tumah* of a *sheretz*, and then later a corpse was discovered floating in the water near the cave's opening. It rules him *tamei*, presumably due to the shared roof of the cave. If, however, the corpse was discovered beneath the base of the pool in the cave, where no one could have known of its presence at the time, then at a later date—and the *nazir* had submerged in the pool in an effort to cool off while still *tahor*—he remains *tahor*. If he submerged because he was already *tamei* from a corpse and was doing this as part of his purification, he loses his entire *nezirut* count. So, *tumah* from an unknown source revealed after a *nazir*'s final rituals may not cause one to lose his accrued *nezirut*, but if he was already *tamei*, he remains *tamei*— just as someone *tahor* remains *tahor*—even if such a hidden *tumah* was later uncovered. The law governing the latter form of *tumah*—often dubbed "*tumah* of the deep"—is said to have been initially taught to Moses at Sinai, although the Mishna ends by noting that it is logical (at least in part) as well.

The Gemara starts off by wondering how it is that "*tumah* of the deep" has no serious consequences. R. Elazar is cited invoking *Numbers* 6.9: "should a dead person die near by him all of a sudden." (Alter, p. 712) This clearly refers to one who is cognizant of corpse *tumah* in his immediate vicinity, and by

implication it differentiates itself from unknown *tumah*. Reish Lakish interprets another verse (*Numbers* 9.10) in such a way as to add to this argument.

Now, the Gemara just outright asks what this "*tumah* of the deep" (*tumat hatehom*) is. It answers, via a *baraita*, that it is a *tumah* that is so concealed from view that likely no one knows about it. Indeed, if anyone is cognizant of it, it no longer may be dubbed "*tumah* of the deep." The Gemara then tries to derive the Mishna's ruling on the basis of logic, but it quickly runs into a dead end and decides that, in fact, "*tumah* of the deep" is (as noted above) a law taught to Moses at Sinai.

The Mishna made a point of pointing out that the timing of the *nazir*'s shave is critical to determining whether defilement has occurred. R. Yochanan states that R. Eliezer was the sage who made this ruling. Our Mishna indicates that both ordinary observable corpse *tumah* and "*tumah* of the deep," if uncovered prior to the *nazir*'s head shave, lead to a *nazir*'s loss of his period of *nezirut* which he must repeat after purification. Time for a bit more analysis. Rami bar Chama concocts a situation and then asks about its verdict: A *nazir* con-tracts *tumah* (either kind) before he finishes his period but only discovers this fact after finishing but before carrying out his closing rituals. Is the crucial point when the *nazir* became aware of his contracting *tumah*, a point signifi-cant for whether or not he loses his accrued period of *nezirut*?

63b

Rava to the rescue to answer this query, and he begins with the forty-sixth and last use in our tractate of the expression "ta shma." The Mishna stated that, if he became aware of contracting *tumah*, no matter which kind, prior to that final shave, his *nezirut* is lost. As Rava explains, if he contracted the *tumah* and became aware of it during his *nezirut* period, it's obvious that his period is a goner. So, it must be that, while contamination took place within his period, he only became aware of his defilement after he finished his period of *nezirut* commitment. That's what the Mishna's statement is all about.

Maybe, though, we don't have all the details of Rami bar Chama's query. Maybe he wanted to know if a *nazir* in such a position loses his entire period or whether he only loses seven days—the former being like defilement con-tracted within a period of *nezirut*, the latter like it after the period but before final rituals. The rabbis deem it all a lost cause and that he must do it all over again, while R. Eliezer deems it a seven-day loss, because it was contracted after fulfillment of a committed period. R. Eliezer, upon a closer look, is dis-tinguishing the point of contracting *tumah* and the point of awareness there of. If our *nazir* only learned of his defilement (which transpired during his period) after he completed that period, then only a seven-day loss is indicated. Back to Rava's explanation, for he makes clear that the Mishna did not differentiate between the two kinds of *tumah* nor if the *nazir*'s defilement transpired during or after the completion of his period.

The Gemara now marshals a *baraita* to examine this whole business of "*tumah* of the deep." Suppose a corpse is discovered under the ground beside a road and in a position such that one cannot walk along this road without going over where that corpse is buried; he is *tamei* vis-à-vis consumption of *teruma*, but a *nazir* remains *tahor*. Further elaboration in the *baraita* points out that one could not walk along this road without traversing the burial spot. Now, if there was space to walk around this spot, then he remains *tahor* even vis-à-vis *teruma*. Further explanation: The corpse needs be intact. If it was broken up in some way, the assumption is that one dodged walking directly over its pieces, and thus he remains *tahor* on all fronts. If, however, the corpse was in any sort of tomb or grave, then our traveler is *tamei*, for even if the corpse is broken up, the tomb joins the pieces. Further explanation: This exemption from contamination applies only in cases when he was walking and only if he was unencumbered with a weight he was carrying or if he was riding. Presumably, the weight would force him at some point to bend over and thus form a roof over a corpse, rendering him *tamei*.

More explanation: When one walks, one can avoid contact or roofing of any sort with a corpse. Burdened with a load or riding, we enter the realm of definite defilement. This all refers to "*tumah* of the deep," meaning our *nazir* still remains *tahor*. When that *tumah* is known, contamination ensues. So, what then makes up "*tumah* of the deep"? Answer: No one anywhere is cognizant of it; if there is a soul somewhere who is, then this does not constitute "*tumah* of the deep." Assuming what we have been describing is a corpse buried beneath a dirt roadbed, the *baraita* explains that even if a corpse is discovered under straw or pebbles, that's enough to qualify as "*tumah* of the deep." Several further "possible" cases are suggested but then quickly rejected as instances of "*tumah* of the deep."

The Mishna differentiated between the two types of *tumah* we have been analyzing with the case of a floating corpse. The Gemara at this point wants to delve more deeply into the issue of floating *tumah*. If someone comes into contact with a source of *tumah* floating in water, the Tanna states that he remains *tahor* no matter if the water was in a pool on the ground or in a restricted space like a vessel of some kind. R. Shimon disagrees and argues that, if the water was on the ground, he is *tahor*, but if in a vessel he's *tamei*.

64a

How does the Tanna come to such a conclusion? R. Yitzchak bar Avudimi cites two places in chapter 11 of *Leviticus* (verses 43 and 29) to demonstrate that, be it floating on water or on the ground, doubtful contact with *tumah* does not constitute contamination. The person remains *tahor*. So, how does R. Shimon come to his conclusion? Ulla cites another verse in *Leviticus* 11 (verse 36) which appears to hold contradictory rulings, but he uses it to distinguish contact with a dead *sheretz* in water on the ground which does not cause contamination with contact with same in a vessel which does.

On the subject of floating *tumah*, the Gemara goes to the next stage, as it were, by examining the situation where a *tumah*-producing entity rests atop an item floating on water. This may sound a bit strange, but Rami bar Chama starts off with a question that makes some sense. Imagine, if you will, a corpse in some sort of a vessel, perhaps a lightweight casket, floating on water. If someone touches the vessel from above, is he *tamei*? If we judge on the basis of the floating vessel, he remains *tahor*; if we judge on the basis of the dead body which is presumably lying flat along the base of the vessel, it is considered to be stable and not floating and would thus be a source of *tumah*.

What began as a reasonable question, though, soon begins to spin out of control, as postulations of all manner of *tumah* sitting above other sources of *tumah* are considered in the context of floating on water, such as corpses atop *sheratzim* or one *sheretz* atop another. These various *tumah* sources carry different potencies and different periods of time before returning to *tahara* for the person who has contact with them. There is also the issue of decomposing bodies of *sheratzim* that merge to form some sort of gooey mess which appears more like a liquid than a solid entity. There are more considerations, but I'm sure readers will get the picture. And, thankfully, the Gemara leaves it there by stating that it cannot answer all these queries and thus chooses to leave them all as they are.

64b

The Gemara pivots now to Rav Hamnuna who offers the following judgment: A *nazir* who, unbeknownst to him, walks over a buried corpse on the seventh day of his purification from corpse *tumah*; such a person remains *tahor* and does not lose his accrued *nezirut*; all this is due to the fact that "*tumah* of the deep" cannot under such circumstances lead to loss of a period of *nezirut*. This judgment is questioned by Rava who notes that, if our *nazir* had yet to submerge as part of his purification, he is still *tamei*. Rav

Hamnuna does not disagree and adds that only if the experience of "*tumah of the deep*" occurs after the purification rituals are completed and the *nazir* is *tahor*, does that experience have no impact on his losing his accrued *nezirut*. In an uncommonly genial resolution, Rava retracts his difficulty with Rav Hamnuna's judgment. Both sages agree that if a person is *tahor*, he is assumed to continue being *tahor*, and ditto *tamei*. And, as if courtesy is contagious, Abaye poses what he finds difficult in this judgment, only to withdraw it soon after Rava explains.

Abaye's concern had to with the fact that completion of purification can only transpire with the setting of the sun on the final day of the ritual. This leads to a detailed comparative discussion with a woman who miscarries. This goes down an unrelated rabbit hole and then abruptly comes to an end before a new Mishna.

Back on 63a, the previous Mishna laid out the general ruling that a presumption of *tahara* remains intact, as does a presumption of *tumah*. We now get a sequence of Mishnayot which employ this general perspective but have no other direct connection to the matter at hand. So, if a person were to discover and unearth a corpse while digging in a place that had hitherto never been used for burial, buried as corpses ordinarily were, it may be removed (with the dirt encompassing it) for proper burial. Inasmuch as this is not ordinary Jewish burial practice, one must assume that it was temporarily laid to rest there, and one is thus allowed to rebury it properly in a graveyard. Even if two such corpses are unearthed at a hitherto unexpected site, they may be removed for reburial (again, with the dirt encompassing them).

However, what happens when three corpses are located is different. If the distance between the two furthest apart is between four and eight cubits (each cubit is reckoned at between 18 and 23 inches), then one has happened upon an unmarked cemetery. Now things get considerably more complicated.

65a

The person doing the "excavating" is required at this point to measure from the center of the site outward for twenty cubits in all directions. Should he come upon as few as one additional corpse within that radius, he is required to explore another twenty cubits further. Now that he has unearthed these other graves, he cannot simply remove the corpses for reburial. Although we have, for now, departed the realm of *nezirut*, the issue of *tumah* and *tahara* with respect to a corpse or corpses remains front and center.

Rav Yehuda gets the Gemara's discussion started by noting that the Mishna indicated someone who discovered a buried corpse; that would mean it wasn't known beforehand. Also, the fact that the text referred to a "corpse" indicates that it was the body of someone who died of natural causes, not someone cut down. Were it the body of a murder victim, it would very likely be missing some part or at least a quantity of blood. And, the corpse was found in a reclining position (meaning it wasn't sitting up) and laid out in what the Mishna dubbed the usual way (presumably for a Jew).

We move now to the discovery of two graves, and the Gemara quotes from a *baraita*. If two corpses there were next to one another and facing opposite directions, this would indicate a pagan burial site, as graves in regular Jewish cemeteries face the same direction. They would thus be exempt from the rule of encompassing earth when reburied elsewhere. If three graves were discovered, one of them known beforehand though unclear if it was a permanent or provisional gravesite and the other two only just uncovered (or two known and one heretofore unknown), the rule that the encompassing earth must be removed remains in place, and the rules of a cemetery area are not.

The business about the dirt encompassing the newly discovered corpse is now discussed further. The Mishna indicated that it must be removed along with the corpse, but why? Rav Yehuda explains that this is derived from *Genesis* 47.30, where Jacob asks Joseph to be sure and bury him not in Egypt but in the land of Canaan: "carry me from Egypt." (Alter, p. 276) That seems odd as an explanation, until we read into it that mention of "Egypt" is unnecessary and thus is interpreted to mean some part or some bit of Egypt, and thus some dirt of Egypt.

In actual terms, how much dirt are we talking about? Well, claims R. Elazar, it means all the soft earth around the body and then the three fingers-worth of earth beneath it. There is a similarly named R. Elazar, son of R. Tzadok, whose view is cited within a *baraita* to the effect that one also takes any bits of wood from a decomposing coffin along with dirt mixed with decomposing flesh, while discarding anything clearly alien to the corpse and leaves what might be dubious along with it. It goes on to list, somewhat ghoulishly, the defiling amounts and measures of body parts, but no mention of the soil to three fingers' depth. It's as if the two rabbis are operating on two qualitatively different scales. This piece of analysis ends with another *baraita* supporting the first R. Elazar.

65b

Rava poses a scenario that complicates things. A man discovers a corpse in a field and, following the ruling of the Mishna, removes it properly; then, he goes back and discovers a second corpse which he also removes in proper fashion. So far so good, but then he happens upon a third corpse within the spatial parameters set out by the Mishna, and that means the entire area was actually a proper burial site from which bodies should not have been moved. He must then not move that third corpse, nor may those first two be returned to this original place. He did nothing wrong in moving the first two, but now that they have been properly buried elsewhere, they can't be moved again.

The Mishna also ruled that, once three (or presumably more) corpses are uncovered meaning the area was a proper burial site, one is to dig twenty cubits around the site for other bodies. What is to be done if none are discovered, suggesting that this might not really be a burial site after all? Rav Menashya bar Yirmeya, channeling Rav, claims that the three graves unearthed nonetheless still constitute a gravesite.

A new Mishna continues discussion of topics at best indirectly tied to the main topic of our tractate. It examines doubts about *tzaraat* as it may affect changes in one's skin color. If there is any question of *tzaraat* which appears early on, before *tzaraat* has been checked and confirmed by an expert, it is deemed *tahor*, until such time as the affliction is confirmed to be *tamei*. After that point, any doubt about it being deemed *tamei* dissolves.

As we have seen many times, the Gemara begins by wondering where in scripture there is support for such a ruling. Rav Yehuda, channeling Rav, cites a verse from *Leviticus* (13.59): "to render it clean or unclean" (Alter, p. 598), meaning *tahor* or *tamei*. *Tahor* precedes *tamei*, so presumably in initially doubtful cases, we go with *tahor*. Shouldn't we, then, question the Gemara, continue to stand with *tahor*, even after it has been confirmed to be *tamei*? This is followed by a discussion of details of skin discoloration and white hairs growing from them—and which appeared first—but the Gemara ultimately reverts to the same citation invoked by Rav Yehuda citing Rav.

The next Mishna moves on to discuss *zivah* (a seminal emission leading one to be dubbed a *zav*) brought on by various factors and a *tumah* determination. Should he have two such discharges, purification requires seven days without further discharge and then submerging in a pool of spring water. It gets more onerous with three discharges. A *zav* undergoes assessment for the cause from seven possible sources: foods (various fatty items, eggs, and the like), drink (too much of it), bearing heavy burdens or jumping (meaning hard work), sickness, visual sights (such as beautiful women causing arousal), or thought (ditto). Once he has been confirmed to be a victim of *tumah*, two discharges, he no longer is assessed, everything preceding this array is judged *tamei*. The presumption of *tamei* remains intact.

The same Mishna now segues abruptly to a piece from tractate *Sanhedrin* (Assembly of judges) which is the actual name of the high rabbinical court and which deals with numerous common law proceedings. Here it looks at the law regarding an assailant's quarry who is at the point of death but wavering. If a man attacks another, and the doctor says the victim is doomed, but he rallies from being on the verge of death, only shortly thereafter to succumb, the assailant has committed capital murder and is accountable for the death penalty. R. Nechemya demurs and says the death penalty should be off the table, because when the victim rallied, that state of affairs stands, and his ultimate death must be attributable to external causes.

The Gemara has two, very different topics with which to deal. It starts by analyzing the distinction implicit in the Mishna between a second and third discharge experienced by a *zav*—with a third discharge, no assessment of the seven possible external stimuli is undertaken. R. Natan starts us off with a scriptural reference to substantiate this distinction, *Leviticus* 15.33: "about the person with flux [what we have been calling 'discharge'], whether male or female." (Alter, p. 610) It's a bit mystifying how this is related to the question at hand, but a *baraita* is cited that may help: R. Eliezer claims, contrary to what we have determined earlier, that if a man experiences a third discharge, he is assessed, but for the fourth discharge, no need. The difference here surrounds the particle *et* (a direct-object marker in Hebrew) in the phrase in *Leviticus*—we're really getting into the weeds here.

The next segment of the Mishna concerns all the doubts and the like that may have come up and fall by the wayside, as he is *tamei*.

66a

Rava tries to clear up what "doubt" refers to in this context, and it turns out that uncertainty here seems fairly tangential to the issue at hand.

The Mishna went on to state that a *zav*'s seminal flow is contaminating, but the question is how. We already know that contact with the semen emitted by a *zav* would be *tamei*, but the point of the ruling is that that same semen defiled via carrying. Yet, we are immediately then confronted with a *baraita* in which R. Eliezer states precisely the opposite—namely, that a *zav*'s semen does not defile via carrying. And, by the same token, R. Yehoshua says that it does, because that semen, given its source, inevitably contains tiny amounts of *zivah*. The point is that, even in R. Yehoshua's case, it's this tiny amount that is the problem, but a *zav* may also conceivably have pure semen which would not be defiling. The Gemara continues with various issues concerning semen, *zivah*, and the like, but it ultimately returns to Rava's point about the semen of a *zav* defiling via carrying, though it explains further now that that period of its possible contamination lasts for twenty-four hours after the discharge of *zivah*.

On to the final Mishna in tractate *Nazir*. The topic returns to *nezirut* and concerns whether the prophet Samuel was a *nazir*. According to R. Nehorai, he was indeed a *nazir*, and he cites an early verse in *I Samuel* regarding a vow before God from Hannah, Samuel's mother who had long been unable to become pregnant, that she would see to it that a *morah* would ever "come upon his head." R. Nehorai apparently takes the word *morah* to mean a razor, and to explain how he comes to such a conclusion, he notes that the same word was used in the context of Samson, who we all known was a lifelong *nazir*. Thus, Samuel must also have been a *nazir*.

R. Yose has a different understanding of the term. He associates it with *mora* (pronounced the same but spelled slightly differently) meaning fear. Thus, the verse in *I Samuel* would mean that the prophet would never fear any flesh and blood (meaning any other man), and thus it bears no connection to *nezirut*. R. Nehorai retorts that the well-known verse in which God entrusts Samuel with the task of anointing David as king, and Samuel responds that he fears that, if Saul learns of this, he will have Samuel killed. If that's not fear, what is?

The Gemara seemingly has no relationship whatsoever to the Mishna, except that two of the rabbis involved are R. Yose and R. Nehorai. Otherwise, you got me. Rav instructs his son Chiyya,

66b

just as Rav Huna instructs his son Rabbah, to be prompt in raising the cup of wine and reciting the blessing—better to be the one who recites the blessing than one of those who respond with *amen*. Maybe that's the wrong implication, as we next meet a *baraita* in which R. Yose states affirmatively that responding *amen* is greater than reciting the blessing. And, R. Nehorai agrees completely. Another *baraita*, however, valorizes the blesser over the *amen* responders.

The tractate ends with a lovely teaching from R. Elazar to the effect that peace in the world is enhanced by those who study Torah. He invokes *Isaiah* 54.13: "And all of your children shall be disciples of God, and great shall be the peace of your children."

Glossary

amud (pl. *amudim*): single side of a page (two per *daf*), verso or recto

asham: guilt offering

baraita (pl. *baraitot*): an oral law not codified in the Mishna but with the authority of a Tanna

bechor: a male first-born kosher animal

chatat: sin offering

daf (pl. *dapim*): Talmudic folio

erech: self-assessment (in monetary terms)

gezera shava: explication of a word or phrase in scripture by comparison with the same word or phrase elsewhere in scripture

halacha (pl. *halachot*): legal ruling derived from the Mishna

kal vachomer: *a fortiori* reasoning

klal ufrat: general and particular, a hermeneutical tool used in the Talmud

metzora: one afflicted with *tzaraat*

mikveh: ritual purification bath

mitzvah (pl. *mitzvot*): commandment, good deed

neveilah: the corpse of an animal not properly (ritually) slaughtered

nezirut: vow of abstinence from grape products, shaving, and contact with human corpses

olah: burnt offering

prat uchlal ufrat: specification-generalization-specification, a hermeneutical tool used in the Talmud

R.: rabbi

seder (order): one of the six groups of tractates of the Talmud

shelamim: peace offering

sheratz (pl. *sheratzim*): creeping or swarming creature (certain rodents and bugs)

shiva: seven-day mourning ritual following the death of a close relative

sotah: suspected adulteress

tahara: state of ritual purity

tahor: ritually pure

tamei: ritually impure

Tanna (pl. Tannaim): commentator on the Mishna, ca. 70–200 C.E.

teruma: food given to and only consumable by a Kohen

todah: thanksgiving offering

tumah: ritual impurity

tzaraat: impurity manifested as a skin discoloration

zav: a man who experiences a seminal discharge

zavah: a woman who experiences bleeding on three successive days

zivah: a contaminating discharge, seminal for a man and vaginal blood for a woman

Index

Biblical and Rabbinic Reference Index

About the Author

Joshua A. Fogel is professor of history at the York University in Toronto and a fellow of the Royal Society of Canada. He previously taught at Harvard University (1981–1988) and the University of California, Santa Barbara (1989–2005). He specializes in Chinese and Japanese intellectual history and is the author, editor, or translator of over seventy volumes over the course of more than forty years. This work is the sixth of his writings on tractates of the Talmud, all published by Hamilton Books. Recent work of his in East Asian studies include: *A Friend in Deed: Lu Xun, Uchiyama Kanzō, and the Intellectual World of Shanghai on the Eve of War* as author; and *Sino-Japanese Reflections: Literary and Cultural Interactions between China and Japan in Early Modernity* and *Time and Language: New Sinology and Chinese History* as editor.